W9-BNE-797

PSYCHOLOGICAL ISSUES

VOL. III, No. 3   MONOGRAPH 11

EGO AND REALITY IN PSYCHOANALYTIC THEORY

A Proposal Regarding Independent Ego Energies

by

ROBERT W. WHITE, Ph.D.

WITHDRAWN

Theodore Lownik Library
Illinois Benedictine College
Lisle, Illinois 60532

INTERNATIONAL UNIVERSITIES PRESS, INC.

239 Park Avenue South • New York, N.Y. 10003

Copyright, 1963, by International Universities Press, Inc.
Library of Congress Catalog Card Number: 63-19631

PSYCHOLOGICAL ISSUES

154.22
W587e

GEORGE S. KLEIN, *Editor*

Editorial Board

MARGARET BRENMAN   ROBERT R. HOLT

ERIK H. ERIKSON   MARIE JAHODA

SIBYLLE ESCALONA   GEORGE S. KLEIN

CHARLES FISHER   GARDNER LINDZEY

MERTON M. GILL   ROY SCHAFER

ROBERT S. WALLERSTEIN

SUZETTE H. ANNIN, *Editorial Assistant*

CONTENTS

1

STATEMENT OF PURPOSE

I should like to begin by giving as clear a statement as possible concerning the purpose of this essay. It is an attempt to make progress in psychoanalytic ego psychology by examining the concept of independent ego energies and by working out the consequences of this concept for the theory as a whole. My thesis is that the idea of ego energies independent of libidinal and aggressive instincts need no longer be regarded as a vague notion, that it is receiving substantial support and definition from research in animal and child behavior, and that if taken seriously it brings about significant improvements in psychoanalytic ego theory. I shall try to show what these changes are and why I believe them to be valuable for the further growth of ego psychology.

During the years since Freud's death there have been many attempts to push forward the line of inquiry with which he became concerned rather late in his career. These efforts have done a good deal to transform psychoanalysis from a theory of neurosis into the general theory of personality he hoped it would become. They have also reduced the gap between clinical and academic child psychologies, thus giving promise of still greater generality in our understanding of development. I believe, however, that the forward movement has been handicapped, and might even be brought to a halt, by conceptual difficulties having to do with the energies of the ego. Because energy is vested in instincts, and because the activities of the ego are clearly not instinctual, there has been an enduring problem of explaining the sources of power behind the vital and varied functions the ego performs. Quotations scattered through Freud's work show that he always entertained the possibility that the ego might have energies and satisfactions of its own, but nowhere is this thought developed beyond a sentence or two. On the

1

contrary, he spared no pains to derive everything possible from instinctual energies. What would happen if we tried it the other way around, so to speak: if we sought to form an intelligible idea of the nature of ego energies and showed what they could be expected to do by themselves or in conjunction with instincts? That is what I want to try in this essay.

In pursuit of this purpose it will be necessary first to examine the present position of psychoanalytic ego psychology. It would not be in point to reconstruct the entire history of this line of investigation, but something may be gained by looking at the current content of ego psychology, noticing the facts that have chiefly commanded attention, and considering the methods of observation that have yielded this body of facts. The psychoanalytic method, superbly designed to disclose the operations of id and superego, must be weighed afresh as an avenue to knowledge about the workings of the ego.

As a second step in this undertaking I shall briefly review those findings of recent research in animal and child psychology that bear on the concept of independent ego energies. It seems to me possible now to give a fairly specific content to this concept, organizing it around the idea of the attainment of competence through action and through learning about the consequences of action. The ego has always been understood to be that part of the personality that is in contact with reality and is modified by reality, so that it can exercise realistic control over the expression of impulse. I shall argue that an action theory is best equipped to make such attainments understandable, and I shall also try to show that the energies involved cannot be very well derived from erotic and aggressive instincts.

From this point onward my purpose will be to take up some of the main concepts and problems of psychoanalytic ego psychology and to show how they are affected by introducing the idea of an active ego serving the biological purpose of competence. Can we by this means improve our understanding of reality testing, control by reality, and the construction of a stable objective world? Can an action theory elucidate early ego deviations and define for us more precisely the place of the mother in the infant's early development? Can it help us with concepts such as identification? Can we form a more detailed picture of the sources of self-esteem, of ego strength, and of the history of fantasies of omnipotence? Can we, finally, attain a better grasp of such difficult concepts as anticathexis, the growth of structures, neutralization, and sublimation? I would not have embarked upon this essay if I were not convinced that ego psychology can be made simpler, more consistent, and more useful by introducing the idea of ego activity which I shall shortly describe. And if the result of this effort should be to diminish further the sense of separation between psychoanalytic and academic students of child development, we might look forward to faster collaborative progress in understanding the growth of personality.

While my case obviously rests on the whole content of the following chapters, readers will find at the end a condensed version of the argument.

2

THE CONTENT OF PSYCHOANALYTIC
EGO PSYCHOLOGY

The concept of the ego had a curious history in Freud's intellectual career. It made its appearance in his earliest writings on hysteria, where it was held responsible for defense against painful memories and affects. In a sense, the ego of this period anticipated Freud's final conception, advanced in 1923 in *The Ego and the Id*. Hartmann (1956a) finds strong intimations of the future in the "Project for a Scientific Psychology" (Freud, 1895), where the ego is characterized by a variety of functions, such as perception, memory, and thinking, that serve to establish relations with the external world. But these ideas, which belong in Freud's "prepsychoanalytic" stage and which represented no particular advance over prevailing conceptions, were in any event destined for almost complete eclipse during those years of rich discovery when the psychoanalytic method began to lay bare the astonishing secrets of sexuality and the unconscious. For a while the ego was turned into a class of instincts, standing in opposition to sexual instincts. Then came Freud's discoveries concerning narcissism, as a consequence of which the sexual instincts largely absorbed the ego instincts. Fortunately, psychoanalytic theory soon escaped the danger of drowning in instinctual dynamics. Defense emerged again as a major concern, and the ego made its return as a structural aspect of personality.

If the new ego of 1923 was in some respects like the old one of 1895, it yet represented a striking theoretical advance. The intervening years had provided the dynamics without which any psychological theory of the ego tends to be superficial and almost obvious. The relation of the ego to instinctual urges, the constant mediation between drives inside and conditions outside, could now for the

4

first time become objects of effective study. The conception of what the ego had to deal with had been revolutionized.

Freud was led back to the ego by his interest in the processes of defense, but he saw clearly that its central functions always turned upon the relation to reality. The ego, he wrote, "is that part of the id which has been modified by the direct influence of the external world . . . the ego seeks to bring the influence of the external world to bear upon the id and its tendencies, and endeavours to substitute the reality principle for the pleasure principle which reigns unrestrictedly in the id" (1923, p. 25). The statement is amplified but not basically changed in that brief work of his last years, *An Outline of Psychoanalysis:*

> The principal characteristics of the ego are these. In consequence of the relation which was already established between sensory perception and muscular action, the ego is in control of voluntary movement. It has the task of self-preservation. As regards *external* events, it performs that task by becoming aware of the stimuli from without, by storing up experiences of them (in the memory), by avoiding excessive stimuli (through flight), by dealing with moderate stimuli (through adaptation), and, finally, by learning to bring about appropriate modifications in the external world to its own advantage (through activity). As regards *internal* events, in relation to the id, it performs that task by gaining control over the demands of the instincts, by deciding whether they shall be allowed to obtain satisfaction, by postponing that satisfaction to times and circumstances favorable in the external world or by suppressing their excitations completely [1940, p. 15].

The conclusion is obvious; Freud stated it in yet another place when he wrote: "This relation to the external world is decisive for the ego" (1932, p. 106).

This conception of the ego serves to define the task of psychoanalytic ego psychology. An explanation must ultimately be found for the many and varied processes whereby the ego mediates between personal need and surrounding reality. It is possible to look upon this task as a logical extension of psychoanalytic theory designed to account for facts neglected in the excitement of opening the door on instinctual dynamics. This is quite in line with Freud's aspiration that psychoanalysis should provide a complete theory of personality and its development. But if we look upon the matter in this light, we must be careful to avoid a dangerous pitfall concerning method. To what extent can the ego be investigated by psycho-analytic methods? To what extent can a technique based on free association, superbly adapted to uncovering unconscious instinctual processes, be expected also to disclose the rather different activities of the ego?

This is not a simple question. Only a careful, discriminating answer can help us in our quest. I believe that we can arrive at such an answer by examining first the content of ego psychology at the time of Freud's death, when analytic therapy was still the chief source of information; then by considering the progress that has been made since 1939, looking especially at the assumptions that have seemed necessary, and at the additional information that has been consulted, in order to make ego psychology more equal to the tasks Freud assigned it.

EGO PSYCHOLOGY AT THE TIME OF FREUD'S DEATH

The Reality Principle

Freud's ultimate return to an interest in the ego was perhaps heralded in his paper of 1911 on the two principles in mental functioning, the pleasure principle and the reality principle. Although the paper was brief, and its author apologized for his "few remarks" (1911, p. 226) on so important a topic, the statement covers most of what he was ever to say specifically about the manner in which the ego learns about the nature of reality. The initial situation that prompts a break from the pleasure principle is one in which both gratification and hallucinated gratification fail. "Instead of it, the psychical apparatus had to decide to form a conception of the real circumstances in the external world and to endeavour to make a real alteration in them. . . . This setting-up of the *reality principle* proved to be a momentous step" (1911, p. 219). He went on to enumerate the requisite adaptations in the mental apparatus: the heightened importance of the sense organs and of consciousness, the activity of attention which "meets the sense-impressions half way" (p. 221), the storage of impressions in memory, the "impartial passing of judgement" (p. 221) instead of repressing unpleasant ideas, the use of motor discharge to alter reality, and the restraint of this activity by the processes of thought, which became possible through "raising the level of the whole cathectic process" (p. 221) and thus binding the energies. At the time, Freud thought of all this as going on in the ego instincts, but it will be noticed that he spoke of a *mental apparatus,* to which fairly consistently throughout his life he attributed certain functions that were not instinctual (Bibring, 1936).

We may regard these statements as ones of principle rather than of specific findings. He was not undertaking to explain, except by the barest suggestion, how such important business was carried on. Rapaport (1960) has pointed out that Freud in *The Interpretation of Dreams* (1900) worked out an explanation of attention and consciousness in terms of cathectic energy, though the energy in question was treated as a reservoir somewhat separate from the main sources of instinctual drive. Hints of this interest are found in his later writings (1925a, 1925b); in "Negation" he attempted to derive an intellectual function, judgment, "from the interplay of the primary instinctual impulses" (1925b, p. 239). But we know that his paper on consciousness, intended to form part of the series on metapsychology, was one of the manuscripts he did not find worthy of preservation (Jones, 1955). Thus it happened that learning about reality, and making reality effective in the guidance of behavior, never became more than minor and merely schematic parts of Freud's ego psychology.

Defense

The outstanding content of ego psychology, of course, was defense. Two of the most important books in the psychoanalytic literature, Freud's *Inhibitions, Symptoms and Anxiety* (1926) and Anna Freud's *The Ego and the Mechanisms of Defence* (1936), deal with this subject in great detail. It is clear that once Freud had arrived at his structural conception of id, ego, and superego, the problems of anxiety and defense were liberated for a major recasting. The gain for ego psychology is possibly best shown in Anna Freud's felicitous account of the conditions during analytic therapy under which it is possible to observe ego defenses directly, instead of reconstructing them long after they have happened. When the ego is in harmony with an id impulse and tries merely to promote it, we learn something about our instinctual life but little about the ego.

It is only when ego and id are in conflict that we can briefly catch the ego in its defensive operations. But this situation occurs often during analysis when an unwelcome id impulse forces its way into the free associations and the ego, no longer able to stand aside, institutes defensive steps that appear as resistances. At such moments the ego betrays its defensive secrets directly to the observer.

The briefest reminder of Freud's own work on defense will be sufficient at this point. Increasingly impressed by the central importance of anxiety in neurosis, he came to feel that he had not done justice to anxiety when he derived it by an economic process from the instinctual energies that were blocked by repression. He retracted this formula and replaced it by the theorem that anxiety is the cause of both repression and symptom formation. He further specified that anxiety is not to be conceived of as a phenomenon of the id but as an affect experienced by the ego. The anxiety pattern may be aroused at first automatically, as on the occasion of birth, but as we see it at work in repression the process has become rather different. The ego, being now somewhat organized, is usually able to perceive in advance the danger entailed by an impulse. In accordance with its tendency to repeat actively the situations in which it has been passively helpless, it now utilizes the incipient anxiety response as a danger signal and as a means of achieving timely repression. This is possible because the signal releases a mechanism of great power: the ego "has only to give a 'signal of unpleasure' in order to attain its object with the aid of that almost omnipotent institution, the pleasure principle" (1926, p. 92). Repression ensues through the normal operation of the pleasure-pain mechanism.

Freud was well aware that these assumptions put enormous power at the disposal of the ego. Using his earlier metaphor of the rider and the horse, in which the horse often carried the rider wherever it wanted to go, we must say that he had come to have a much greater respect for the ego's horsemanship. He saw that "the affect of anxiety occupies a unique position in the economy of the mind" (1926, p. 150). Through its use of the anxiety signal and the pleasure-pain mechanism the ego could bring about the total suppression of an instinctual impulse or, if not this, a major deformation of the impulse so that it must thereafter appear only in remote and unsatisfying derivatives. Freud had been gingerly about its power when he first introduced the ego as a structure or institution, but he soon recognized that in its defensive operations it was capable of tremendous influence over the instincts.

Neutralized Energies

This recognition did not, however, lead Freud to change his conception of the energies inherent in the ego. The pleasure-pain mechanism had always been conceived of as an affair of the id, indeed as its sole way of functioning. If the ego scanned the environment, inner or outer, and scented danger there, it used only such forces of its own as might be implied in the metaphor of an apparatus conveying signals to the dynamos of power in the id. But in *The Ego and the Id* Freud had been led to an additional hypothesis concerning ego energies. He arrived at his idea by considering cases in which love changed suddenly into hate, or hate into love—a difficult problem now that he had adopted the theory of Eros and Thanatos. He reflected, for example, on the instance of rivalry changing to homosexual love, which seemed to present an inexplicable direct transformation of one instinct into another. The difficulty could be solved by assuming an ambivalence from the start, and then by the further assumption that energies could be brought in to reinforce one side or the other. "We have reckoned," Freud wrote, "as though there existed in the mind—whether in the ego or in the id—a displaceable energy, which, neutral in itself, can be added to a qualitatively differentiated erotic or destructive impulse, and augment its total cathexis. Without assuming the existence of a displaceable energy of this kind we can make no headway" (1923, p. 44). As to the source of this neutral energy, he concluded that it "proceeds from the narcissistic store of libido—that it is desexualized Eros" (p. 44). Wherever located, this energy seems to be very much at the disposal of the ego, which alone can apprehend the circumstances, within and without, that would determine which side of the conflict should be favored.

The idea of neutralized energies seems to have grown rapidly in Freud's mind. In *Inhibitions, Symptoms and Anxiety* we find him using it to account for the attempts made by the ego to bind even the neurotic symptom into its coherent organization: "Its desexualized energy still shows traces of its origin in its impulsion to bind together and unify" (1926, p. 98). This concept represents his

nearest approach, except for scattered remarks that remained unde-
veloped, to attributing to the ego independent energies of its own.
He gave several reminders that the ego was, after all, basically a
part of the id, and this presumably gave it certain rights in the
energy system as a whole.

Identification

The desexualizing of an energy originally erotic would seem to be
a rather radical process deserving some explanation. The nearest
thing to an explicit statement lies in Freud's account of identification, which is of interest here also because he thought of identification as a very important process in the growth of the ego. The
original clue came from his study of melancholia in 1917, a dis-
order which he explained "by supposing that . . . an object which
was lost has been set up again inside the ego—that is, that an object-
cathexis has been replaced by an identification" (1923, p. 28). In
terms of energy this meant a "transformation of object-libido into
narcissistic libido which . . . obviously implies an abandonment of
sexual aims, a desexualization—a kind of sublimation, therefore"
(p. 30). This might be taken to imply that neutralization depends
upon a regression from object choice, but this merely states a condition rather than explaining a process.

In *The Ego and the Id* Freud stated that identification is frequent
and important especially in the early stages of development. It
entails a modification of the ego, which becomes more like the
object, and this allows one to say that "the character of the ego is
a precipitate of abandoned object-cathexes" (1923, p. 29). Freud
had already proposed in *Group Psychology and the Analysis of the
Ego* (1921) that identification is the earliest form of relation to an
object, preceding object cathexis. From these premises he developed
his well-known ideas concerning identification and love in the family
circle, culminating in the oedipus complex and the formation of
the superego.

Further Topics

The contributions to ego psychology made by Freud's colleagues
up to the time of his death consist mostly of elaborations of points
already made in his writings. Such, for example, was Ferenczi's
essay on "Stages in the Development of the Sense of Reality"

(1913), inspired by Freud's remarks about the reality principle together with his observation of the "omnipotence of thought" in obsessional neurotics. Ferenczi hypothesized a state of complete omnipotence—that is to say, wish fulfillment—in the womb, and traced three stages in the renunciation of this omnipotence through the influence of real situations in the baby's life. "In general the development of the reality-sense," he wrote, "is represented by a succession of repressions, to which mankind was compelled, . . . through adjustment to a demanded renunciation" (1913, p. 236). The theme was taken up by Fenichel (1937) who postulated "an eternal longing" to recover past states of omnipotence, a basic human need that is closely related to self-regard. Although self-regard is regulated by our sense of closeness to omnipotence, Fenichel reasoned that, since omnipotence originally implied the elimination of tension through wish fulfillment, we can conclude that supplies of nourishment and supplies of affection will become the actual regulators of self-regard.

Fenichel's paper was an attempt to summarize what had been learned up to 1937 about early ego development. Besides topics already mentioned, he took up the question of the earliest object and first cathexis of external objects. When the infant becomes capable of "realization of the fact that it takes an intervention by the external world to eliminate his hunger," this "leads to his first cathexis of longing in regard to the external objects in question." But since what is longed for is satisfaction, cathexis vanishes and sleep supervenes as soon as the object provides nourishment; hence, "the first 'affirmation' of the world is an intermediate aim on the way to its 'negation' " (1937, p. 29). Fenichel concerned himself also with other earliest manifestations: putting in the mouth and spitting out as the "basis of all perception"; introjection and projection in the course of separating ego and nonego; oral incorporation as the first model for identification.

Such, then, was ego psychology at the time of Freud's death. The relation to reality was agreed to be the central problem. Defense had been studied in detail and seemed well understood. The origins of omnipotent fantasies had been pointed out, the first knowledge of objects had been examined, and identification had been postulated as a prominent mechanism in the shaping of the ego. A variety of ego functions such as judgment and thought had been sketched in schematic fashion. Independent energies in the ego were mentioned only as a possibility, but Freud's theory of neutralized libidinal energies came close to providing the ego with a power station of its own.

LIMITS IMPOSED BY METHOD AND THEORY

Science deals with what can be observed, not with everything it would be nice to know in order to fill out a satisfying theory. We cannot hold it against the ego psychology of 1939 that it left a great many problems untouched. Freud's genius for discovery had continued to work; the findings on defense alone were a monumental scientific achievement. But it is also true of science that it has to keep up a pitiless self-criticism. It is never enough to defend the incompleteness of a set of discoveries by implying that more research in the same direction will presently solve all the puzzles. There is always another possibility, which is that the results are incomplete because of limits inherent in the method of observation or in the concepts used to support them. To know when this is so is of the utmost importance, because in these circumstances the optimistic belief that all will presently be revealed is simply not justified. It is possible that nothing more can be learned, and even that serious errors will be perpetuated, unless the limits of method and theory are recognized and the search is put upon a broader basis.

Examined in this spirit of scientific self-criticism, the ego psychology of 1939, it seems to me, was heading into great difficulties. The strongest testimony for this is the changes introduced by the next generation of psychoanalytic workers, whose ideas we shall presently examine. But the trouble already proclaims itself if we simply compare the content of ego psychology with the definition of the ego as Freud gave it.

The central function of the ego was the mediation between instinctual drive and surrounding circumstances. The ego was held to be modified by its contact with the environment. It came to understand the environment and to represent it so that its requirements would be taken into account in behavior. The processes whereby the ego achieved this relation to reality should thus have been a central concern. But they were not. The most remarkable feature of the ego psychology of 1939 is that it rarely aimed at this target and produced little information about it.

The great discoveries about defense show us how the ego musters energies and uses mechanisms to check and distort instinctual expression. The ego's relations to id and superego are worked out in detail, but its relation to reality, here chiefly the recognition of danger, is pretty much taken for granted. Indeed the defense mechanisms of the ego, as seen in neurotic patients, are primitive and inappropriate, being used on the basis of a very poor appreciation of current reality. The findings on defense thus deal mainly with what the ego does when terror has reduced it to primitive mechanisms. Identification is seen as an important principle of development, but how the ego changes itself to be like another person is not explained at all; the findings bear entirely on the situations and motives that elicit the process. The growth of the sense of reality is treated as a problem in instinctual frustration. Ferenczi dealt with it as a series of repressions of fantasies of omnipotence, as if the elimination of such fantasies automatically guaranteed an accurate, objective appraisal of reality. We find the ego deciding to form a conception of reality, recognizing that an external object intervenes to satisfy its needs, reliving actively what it has experienced passively, and synthesizing its various parts; but these significant activities, if explained at all, are interpreted only in terms of the expenditure of instinctual energies.

With the benefit of hindsight it is not hard to detect the reasons for this shooting around, rather than straight at, the target. I suggest two such reasons. The first is a question of method: the psychoanalytic method of observation is in most respects unsuitable for learning about the adaptive activities of the ego. The second is a question of concepts: certain of Freud's theories, derived only in part from the method, constitute real obstacles to thinking about the adaptive process.

Concerning the *psychoanalytic method of observation,* we must always bear in mind that it explicitly aims to reduce the activity of the ego. As Anna Freud expresses it, the ego "is required to eliminate itself, to refrain from criticizing the associations and to disregard the claims of logical connection, which are at other times held to be legitimate. The ego is, in fact, requested to be silent . . ." (1936, p. 12). Of course, the ego is unable to maintain this silence, but what calls it to action is a threat of some kind, usually the emergence of a dangerous id derivative or a threat to its protective organization. This creates the perfect laboratory for observing defensive operations. But we can hardly expect to learn in this way about the long historical course of adaptations that goes on in every person's life, adaptations which, when successful, often make the use of primitive defense mechanisms unnecessary.

The difficulty concerning method can be expressed in another way by saying that psychoanalysis was from the start an uncovering technique. Its momentous scientific triumphs were won by revealing what is unconscious. Freud, who had once criticized Adler for having a "mere ego psychology" (Jones, 1955), later wrote: "We should like to learn more about the ego, now that we know that it, too, can be unconscious in the proper sense of the word" (1923, p. 19). Freud thus recognized that the special genius of psychoanalysis lay in uncovering. But uncovering, in the proper psychoanalytic sense of the word, implies the removal of resistances and repressions so that impulse and fantasy can make their way into consciousness. It is wishes and fantasies that can be uncovered, and while some of them will shed light on certain aspects of the ego, they will clearly not have much to say about the processes whereby we develop a sense of reality. These may be unconscious, but not in the main because anxiety and defense have made them so.

Concerning the *concepts* used to explain the findings of psychoanalysis, we have to notice certain implications of a theory that places unusual emphasis on instincts. Freud conceived two basic instincts, Eros and Thanatos, to be "the ultimate cause of all activity" (1940, p. 19). Instincts supplied the energy for everything that was done by the mental apparatus, and the apparatus thus functioned in the service of instinctual aims. This exclusive powering of behavior by erotic and destructive instincts, to which an inherently powerless mental apparatus is at first subservient, leads straight into a serious difficulty about the development of a sense of reality. The full force of this difficulty is shown in Fenichel's idea that object cathexis vanishes with need reduction and that " 'affirmation' of the world is an intermediate aim on the way to its 'negation.' " If our interest in reality is the always transient one of gratifying an instinct, it is hard to explain the progress from knowledge of the world in its instinct-gratifying properties to knowledge of the world in its objective properties independent of our needs. The strongly instinctual trend in Freud's theory served, I believe, to discourage interest in studying anything beyond the very first steps in reality testing.

Another feature of the theory, this one closely tied to the method, may well have had an even more discouraging effect. Freud's theory of development placed very great emphasis on the earliest experiences. This emphasis is expressed in the concepts of fixation and regression, which so aptly accounted for the infantile character of neurotic symptoms and fantasies. It can indeed be said that a very important aspect of explanation in Freud's system is the showing of genetic roots: the demonstration that a piece of behavior, now troublesome and unrealistic, contains significant elements of repetition from an earlier time in life, when perhaps such behavior was appropriate. The possibility of interpretation in psychoanalysis depends upon these repetitive elements. Today's reaction to the analyst repeats yesterday's to the employer, last year's to the business rival, an earlier year's to the teacher, and a much earlier year's to the father in the oedipal situation. The search for the earliest experience as the pattern for later behavior was thus greatly encouraged: the first object choice, the first cathexis of an external object, oral incorporation as the model for identification, the experience of birth as establishing the anxiety reaction, the omnipotence of the child in the womb. We have all been made shrewd about the repetitive elements in human behavior.

The trouble is that adaptive behavior implies not repetition but change. Adaptive behavior does not literally repeat earlier patterns: it includes an accommodation to the present circumstances. This concept of normal growth through reality testing and change is implicit in psychoanalytic theory, but it came under direct observation only in the special case of the patient's improvement during treatment. The set established by the method was all in the opposite direction. What would there be to interpret if a person had responded differently to father, teacher, business rival, and employer, each time accommodating himself to the real differences among them? Obviously a therapist has little interest in searching for this kind of sequence, which does not produce illness or require treatment. Yet it is just such sequences that one would have to look for in order to understand ego development. Repetitions merely show the ego at its weakest moments.

The ego psychology of 1939 had made great progress in uncovering what there was to be uncovered about the ego. But it had not transcended the limits imposed by the psychoanalytic method of observation and by the supporting conceptual scheme. The need to break through these limits appeared almost at once in the work now to be reviewed.

EGO PSYCHOLOGY SINCE 1939

In glancing at what has happened to ego psychology since Freud's death we shall be concerned mainly with two questions. First, what new content has been introduced into psychoanalytic ego psychology? Second, how has this new content been related to the older parts of the theory, particularly to instinctual energies?

Hartmann's Contributions

In 1939 Heinz Hartmann published an essay now translated into English under the title *Ego Psychology and the Problem of Adaptation*. This essay, subsequently amplified by the author in a long series of theoretical papers, was a searching attempt to bring ego psychology back on target by emphasizing "those processes and working methods of the mental apparatus which lead to *adapted achievements*" (p. 6). Hartmann listed a number of such achievements: "perception, intention, object comprehension, thinking, language, recall-phenomena, productivity, . . . [the] phases of motor development, grasping, crawling, walking, . . . the maturation and learning processes implicit in all these" (p. 8). He pointed out that such developments take place to a substantial degree quite apart from instinctual conflicts. He urged that serious consideration be given in psychoanalytic theory to the many developmental events that take place in a "conflict-free ego sphere" (p. 8). His emphasis on adaptation gave a new prominence to the mental apparatus. The instinctual drives alone could not guarantee survival; one has to assume mediation by an innate ego apparatus if the infant is to meet successfully the "average expectable" environmental conditions (p. 23). The apparatus develops through maturation and learning, partly in situations of conflict but partly in circumstances that are conflict-free. The growth of locomotion, for example, is not necessarily caught up in struggles to obtain erotic or aggressive gratification or to avoid anxiety. Anna Freud (1952) has observed that walking becomes independent of instinctual conflict a few weeks after its beginning, thereafter serving the child impartially in conflictful and conflict-free situations.

In "Notes on the Reality Principle" (1956b), Hartmann pointed out that Freud's account of the transition from the pleasure principle to the reality principle contained important hidden assumptions. Putting off a present for a future pleasure implies two processes, postponement and anticipation, that cannot be conjured up from the mere fact that an instinctual drive is frustrated. The function of postponement or control of discharge may be a very elementary one, but its presence demonstrates that "some preparedness for dealing with reality precedes those experiences Freud referred to" (p. 35). The developing ego apparatus, in short, makes an independent contribution to the growth of a sense of reality, not only at the beginning but throughout life. It is obvious what this implies for the content of ego psychology.

With respect to the energies involved in autonomous ego development, Hartmann seems hospitable to the idea that the ego apparatus might have energies of its own and that "the activities . . . that constitute the reality principle can be pleasurable in themselves" (1956b, p. 33). He is not, however, more hospitable than Freud, who admitted such possibilities without turning them to systematic use. For the purposes of systematic theory Hartmann has consistently preferred to employ Freud's idea of neutralization. In conjunction with Kris and Loewenstein (1949), he carried this idea a logical step forward by proposing that the energies of both erotic and aggressive instincts could be neutralized and thus placed' at the disposal of the ego for purposes more complex than immediate gratification. It is through neutralization of instinctual energies that we are able to be interested in the environment in its own right, according to its own lawful connections. Elevated to a general principle rather than an occasional happening, the doctrine of neutralization permits the ego to have independent energies without challenging Freud's theory of the instincts.

Hendrick's, Kardiner's, and Mittelmann's Contributions

To the minds of certain other workers the problem of ego energies has seemed to require a more revolutionary solution. The strongest move in this direction was made by Hendrick (1942, 1943a, 1943b), who proposed an *instinct to master*. It is interesting to notice that Hendrick suggested an enlargement of the content of ego psychology that is very similar to Hartmann's suggestion. To him, the ego is eventually integrated out of functions such as learning to suck, to manipulate, to walk, to speak, to comprehend, and to reason. These functions all have to do with mastering some aspect of the environment, and they yield "primary pleasure" when efficient action "enable[s] the individual to control or alter his environment" (1943a, p. 311), quite apart from the sensual value of his activity. Hendrick believed that theory would be clarified by postulating "an inborn drive to do and to learn how to do" (1942, p. 40), a mastery instinct that supplied the power for those numerous and extended feats of learning whereby the helpless infant turns into the skillful, adapted adult.

Kardiner's work on the development of the effective ego represents a similar expansion of content, though no explicit hypothesis is proposed concerning energy sources. The traumatic neuroses of war, wherein the dominant threat is to self-preservation and the symptoms are often lodged in action systems, convinced him that study should be directed to the growth of adaptive behavior. Action systems gradually become integrated so as to maintain "controlled contact" with the environment and "controlled exploitation of objects in the outer world" (Kardiner and Spiegel, 1947, p. 260). Such integration is favored by successful and gratifying experiences of mastery; it is injured and disrupted by frustrations. Kardiner's thinking thus takes a line similar to Hartmann's concerning the "conflict-free ego sphere."

In like vein, Mittelmann (1954) drew attention to the importance of motility in the growth of personality. He pointed out the "driven" character of motor behavior, such as manipulation and locomotion, during the second and third years. He showed further that the child's motility has much to do with the evolution of assertiveness and self-esteem, and that it is "one of the most important aspects of reality testing" (pp. 159-160). On the question of energies he regarded motility as an urge in its own right analogous to oral, excretory, or genital urges, a partial instinct which for a period of life "dominates all other urges" (p. 145). Once again we find the content of ego psychology expanded in a now familiar direction, and we confront yet another solution to the problem of energies thus created.

Erikson's Contributions

Erik H. Erikson has gone much further than anyone else in filling out a picture of ego development. His well-known eight stages, presented first in *Childhood and Society* (1950) and amplified in *Identity and the Life Cycle* (1946-1956), are the result of a searching attempt to establish the part played by the surrounding culture in individual growth. Erikson sees parents not only as individuals with their own traits but also as transmitters of cultural expectations. In both capacities they undertake to regulate the child's behavior, but in view of the interactive nature of all human relations this is seen as a process of *mutual regulation* to which the child's activity makes a significant contribution. In the back of the parents' minds there may be a cultural timetable of what to expect of the child at each stage, but the child's developing behavior plays an indispensable part in evoking these successive expectations. The stages in the growth of the ego are thus determined from the child's side by his evolving sensorimotor capacities and cognitive grasp as well as by the instinctual developments postulated by Freud. Once more we find the facts of sensorimotor development being summoned to assist in building psychoanalytic ego psychology.

Erikson's account is the first one to do justice in more than a schematic way to both the processes of inner development and the influence of the social and cultural surroundings. He has not been explicitly concerned with the energies involved in sensorimotor growth, but he has undertaken to place the whole problem on a much broader basis than the one specified in Freud's stages of libidinal development. Erikson sees Freud's formulation as one that was too narrowly conceived in terms only of pleasure seeking and erogenous zones. In his own analysis he introduces the concept of *modes*, referring to generalized patterns of behavior in the motor and cognitive spheres. Zone and mode are all of a piece, so to speak. Hence the progression from oral to anal to phallic stages is rather strongly determined by a general ripening of sensorimotor capacity as a whole, with harmonious cooperation from changes in zonal sensitivity. The first predominant mode of behavior is incorporative; then, as manipulative and motor prowess grow, there is an advance to retentive and eliminative modes; a little later, with increasing mastery of locomotion and language and with an expanding imagination, the child's behavior as a whole becomes dominated by the intrusive mode. The next stage, one of latency in Freud's zonal conception, is for Erikson highly important in its own right, being the time when the child, no longer satisfied with play and make-believe, wants to be able to participate in actions having significance in the adult world—to develop a *sense of industry*. At this point the zonal contribution to ego development seems to be of small importance, though it reappears again at puberty.

It is not easy to interpret this account in terms of the psychoanalytic theory of energies. The growth of motor and cognitive capacities would appear to be "neutral" with respect to instinctual aims, but the obvious similarities between modes and zonal impulses suggest some subtle kind of libidinal involvement. Perhaps Freud's idea of Eros is broad enough to wrap around this whole thing, but then the concept of instinctual drive becomes vastly generalized and cannot any longer be defined in terms of specific aims and somatic sources. Erikson's contribution, so vital in scope and rich in detail, has had such a strong and favorable effect on ego psychology that one cannot hold this one point of unclearness very much against it. But the unclearness happens to come just at the spot which is the central problem of this essay.

Conclusions

In this rapid glance at the progress of psychoanalytic ego psychology since 1939 I have attended particularly to two points: the additional content brought in for fuller understanding of the ego, and the relation of this content to the earlier conceptual scheme, especially to the theory of instinctual drives.

With respect to the first point the contributors are in conspicuous agreement. They leave little doubt about what must be introduced if the ego's relation to reality is to be fully grasped. Everywhere the story is the same: we must draw into the picture the facts of manipulation, locomotion, language, the mastery of motor skills, the growth of cognition, the emergence of higher thought processes, indeed the whole putting together of man's complex repertory of adaptive behavior. Only thus can we direct our efforts at the target indicated in Freud's concept of the ego. These facts are, of course, to a considerable extent the familiar materials of academic child psychology. To admit them implies that the psychoanalytic method has to be supplemented by other methods of observation. Various writers in the psychoanalytic tradition have begun to examine seriously the work of developmental psychologists such as Piaget; others have adopted experimental methods; and some have undertaken systematic direct observation of growth, hoping to surprise new secrets by looking simultaneously with the eyes of Gesell and of Freud. The direction in which one must move in order to build an ego psychology is no longer in question.

With respect to theory, however, there is very little agreement. The attempt to accommodate the new content in traditional psychoanalytic theory has not produced a chorus of harmonious sounds. It is not hard to see why. The adaptive activities of the ego do not on the face of it show any clear and regular relation to instinctual aims. When a child plays for a solid hour with shovel, pail, and sand, digging and transporting the sand, pouring and piling it, fashioning roads and mountains and castles, when he struggles laboriously to climb a steep bank or get into the upper branches of a tall tree, when he experiments with speech sounds and tries out the effects of new combinations of words, it is not in the least obvious that these actions constitute a movement toward erotic or aggressive goals. What seems to be most clearly accomplished by the child's persistent activity is a steady gain in dealing effectively with the environment. Adaptive activity often appears to go on under its own power, as if it were an end in itself.

To say this is not to deny the possibility of an ultimate connection. The symptoms of neurosis had no obvious connection with instinctual drives until psychoanalysis disclosed the underlying erotic and aggressive fantasies. But it does not follow automatically that the same type of connection can be shown for ego functions, and in any event the problem remains one of establishing a relation between the instinctual aims that Freud considered basic and a whole realm of behavior that does not seem to work in the service of these aims. We can expect disagreement over such a task.

Some of the contributors evidently believe that the connection is impossible. Hendrick by postulating an instinct to master, and Mittelmann by hypothesizing a partial instinct of motility, take the stand that erotic and aggressive instincts in their usual meanings cannot be conceived of as supplying all the energy for the growth of ego functions. Others, like Erikson and Kardiner, pursue their study of the ego without taking any stand on energy sources; they seem to feel no compelling necessity to square things with Freud's instinct theory. But there are still others who support the connection and undertake to elucidate its nature. They accomplish this in one or more of three ways. (1) Encouraged, perhaps, by Freud's speculations, they give erotic and aggressive instincts a greatly expanded definition, making it possible to include certain kinds of adaptive behavior as direct expressions of instinct. Spitz (1953), for example, includes grasping under aggression even when it is not experienced as hostility and does not aim at destruction, while Kardos and Peto (1956) identify all play with pregenital libidinal activity. (2) Encouraged, perhaps, by Freud's perspicacious observations on play (1920), they hypothesize a symbolic erotic or aggressive meaning behind all the actions that contribute to the building of ego functions. The child's play with sand, for example, will symbolize from moment to moment the oral, anal, and sadistic urges that are basic to his being. (3) Finally, this time clearly encouraged by the lead Freud gave, they postulate a process whereby erotic and aggressive energy can be neutralized or divested of its original aim so that it becomes available for ego functions. Hartmann especially has developed this idea, which can be seen to involve a certain concession to the doubters: if we are to power ego activities with instinctual energy, we must somehow get rid of instinctual aims.

Such diversity of opinion surely signifies that the energy problem is difficult. The one hypothesis that has not yet, it seems to me, been given a sufficient trial is one that assumes independent ego energies but does not try to give them the character of instincts. This hypothesis has enjoyed an active life in Freud's and Hartmann's footnotes. I shall now try the experiment of putting it in the main text. It lies, I should say, directly between Hendrick and

Hartmann: it assumes an independent source of energy without casting it as an instinct, and it assumes "neutral" energies without deriving them by transformation from erotic and aggressive instincts. The plausibility of such an assumption has been greatly increased in the last few years by new turns of events in the study of animal behavior and of child development. Let us see what assistance they can bring.

3

A WAY OF CONCEIVING OF
INDEPENDENT EGO ENERGIES:
EFFICACY AND COMPETENCE

In this chapter I shall try to develop a conception of independent ego energies that can be of use to psychoanalytic theory. In calling such energies "independent" and in connecting them particularly with the "ego" I am following customary psychoanalytic usage. Energies can be described as pertaining especially to the ego when they have to do with adaptation and with the governing of behavior by reality. They can be described as independent if they do not come from either erotic or aggressive instincts, in other words, if they are not part of the two fundamental instinctual drives postulated by Freud. In the terms of drive theory in academic psychology, it would be said that the energies in question do not come from the commonly recognized primary drives such as hunger, thirst, sex, and the avoidance of pain. Recognizing this independence should not be taken to imply that we are concerned with forces which are somehow not fundamental or primary, nor should it be interpreted as an attempt to depart from a biological framework. I shall try show that independent ego energies are as basic as anything in human nature, and that they have a clear significance for survival.

While our concern is mainly with human beings, it is worth pointing out that some of the same problems have recently been under discussion in animal psychology. It will profit us to start with animal behavior where the issues can be more sharply drawn.

24

Exploration and Play in Animals

It requires no special study to appreciate the fact that many animals are given to exploration, manipulation, and playful activity. If there is a puppy in the house its playfulness will detract noticeably from one's scholarly work, and even if one allows a quiet, well-fed cat to sit purring on one's writing table it will not be long before pencils and erasers are delicately moved into a position where they may serve to demonstrate the properties of freely falling bodies. Keen observers of animals have often recorded more extensive examples of this propensity to play. Konrad Lorenz (1952), for instance, gives a memorable description of the games played by jackdaws in high winds. Far from seeking cover, the birds can be observed shooting up, down, and around at amazing speeds.

> . . . it is a game, in the most literal sense of the word: practised movements, indulged in and enjoyed for their own sake and not for the achievement of a special object. And rest assured, these are not merely inborn, purely instinctive actions, but movements that have been carefully learned. . . .
>
> And look what they do with the wind! At first sight, you, poor human being, think that the storm is playing with the birds, like a cat with a mouse, but soon you see, with astonishment, that it is the fury of the elements that here plays the role of the mouse and that the jackdaws are treating the storm exactly as the cat its unfortunate victim. Nearly, but only nearly, do they give the storm its head, let it throw them high, high into the heavens, till they seem to fall upwards, then, with a casual flap of a wing, they turn themselves over, open their pinions for a fraction of a second from below against the wind, and dive—with an acceleration far greater than that of a falling stone—into the depths below. Another tiny jerk of the wing and they return to their normal position and, on close-reefed sails, shoot away with breathless speed into the teeth of the gale, . . . this all playfully and without effort. . . . [The wind] itself must perform the work of propelling the birds through the air at a rate of well over 80 miles an hour; the jackdaws do nothing to help beyond a few lazy adjustments of their black wings. Sovereign control over the power of the elements, intoxicating triumph of the living organism over the pitiless strength of the inorganic! [pp. 128-129].

Gavin Maxwell, in *Ring of Bright Water* (1960), speaks of the "perpetual play" of otters, observable both in the wild state and when they are kept as pets.

Mij would spend hours shuffling a rubber ball around the room like a four-footed soccer player using all four feet to dribble the ball, and he could also throw it, with a powerful flick of the neck, to a surprising height and distance. These games he would play either by himself or with me, but the really steady play of an otter, the time filling play born of a sense of well-being and a full stomach, seemed to me to be when the otter lies on his back and juggles with small objects between his paws. This they do with extraordinarily concentrated absorption and dexterity, as though a conjurer were trying to perfect some trick, as though in this play there were some goal the human observer could not guess [p. 86].

In the heyday of the theory that animal behavior is motivated exclusively by the primary viscerogenic drives, this kind of activity was not seen as challenging the basic proposition. There was always the possibility that some visceral drive was obscurely at work, that some subtle avoidance of anxiety was involved, or that the behavior had been secondarily reinforced because of a previous connection with drive-reducing consummations. When most research on animal learning was being done with hungry, sexually aroused, or frightened animals, the facts of play and exploration did not strongly obtrude themselves, and hypotheses like secondary reinforcement could hopefully be supposed to cover all contingencies.

About twenty years ago, however, there was a marked renewal of interest in animal curiosity. Primary-drive theory was first somewhat shaken by a series of findings on "incidental learning." If well-fed, sexually satisfied, comfortable animals were allowed to wander in mazes or problem boxes, they learned something about them and could deal with them more effectively on a later occasion when a primary drive was active. Since drive reduction was held to be essential for learning, these results offered something of a paradox and led to considerable controversy (Thistlethwaite, 1951). Older ideas concerning an instinct of curiosity and an exploratory drive were brought back to life, and a whole series of investigations was directed at this aspect of animal behavior. Summaries of this now extensive work can be found in Butler (1958), Berlyne (1960), and Welker (1961).

Exploratory behavior on the part of rats was studied by Berlyne (1950) by putting the animals in unfamiliar places and later introducing a variety of unfamiliar objects. Each novelty evoked characteristic behavior of approaching, sniffing, and examining from all sides. Interest in any one object lasted only for a short while, but the introduction of a fresh novelty brought an immediate renewal of exploratory action. Montgomery (1954) placed rats in a simple maze offering the choice between a blind alley with quick return to the living quarters and another alley that led into further unfamiliar maze territory suitable for exploration. The animals learned to favor this second alley in preference to the first. With a similar design Miles (1958) has shown that kittens reared in small cages, which more or less prevented play, would learn to prefer the route that led them to balls of paper, pieces of string, and other choice feline toys. Young chimpanzees were used as subjects by Welker (1956), who gave the animals various pairs of objects to see what they would do with them and which ones they would prefer. Initial uneasiness was sometimes apparent, but eventually each object would be picked up and carefully explored, then discarded. More time was spent upon objects that were big and bright and that could be moved, changed, and made to emit sounds and light.

In such experiments the attempt is made to rule out the participation of primary drives by satisfying them beforehand. When the animal subjects are tested they are well fed, sexually inactive or satisfied, apparently comfortable, and not noticeably anxious after the first few moments in a new situation. Yet their behavior cannot be properly described as merely random, idle, or restless, nor can it be interpreted simply as responses to proffered stimulation. It exhibits qualities of direction, selection, and persistence that are generally taken as signs that behavior is motivated. Given a choice, the animals elect to go where they will encounter objects and novel surroundings, where there will be an increase of stimulation rather than the quickest possible return to inactivity. It has been shown by Butler and Harlow (1957), in an experiment with monkeys, that a whole series of learned discriminations can be built up on the basis of a reward which consists only of opening a window so that the animal can look out at the normal comings and goings of the entrance room to the laboratory. The learning pattern is highly similar to what has often been produced by sexual or food rewards.

It is never possible, of course, to prove beyond peradventure that no primary drive has been at work in a given experiment of this kind. Critics have argued that the monkeys in Butler and Harlow's experiment might feel isolated and anxious in a closed cage and might experience a reduction of anxiety through the opening of the window. But similar results have by now been produced many times under different conditions; criticism of individual experiments cannot easily blind us to the weight and trend of the evidence.

Moreover, it is possible to discern certain common features in what seems to be sought in manipulative and exploratory behavior. When novelty is involved, the animal behaves in such a way as to establish a new relation between himself and the object, a relation in which actions have been tried and their consequences discovered so that he knows what he can do with the object and what it will do to him. Furthermore, acting in this way upon objects does not necessarily cease when the novelty has worn off. Harlow (1953) reports upon an experiment in which rhesus monkeys showed a rather striking persistence of interest in a manipulative problem even though it led to no reward beyond itself. He installed in the living cage a hasp that could be raised by removing both a hook and a pin. In spite of the fact that the hasp opened no doors and produced no extraneous rewards, the monkeys would return to it and solve it afresh as many as seven or eight times in the course of several days. Doing something to the environment, producing effects upon it and changes in it, seem to stand in this experiment as rewards in their own right. This is even more striking when we notice the preference displayed by animals like Welker's chimpanzees for objects upon which it is possible to have large effects. Monkeys prefer paper and wood, which can be torn or bitten, to more refractory objects made of plastic or metal (Carr and Brown, 1959; Cho and Davis, 1957). The most striking illustration of this principle is provided by a series of experiments summarized by Welker (1961, p. 210) showing that mice, rats, and monkeys can all learn to push levers or take some other form of arbitrary action when the only consequence is either an increase or a decrease in the intensity of light. The animals, we might say, like bored children, amuse themselves by snapping the light switch on and off just for the fun of having some effect upon something.

In trying to conceptualize this body of new findings about exploration and manipulation in animals, many workers have proposed that we simply assume an additional primary drive, an exploratory drive, or perhaps a manipulative one. It is worth noticing that this procedure is strictly parallel to Ives Hendrick's procedure in assuming an instinct to master. I shall consider presently, after I have examined material from child development, the difficulties created by this solution to the problem. Suffice it to say here that the assumption of a new drive, justified as it may seem to be by the directionality and persistence of exploratory behavior and by the manner in which learning is reinforced, raises great difficulties concerning the substantive meaning of drive. This is a problem for academic drive theory and psychoanalytic instinct theory alike. Exploration does not resemble any other primary drive with respect to somatic sources, specificity of aims, or the pattern of consummation and drive reduction. It can scarcely be defined at all in these terms. For the moment let us assume merely that animal play and exploration may have to be referred to an energy that is independent of drives.

PLAY AND INVESTIGATION IN YOUNG CHILDREN

When we turn our attention from animals to young children we are at once confronted by certain striking similarities. Children also engage in manipulative and exploratory activity which in the earliest years is not unlike that of the animals. They investigate novelties, they try to produce effects on the environment; they tear paper, experiment with locks, and play with light switches. In a book that has become a classic, Karl Groos (1901) spoke of the child's "joy in being a cause," shown in his delight in making a lot of noise, moving everything around, and playing with mud, sand, and puddles where extensive effects could be produced. Intensive observational studies such as those of Preyer (1888), Sully (1896), and Stern (1914) continue to be of value with respect to such behavior, but there are also more recent systematic studies of growth such as those of Gesell and his associates (1943, 1946) and the very fine experimental work of Jean Piaget (1936, 1937, 1945). A substantial amount of this work bears in one way or another on behavior that can be classified as play, exploration, or manipulation. A brief sampling of observations will assist our present inquiry.

Much as the newborn infant is dominated by needs for food,

avoidance of pain, and oral-erotic pleasure, there are times in his waking life when he seems to be functioning merely as an explorer. Wolff (1959) finds evidences of this kind even in the days immediately after birth. Gesell and Ilg (1943) call attention to a kind of visual exploration at four weeks, shown in staring at lights and windows; sometimes there are signs of anger if the baby is turned on the side away from the light. A few weeks later there will be an interest in strong colors: "Intense crying may be controlled by having a bright-colored cretonne pillow to gaze upon" (p. 99). At sixteen weeks the infant spends a certain amount of time in physical activity such as kicking, clasping the hands, rolling to one side, and rotating the head from side to side; he also appears to take delight in vocalizing. Such activity is often accompanied by signs of pleasure such as gurgling and laughing, and it occurs typically in spare time when hunger and other discomforts are not in evidence. The available amount of spare time increases steadily until at the end of the first year it comes to something like six hours a day. The year-old child makes a substantial investment of his time in the playful exploration of his surroundings.

Around the middle of the first year comes what Gesell and Ilg call "the heyday for manipulation," when grasping becomes an eager and intent business. At twenty-eight weeks one can observe something like the following as the child plays with a clothespin:

> [The child] wants to finger the clothespin, to get the feel of it. He puts it to his mouth, pulls it out, looks at it, rotates it with a twist of the wrist, puts it back into his mouth, pulls it out, gives it another twist, brings up his free hand, transfers the clothespin from hand to hand, bangs it on the high chair tray, drops it, recovers it, retransfers it from hand to hand, drops it out of reach, leans over to retrieve it, fails, fusses a moment, then bangs the tray with his empty hand. . . . He is never idle because he is under such a compelling urge to use his hands for manipulation and exploitation [1943, pp. 108-109].

As his expertness develops, the child complicates the process of feeding by exploring the utensils, playing with spilled food, and busying himself with toys, as if the slow process of eating were not sufficient to occupy his energies. In due course his accomplishments will extend to creeping, then walking, then all kinds of more complicated and athletic methods of locomotion. These things, too, have the quality of eager and intent business, as Mittelmann

(1954) pointed out so clearly. When successful they are likely to be accompanied by signs of delight, and failure or frustration may elicit strong evidences of anger.

The nature of manipulative activity is illuminated by Piaget's highly detailed observations of his own three children. Watching his infant son Laurent, then three months and ten days old, he saw him capture by chance a chain connected with suspended rattles; this was followed by gazing at the rattles, repeating the movement many times, and accompanying the peals of the rattles with peals of laughter. Three days later the following observation is recorded:

> . . . Laurent by chance strikes the chain while sucking his fingers . . . he grasps it and slowly displaces it while looking at the rattles. He then begins to swing it very gently which produces a slight movement of the hanging rattles and an as yet faint sound inside them. Laurent then definitely increases by degrees his own movements: he shakes the chain more and more vigorously and laughs uproariously at the result obtained [1936, p. 185].

Laurent's return to the rattles may well remind us of Harlow's monkeys returning to the problem of the hasp. Piaget's descriptions of young children exploring the properties of new objects can be matched with Welker's account of young chimpanzees when similarly confronted by novelties. No doubt the activity of somewhat older children on playground slides and jungle gyms can be seen as similar to that of jackdaws in high winds, though here a closer analogy is provided by skiing on steep slopes or canoeing in white water. But Piaget gives us also examples of a kind of graded and persistent experimental activity which, while it may remind us a little of a cat's delicate use of its paws, carries us over quite easily to the behavior of the seasoned adult human scientist. Laurent, for instance, when still a month short of his first birthday, made persistent studies of the behavior of falling bodies. This he did by holding up at arm's length his toy swan, bits of bread, and other convenient objects, and letting them fall first from one position, then from another. Even before thought processes are formed and anchored by language it is possible to display the spirit of Galileo.

The child's playful and exploratory activities can be seen in an even clearer light through a series of observations made by Stott

(1961) on his son between the ages of two and one half and eighteen months. From very detailed records Stott abstracted "those items which seemed unrelated to any organic need," but which nevertheless gave evidence of being motivated rather than random. Motivation was attested by the following types of evidence:

> ... (i) concentration of attention, (ii) perseverance or unambiguous repetition, (iii) expressions of gratification concomitant with a given result, (iv) expressions of annoyance at failure, (v) precedence over satisfaction of organic needs such as eating and drinking or avoidance of physical hurt; or displacement of eating and drinking habits more effective than the new experimental mode in satisfying the need [1961, p. 97].

The behavior recorded by Stott as fulfilling the necessary conditions—motivated, but not by a known organic need—includes a wide range of activity. It begins at twelve weeks with the infant's careful study of his hand movements, continues with various instances of manipulating objects and intently watching the movements of other people, includes successive experiments with crawling, walking, and moving things about, and ends with such items as "tears up paper-covered book," "carries coal-hammer about house and thumps it on floor," and "twists knobs of wireless set." Stott then analyzes these activities in terms of the effects they produce upon the environment and upon the child's relation to the environment. Seen in this way, the behavior promotes "a general *relationship of effectiveness* which the child seeks to maintain or establish between itself and its environment" (p. 103). This is the one thing that is consistent about it. Some of the acts were perhaps socially encouraged, but others were done in defiance of adults and at the risk of punishment. Those acts that were connected with an organic need, such as experimental attempts at self-feeding, resulted in a poorer satisfaction of the organic need. The whole series of behaviors finds its most probable meaning in the forwarding of a relationship of effectiveness.

These studies of playful and investigatory behavior in young children bring us to the same point that we reached with animals. The behavior we have been examining cannot easily be referred to primary drives. It does not conform to the pattern of a drive with respect to such features as somatic source, preferred objects, and consummatory aim; thus we cannot expect to forward our understanding merely by postulating an additional primary drive. If we took the human material alone, we might be inclined to impute symbolic erotic or aggressive meanings to each of the acts, but the strong parallels in animal behavior show that this sort of interpretation cannot be biologically fundamental. Yet the behavior is certainly motivated. It is pursued with concentration, persistence, and signs of satisfaction and frustration, and it occupies a great deal of time in the child's life. Clearly it has to do with effective dealing with reality, and it belongs in just those parts of the human repertory that have recently come to be seen as fundamental for ego psychology.

The playful, exploratory, manipulative behavior of animals and young children provides us, I believe, with the clearest body of facts upon which to build a conception of independent ego energies.

EFFECTANCE AND COMPETENCE

Effectance and Feeling of Efficacy

The thesis will now be advanced that the kinds of behavior described in this chapter are motivated by energies independent of instinctual drives. In psychoanalytic terms we can conceive of them as energies that are inherent in the mental or ego apparatus. They will be claimed and utilized from time to time by the demands of an instinctual drive; all drives must make use of the apparatus on their way to a suitable consummation. When not thus claimed they will operate in their own way, and this way is most plainly revealed in exploratory and manipulative behavior, which seems to perform the service of maintaining and expanding an effective interaction with the environment. Closely studied, such behavior repeatedly shows characteristics of activity, effort, and the production of some kind of effect. Even when the infant is merely fixating an object in vision, he is making an active effort and is producing the effect of a clearer image. When he begins to touch and handle things, the changes in his images will be the consequence of actual effects on the real environment. The inherent energies of the ego apparatus prompt the child to keep trying out the effectiveness of his ripening capacities for action.

For this reason I propose that we refer to the energies in question as *effectance*. Perhaps this will not ultimately seem to be a good word, but as a temporary designation I think there is something to be said for it. In academic psychology, with its strong historical roots in the philosophical problem of knowledge, there has long been a tendency to consider the organism's relation to its environment mainly in terms of cognition. The investigator has asked how knowledge becomes imprinted and stored, as if the biological goal were a bulging warehouse of information to be enjoyed as a miser delights in his gold. The word *effectance* has the virtue of opposing this distortion and, in line with Piaget and other recent workers, placing emphasis on action and its consequences. The living organism does not typically sit and learn. It learns through action, and what it learns is a design or readiness for future action.

Perhaps these statements will arouse misgivings that effectance is going to be used in an old-fashioned teleological sense. I do not want to imply that young animals and children play and explore because of a desire to practice useful skills and prepare for future contingencies. They play and explore because it is fun—because there is something inherently satisfying about it—not because it is going to have value at some future time. The same, of course, is true of the sexual drive. Its biological significance lies in the reproduction of the species, but we do not suppose that animals are influenced by this abstract thought, and there are plenty of times when intelligent human beings forget Nature's larger plan. The dynamics of sexual behavior are basically here and now, consisting of tensions, discharges, and affective experiences of the immediate present. The dynamics of effectance are equally present and immediate. Playful exploration and manipulation take place because one feels inclined toward such behavior and finds it naturally satisfying.

The nature of the satisfaction requires careful scrutiny. It is not possible to assimilate it to any scheme that equates pleasure with the reduction of tension. A generation ago the equation of pleasure, learning, and drive reduction seemed to have the properties of a general law. But Freud in his later years came to doubt the connection, and during the last fifteen years a substantial number of experiments with animals has shown that drive reduction is not an essential condition for learning. Animals will learn, for instance, to choose a sweet-tasting substance that has no food value and thus does not reduce the hunger drive (Sheffield and Roby, 1950).

They will learn, as we have seen, to elect routes that lead them into territory for exploration in preference to routes that lead to quiescence. When we put beside these findings the well-known human tendency to be bored by monotony and to crave variety and excitement, it is clear that in some circumstances satisfaction is correlated with increases of arousal or tension (White, 1959). Theory today has been released from the strait jacket that pleasure and learning must always imply drive reduction.

Thus liberated, we can examine without prejudice the satisfaction that goes with effectance. Taking into account not only stimulation and perception but also action, effort, and the production of effects, I shall call the accompanying experience a *feeling of efficacy*. It might be described as a feeling of doing something, of being active or effective, of having an influence on something; but these phrases probably do not help much to amplify the original expression. My thesis is that the feeling of efficacy is a primitive biological endowment as basic as the satisfactions that accompany feeding or sexual gratification, though not nearly as intense. We are most familiar with the feeling of efficacy at a level of behavior where we act with intentions to produce particular effects. We feel efficacious when we throw the ball over the plate, swim to the raft, or mend the broken household appliance. But the feeling does not have to be connected with the achievement of a particular intended result. With exploratory behavior, where results cannot be anticipated, it seems a better guess to say that feelings of efficacy accompany the whole process of producing effects. The activity is satisfying in itself, not for specific consequences.

The ideas just expressed are congruent with those advanced by Piaget in his discussion of the beginnings of causality in young children (1937, Chapter 3). We recall that Karl Groos had spoken of the child's "joy in being a cause." On the basis of detailed observations during the first few months of life, Piaget concludes that the child's earliest conception of causality arises from feelings associated with his own actions.

> . . . ever since the first contacts with the external environment, the child is active . . . ever since the beginnings of his mental life, [the little child] conceives of his own effort as the cause of every phenomenon. . . . Primitive causality may therefore be conceived as a sort of feeling of efficiency or of efficacy linked with acts as such. . . .

[Since at this time there is no distinction between self and object] the point of departure of causality should . . . be sought in a diffuse feeling of efficacy which would accompany the activity itself but would be localized by the child, not in a self, but in the point of culmination of the action [1937, pp. 225, 227-228].

The existence of energies of the kind here called effectance has a clear meaning in terms of adaptation and survival. Hartmann (1939) has pointed out that instincts alone would not guarantee survival; we have to assume adaptive mechanisms already present in the ego apparatus if we are to explain the child's survival even in average expectable environments. We have to assume in addition, it seems to me, an energy intrinsic to the apparatus that guarantees its constant use in finding out about the environment and in learning what effects can be had upon it. In the human case there are not nearly enough innate patterns of behavior to achieve survival. Only through long-sustained cumulative learning can the child become competent to deal with his surroundings. Studies of the growth of perception led Hebb (1949) to the conclusion that even the recognition of common visual patterns "is possible only as the result of an intensive and prolonged visual training that goes on from the moment of birth, during every moment that the eyes are open, with an increase in skill evident over a period of 12 to 16 years at least" (p. 46). The importance of this cumulative learning is even more obvious in the case of language, which at first is mastered so haltingly and later employed so flexibly. It is apparent likewise in motor skills, where the inept and clumsy toddler may later run championship races or take prizes for acrobatics, and where the awkward manipulations of the first year may turn into skilled craftsmanship or musical technique. Man as a species has developed a tremendous power to use his environment for his own advantage, and each individual has to develop an impressive competence if he is to take part in the life around him.

Part of the necessary learning will take place in the service of instinctual drives. The search for drive satisfactions will confer a considerable knowledge about the environment. But there is bound to be a certain narrowness in the curriculum devised by instincts. The push toward instinctual aims and objects means a restriction of what will be learned. Objects will be examined to see whether they are edible, breakable, or erotically gratifying, but not in the spirit of finding out everything that can be done with them. An organism equipped with effectance as well as instinctual energies will get itself a far more liberal education. By using its spare time between instinctual arousals to try out a large variety of interactions with the environment, seeking nothing more specific than the feeling of efficacy, it will acquire knowledge and skills that will be highly useful in future instinctual crises and especially in situations of danger. We can picture the adaptive advantages conferred by effectance by making the following comparisons. A dangerous enemy enters the territory; which resident will survive, the one that has learned only where to satisfy instinctual needs or the one that has explored the territory out of curiosity? An intruding rival comes on the scene; which animal will survive, the one that has fought only when angered or the one that has playfully practiced the art of fighting with its litter mates? Effectance, through the additional learning it brings about, makes the difference between life and death.

Competence and Sense of Competence

Energies of the kind I am describing as effectance, and satisfactions of the kind I am calling the feeling of efficacy, have appeared a good many times before in psychological theory. Karl Bühler (1918) introduced the idea of "pleasure in functioning" (*Funktionslust*), conceiving of it as a satisfaction inherent in the normal exercise of motor and mental functions. Murray and Kluckhohn (1953) advance a similar concept of pleasure in activity for its own sake. "The infant's mind," they say, "is not acting most of the time as the instrument of some urgent animal drive . . . but is preoccupied with *gratifying itself*" (p. 15). Woodworth (1958), thinking chiefly of the results of experiments with animals, comes to the conclusion that all behavior is directed primarily toward dealing with the environment. French (1952), working mainly from the memories and dreams of psychoanalytic patients, attaches importance to a need for activity and stimulation, arguing that the inherent energy of healthy organs has to be kept in regulation by appropriate amounts of action. "When the pressure of biological needs and of other serious purposes is not high and when one's state of health and rest makes activity pleasurable, then behavior takes on a playful character. A healthy child is active for the very joy of it, his senses are alert, and his mind is spontaneously active with all kinds of questions. If he is not already preoccupied with some task, he is eager to find something to do" (p. 136). French implies an integrated relation between this form of satisfaction and the attainment of instinctual goals: "Normal goal-directed activity requires a happy synthesis between the pressure of a purpose and this pleasure in activity" (p. 136). Considering the facts of frustration and of persistence in the face of obstacles, he proposes that a need to assert ourselves against obstacles must be taken as an elementary endowment of the integrative mechanism or ego apparatus. "Satisfaction of the self-assertive need by success in overcoming obstacles," he says, "is closely related to pleasure in functional activity for its own sake" (p. 145).

In view of these and many other conceptualizations moving in the same direction, I cannot claim originality for the ideas put forward in this chapter. *Effectance* is only a name for a kind of energy that many workers have deemed it necessary to assume; *feeling of efficacy* is but a term for a kind of satisfaction already widely postulated inside and outside of psychoanalysis. If I have added anything up to this point it is perhaps only a stronger insistence that "activity for its own sake" be not conceived of as a minor matter—a playful overflow of superfluous energies or a casual and merely time-killing interest in one's surroundings—but rather as a major aspect of the adaptive process and a vital theme in the growth of personality. Exploratory and playful activity, done "for its own sake," reveals its significance for adaptation and survival when we appreciate that it is through action and the consequences of action that we learn to become effective in dealing with our surroundings. Its contribution to the growth of personality will become evident if we push the thesis a little further and consider the developmental importance of feelings of efficacy.

At this point I introduce two new terms: *competence* and *sense of competence*. This will not, I trust, be seen as a mere whim or a fascination with words. If we could always deal with single experiences and simple levels of organization, it would be quite enough to rest with "effectance" and "feeling of efficacy." But in personality nothing stays simple. In no time we could slide back into the futility of the older academic instinct theories if we tried to isolate in adult personality the aspects that are produced and sustained by effectance alone. I therefore introduce *competence* to describe a person's existing capacity to interact effectively with his environment. Innate abilities play some part in this, but in the human case competence is largely a consequence of learning. Such learning may be the result of exploratory and manipulative behavior motivated wholly by effectance, but it may also have occurred under the influence of instinctual pressure or in some combination of sources of energy. Competence, in other words, is a cumulative result of the whole history of transactions with the environment, no matter how they were motivated.

Sense of competence describes the subjective side of one's actual competence. As we know, our sense of competence does not always accurately reflect what others judge to be our actual competence. Not all experiences are of equal importance, and certain successes or failures may contribute disproportionately to our subjective feelings. William James pointed out the extreme case of the athlete hugely humiliated by losing the championship match, in spite of the fact that he can beat everyone else in the world. These departures from objectivity, however, should not obscure the general proposition that sense of competence is built up from the past history of feelings of efficacy, including those that result purely from effectance and those that are associated with the satisfaction of instinctual drives. We can reserve the term *feeling of efficacy* for what is experienced in each individual transaction, using *sense of competence* for the accumulated and organized consequences in later stages of ego development.

In the mature adult the sense of competence may become well organized and differentiated with respect to different spheres of activity. We learn what we can and cannot do, and we may be satisfied to concentrate on the former. Even so, any serious challenge to competence is likely to be profoundly disturbing. If things happen that make us feel incompetent as a spouse, as a parent, or in our occupation, we discover how powerful is our motive to maintain the sense of competence. Thus it can be said that competence becomes in the course of development a highly important nucleus of motivation. As we shall see in a later chapter, it has a great deal to do with confidence and self-respect.

These concepts are introduced here partly because they hint at the importance of effectance and the feeling of efficacy—of independent ego energies—in the development of personality, and partly because they seem to me valuable in rounding out Freud's conception of anxiety. The use by the ego of anxiety as a signal depends upon a situation being apprehended as one of potential danger. This danger has to be conceived of in terms that include, as one variable, what the person feels he can do about the situation. Danger is spotted when threat exceeds one's sense of competence. This principle is of great value in understanding the nature of danger at different points in development. We well know that certain kinds of events can be traumatic at one age but tolerated relatively well at other ages. Careful study of the growth of the sense of competence in children is thus important for understanding psychopathology as well as ego strength.

Social Competence

The last statement may seem to be too strong if we think of competence wholly in relation to the physical environment. Psychopathologies arise mainly out of human relations, not out of clashes with material surroundings. I must therefore now make it clear that the emphasis placed thus far on interactions with inanimate objects has been only for the purpose of easier exposition. The concepts of effectance and competence apply equally well to other human beings, where the child has the same interest in finding out what effects he can have on the environment and what effects it will have on him. The similarity of problems becomes evident if we include animal pets which, more than inanimate objects but less than human ones, have some power to escape, retaliate, and enforce their own demands. The child has to explore his way to a workable relation with the family cat and dog, the ultimate relation being quite different in the two cases. In like fashion he has to find out what transactions are possible with the human inhabitants of his world.

The child takes an active interest in human beings even when he is free from strong bodily urges. He may conduct an intensive investigation of his mother's face, testing the texture of different features and finding out whether or not they can be detached from the ensemble. He may push and pull at his father's hands and try out the power of sounds and smiles in keeping that entertaining wanderer on the scene. There are many interesting things to be found out about the people who frequent the nursery. If they are at all willing to be affected, they provide a fine range of feelings of efficacy.

Early dealings with the human environment, however, are often dominated by imperious needs such as hunger and acute discomforts. To be sure, the infant is not wholly passive: in the very first days he learns to improve his sucking, and before long he will have found out how to cry more demandingly. These actions produce consequences—arrival of the nipple and more rapid intake of milk —and can be presumed to bring some feeling of efficacy. But they are accomplished under conditions of urgency rather than playfulness; they are dominated by the discomfort of hunger and the gratification of feeding. In these circumstances effectance is swamped by hunger, feelings of efficacy are impossible to disentangle from those of gratification, and gains in competence, if they occur, must be attributed to the transaction as a whole. That there is an intrinsic striving which tends to produce such gains can be clearly observed only during those spare-time activities when bodily cravings are in abeyance.

Most human interactions have both an aspect of need gratification and an aspect of competence. Dealing with a refractory child challenges the mother's competence as well as arousing her aggression. A young man who achieves a successful seduction enjoys both sexual gratification and a sense of social competence; the experience would have been different if he had had to beg for it. Efficacy and competence are thus not at all peculiar to transactions with the inanimate environment. The feeling of being able to have some effect on people, to get them to listen, provide some of the things we need, do some of the things we want, receive some of the love and help we want to give—this feeling of social competence is a substantial foundation stone of self-respect and security.

Relation to Psychoanalytic Theories

At the end of Chapter 2 we saw that psychoanalytic theorists fully recognized the importance of adaptive behavior in understanding the ego, but that they had reached no unanimity concerning the energies involved in such behavior. Some were inclined to cover it with a capacious definition of libidinal energy, seeing manipulation and exploratory play as part of a broad pregenital erotic urge. Others preferred to spread the wide umbrella of the death instinct and look upon adaptive behavior as a kind of prehostile aggression. The symbolic significance that shows itself so often in children's play could be used to increase the plausibility of either or both of these generalizations. We noticed, however, that not all theorists were satisfied with such a simple extension of Freud's dual instinct theory. Several workers were dubious about gathering under the instinctual drives so much behavior that had so little demonstrable relation to instinctual aims. Hendrick adopted the radical solution of assuming an additional instinctual drive, the instinct to master. Hartmann took the somewhat more conservative course implied in the concept of neutralization of drive energies.

At that point I said that the thesis to be advanced concerning independent ego energies would lie somewhere between the views of Hendrick and Hartmann. Effectance as I have described it cannot be usefully conceived of as a derived form of energy, a secondary transformation of instinctual-drive energies. I have tried to show that it is biologically basic and central to the adaptive process. Yet I cannot see that we stand to gain by calling it an instinctual drive in its own right. The danger in such an assumption is that we look for properties similar to those of other instinctual drives and fail to discover the unique characteristics of adaptive behavior.

Freud made a valuable distinction in 1905 in what unfortunately turned out to be only a stray thought in his writings: "If we do not require our mental apparatus at the moment for supplying one of our indispensable satisfactions, we allow it itself to work in the direction of pleasure and we seek to derive pleasure from its own activity" (1905, pp. 95-96). What is important here is the distinction between indispensable gratifications and pleasure in intrinsic activity. This latter "pleasure" I have described as a feeling of efficacy, something that differs a good deal from instinctual gratifications, even the more quiet and extended ones of pregenital sexuality. We stand a better chance of keeping things clear if we take effectance as independent ego energy rather than as a form of instinctual energy.

It would be premature at this point to argue these issues in detail. In the following chapters I shall try to show the use that can be made of effectance, efficacy, and competence in understanding the development of the ego, especially in conceptualizing the relation to reality and the governing of behavior by realistic considerations. Only after making this trial will we be in a position to draw conclusions about the operation of the energies postulated by psychoanalytic theory.

4

REALITY AND ITS TESTING

In the last chapter a thesis was advanced concerning the nature of independent ego energies. It is now in order to begin to apply these ideas to those functions and processes of development that are most characteristic of the ego. The heart of the matter is reality testing. What part can be assigned to effectance in learning about reality and adapting to it? How does behavior come to be guided by realities, so that even strong instinctual impulses are expressed in accord with existing conditions?

The infant does little to control instinctual urges. He does not distinguish what is self from what is not of the self, he has almost no knowledge about the nature of reality, and although he is not altogether helpless his repertory of actions for influencing his surroundings would be far too small for survival if certain people in the environment were not strongly disposed to devote themselves to his care. If we imagine him transformed into a young adult, full of practical knowledge about the world, earning a living, and participating in the care of an infant of his own with all the competence that these activities imply, we can appreciate the vast amount of learning that has been accomplished during the intervening years. If we imagine him as a football player, he can serve to illustrate the channeling of powerful competitive aggression into skilled patterns of cooperative action under a system of accepted rules. If we make him an airplane pilot, one of the many skilled people who participate in the ordered arrival and departure of planes at a big airport with rarely an accident, he can stand as a superb modern symbol of what the ego can achieve in mastering the physical world and governing human whim and carelessness. At its best, the ego is indeed accomplished and versatile in its task of mediating between impulse and reality.

The Beginning of Reality Testing

Freud's essay, "Formulations on the Two Principles of Mental Functioning" (1911), provides a convenient point of departure for the discussion of reality testing. Hartmann (1956b) condenses Freud's idea as follows:

> If the infant finds himself in a situation of need, and if attempts toward hallucinatory gratification have proved disappointing, he will turn toward reality; and the repetition of such situations will gradually teach him better to know reality and to strive for those real changes that make gratification possible [p. 32].

Freud's own wording was more picturesque but startlingly voluntaristic:

> ... the psychical apparatus had to decide to form a conception of the real circumstances in the external world and to endeavour to make a real alteration in them. A new principle of mental functioning was thus introduced; what was presented in the mind was no longer what was agreeable but what was real, even if it happened to be disagreeable [1911, p. 219].

Hartmann points out that Freud's account is not complete. The reality principle implies a delay and postponement of instinctual gratification, and these in turn point to something that cannot be deduced from the collision between pleasure seeking and frustration. The decision taken by the mental apparatus implies, as Hartmann expresses it, "the existence of something in the individual that speaks out for reality—a tendency toward self-preservation which, in the mental life of man, we attribute mostly to the ego and to its precursors" (p. 32). Two ego functions, postponement and anticipation, necessarily enter as independent variables into the model situation described by Freud, and they must be taken to signify a preformed adaptiveness in the ego apparatus. Hartmann points out, of course, that in later writings Freud allowed the ego a more active part in the emergence of the reality principle, but this change of view was not consolidated by recasting the process in detail. Most workers continue to think in terms of the original model situation.

The understanding of this model situation can be improved, I think, by insisting upon the importance of action and the consequences of action. This is not a departure from the intentions of Freud and Hartmann, both of whom use an explicit action theory elsewhere to account for the differentiation between self and outer world, or from the expressed views of Hartmann, Kris, and Loewenstein (1946) on this subject. But Freud's mention of knowing about reality and Hartmann's listing of postponement and anticipation as preformed adaptive functions do not clearly imply what I believe to be the true relation here between knowledge and action. The ability to tolerate delay and to endure postponement of gratification is acquired through learning of a particular kind. The most favorable situation for such learning, as Benedek (1938) has shown, is one in which a fairly prompt gratification can be anticipated, and this in turn depends upon the infant's gaining some experience of the consequences of his own action. He can advance beyond hallucinated gratification most readily when he begins to learn that some action or effort on his part has the consequence of producing real gratification. The interpolation of some such act in the sequence of pleasure seeking represents the first influence of reality on the pleasure principle—the first true concession to reality.

The use of words such as "experience" and "anticipation" in this account is in accord with the usual practice in psychoanalytic theory, but it does not imply an adult conscious experience. Making a connection between action and consequence represents a simple learning mechanism that is in the repertory of many kinds of animal.

In terms of action we can express as follows what happens in Freud's model situation. Frustrated need constitutes a call to action; more specifically, to restless action beyond the preparation and performance of consummatory responses. In the young infant this action may consist of little more than squirming, thrashing, and emitting cries, but the cries at least are likely to have a decided effect on a properly tuned environment. If the cries are soon answered in a way that brings gratification, a basis is laid for the future anticipation that will make it possible to tolerate delay. What the child learns is what he can expect to happen as a consequence of his cries.

In general terms, knowledge of the environment is a consequence of action. It is a knowledge of the effects that can be produced by action. As Schilder (1935) put it, "experience in itself is not a ready-made entity, but gets its shape by active probing" (p. 56). The reality principle can be said to replace the pleasure principle to the extent that actions are interpolated which are not themselves directly need reducing but which affect the environment in some way that favors need reduction.

This minor recasting of Freud's model for the beginning of reality testing does not necessarily require the assumption of energies other than those of the frustrated instincts. In view of what has been said about effectance, however, a deprivation model is clearly not the only possible one. Even Hartmann, no enemy of Freud's theory of instincts, deems it imprudent to exclude the possibility of "primary positive response" to reality, a conception strongly advocated by Charlotte Buehler (1954) on the basis of extensive direct observations of infants. The environment is explored and manipulated even when instinctual needs are quiet. Effectance implies a primary positive interest in the world apart from its drive-reducing properties. This activity and this interest are responsible for important learnings about the ways in which reality can and cannot be influenced. The hypothetical infant whose instinctual cravings are always satisfied without delay would still learn a good deal about reality through playful exploration.

Furthermore, it seems necessary to give a better account of the educative consequences when instinctual needs are active. As Bühler points out, and as Loewald (1951) also has argued, the environment can provide pleasant, need-syntonic experiences; it can also promote opportunities for enhancing and developing the gratification of needs. Certainly there are situations in which an outside stimulus will prove to have need-satisfying properties before the inner arousal of need has become painfully acute. There is one very general, very early situation in the life of newborn infants which we probably should accept as another model for reality testing. The infant sucks virtually from the start, but an improvement in the skill and coordination of sucking is observed to take place over perhaps the first ten days. An utterly fixed reflex would not be presumed to yield a feeling of efficacy, but the evidence shows that learning immediately begins to improve upon the innate pattern. Here is a situation in which gratification is going on, but in which effortful activity increases the quantity or speed of gratification. In the child's universe of action, something important has been learned about reality not simply through the pain of deprivation but rather through discovering the way to increase gratification.

The reality principle is broadly based in action, and action is broadly based not only in instinctual energies but also in the exploratory and manipulative tendencies that spring from the independent ego energies here called effectance. Instinctual frustration provides but one of several inducements to shape behavior in accord with realistic considerations.

DISCRIMINATION OF SELF AND NOT-SELF

Hartmann, Kris, and Loewenstein, in "Comments on the Formation of Psychic Structure" (1946), describe as the "first and most fundamental" step in ego development the learning of the distinction between self and surrounding world. The importance of this piece of learning has long been recognized in academic child psychology, but it assumes an added significance for psychoanalytic theory because of its relation to the distribution of instinctual energies. The externalization of libidinal and aggressive energies depends upon a functional discrimination between the external and internal realms. The nature of this discrimination is also imperative for understanding infantile fantasies concerning internal and external good and bad objects, a theme that became central in the later work of Melanie Klein (1955).

Although some writers seem to treat the distinction as something that is accomplished once and for all very early in life or that is there all the time, Hartmann, Kris, and Loewenstein prefer to conceive of it as a piece of learning that takes place gradually through "ever repeated trial experiences." This view is in accord with what I have been saying about learning through action and its consequences, and it seems to be supported by Piaget's (1927) demonstration that at the more obscure edges where testing through action is difficult—for instance, with respect to the locus of thought and dreams—children may still be confused up to eight or nine years. It is evident that if we conceive of this discrimination as a gradual growth through repeated experiences, we are raising difficult problems for certain other parts of psychoanalytic theory. How firm must the discrimination be before an externalization of libidinal and aggressive energies can take place? Can one speak of the introjection of an object if one also conceives that object and self are not successfully differentiated? Much of the work on these concepts has been cast in language that presupposes the distinction, even very early in life, perhaps because it is so difficult for adults to imagine how things would be if experience were undifferentiated in this fundamental respect.

In the essay just mentioned, Hartmann, Kris, and Loewenstein further propose, entirely in accord with Freud's view of the matter, that the mother will be the first and most important object in the infant's world. They deduce from this that the focus of the child's early reality testing and the main arena for his learning about self and not-self will be the mother, or significant parts of the mother such as the breast. The use of this relation as a model, and as the centrally important feature of growth, leads to a closely interwoven treatment of reality testing, discrimination of self, and the problem of object relations. The child's earliest learning is held to proceed partly by identification with the mother, this being gradually replaced by an object relation with a true libidinal tie. This in turn implies that primary narcissistic cathexis has been transformed into object cathexis.

Hartmann, Kris, and Loewenstein's account makes no use of independent ego energies. This makes for difficulty, I believe, in separating the several strands of development that are implied in it. An action-consequence theory which is like Hartmann's but which also makes use of the concept of effectance will give us a sharper view of the first strand, the distinguishing of self and not-self. We can then consider the part played by the mother as object and the probable chronology of the child's learning through interaction with her.

Freud made a brief contribution to the problem in "Instincts and Their Vicissitudes" (1915a), where he proposed that the antithesis between ego and nonego is learned through the consequences of muscular action. The child learns to classify as external those stimuli that can be escaped or abolished by movement, and as internal those stimuli such as the instincts from which motor escape is impossible. Detailed studies show that this formula is rather too simple, but the main idea, the dependence of learning on action, is in agreement with the work of academic child psychologists from Preyer (1888) to Piaget (1937).

Piaget expresses as follows his conception of the original undifferentiated state.

> . . . at this stage the child does not know the mechanism of his own actions, and hence does not dissociate them from the things themselves; he knows only their total and undifferentiated schema . . . comprising in a single act the data of external perception as well as the internal impressions that are affective and kinesthetic, etc., in nature. So long as the object is present it is assimilated in that schema and could not therefore be thought of apart from the acts to which it gives rise. . . . None of this implies substantial permanence: . . . The child's universe is still only a totality of pictures emerging from nothingness at the moment of the action, to return to nothingness at the moment when the action is finished [1937, pp. 42-43].

At this level of experience, self, action, and object are all of one piece, so that food, for instance, is not distinguished as the object of the wishing, searching, and sucking that bring it into the mouth, nor are these actions known as proceeding from a self that exists apart from what it does. The undifferentiated universe of action comes to have structure only because acts have different consequences depending upon what they encounter.

The child's own body is an important aspect of what will be classified as self. Preyer gave instances from the second year of life in which objects and body were still not sharply differentiated. At fourteen months his child "bit himself on his bare arm so that he immediately cried out with pain."

> Even in the nineteenth month it is not yet clear how much belongs to one's own body. The child had lost a shoe. I said, 'Give the shoe.' He stooped, seized it, and gave it to me. Then, when I said to the child as he was standing upright on the floor, 'Give the foot,' . . . he grasped at it with both hands, and labored hard to get it and hand it to me [1888, p. 190].

The essential point of difference between external objects and the body lies in the double sensations received from contact with one's own body: one set from the touching hand, the other from the part that is touched. Shinn (1898, 1907) described in detail the manner in which her niece explored this problem.

The 181st day her hand came in contact with her ear; she became at once very serious, and felt it and pulled it hard; losing it, she felt around her cheek for it, but when her mother put her hand back, she became interested in the cheek and wished to keep on feeling that [Vol. 1, p. 143].

The discrimination of what is body from what is not body becomes refined through further investigation of the properties of both. According to Charlotte Bühler (1954),

The baby very early appears to make evaluations of what is and what is not his own doing. For example, in the famous fingerplay of the 6 week old baby, it can be observed how the baby experiments and how it discovers what it can do. Studies of the infant in this situation indicated by way of change in facial expression that the child seemed to notice a connection between the finger movement he sees and some inner experience. The wonderment about this experience of causation is still greater when the baby watches his toes move at his volition [pp. 641-642].

A little later, when grasping and manipulation of objects become possible, the exploration will include what happens to objects, and the resistances offered by objects will become an important clue to their separateness from the child's body and from his intentions. The discrimination of other people from oneself and from inanimate objects proceeds on a similar basis of interaction. Both Stern (1914) and Levy (1955) make a point of oppositional behavior or "willfulness," beginning sometimes before the end of the first year and gathering momentum up to the negativism of two and one half, as a means of testing and establishing the degree of freedom available to the self when interacting with others. At twenty-four months, according to Gesell and Ilg (1943), the child attains a correct use of "I," "me," and "you." This verbal achievement probably signifies a considerable firmness in the underlying discriminations established through action.

These excerpts from studies of child development support the idea that the discrimination between self and not-self results from action and its differential consequences. They are in harmony with Hartmann's conception of a gradual learning through repeated experiences. They also seem to me to bring additional testimony in favor of the concept of effectance. Playful exploration makes a substantial contribution to these diverse experiences. It does not stand alone as the sole motive; satisfactions of hunger, expressions of aggression, and eroticism of the lips and skin are certainly involved in some of the situations. But the persistent experimenting with people, things, and one's own body that is required to establish the basic discrimination calls for a steady output of energy during the spare time between instinctual arousals. The contented child is the most versatile explorer of the world at large.

These excerpts also raise a serious question about the centrality of the mother. No one will challenge her affective importance to the infant, but it is not a compulsory deduction from this that she will be the main arena of reality testing and the object most suitable for discriminating self and not-self. Indeed one might consider her, precisely because of her close and intimate interactions with the child, a rather unsuitable object for arriving at cool appraisals of reality. Both common experience and clinical observation suggest that in mother-fixated children the mother continues to be the one object not fully discriminated from the self even when this distinction has been achieved as regards all other objects. It is true that security felt in relation to the mother has an important influence upon the child's behavior in other spheres. Yet it may well be that inanimate objects have to take the lead in establishing the difference between self and not-self, and that minor characters in the world of the nursery can be separated more readily than the person on whom so very much depends.

The relative merits of people and inanimate objects in reality testing are suggested in the following comments by Mahler and Gosliner (1955) on a ten-year-old boy suffering from a severe symbiotic psychosis.

> Aro's restitutive attempts to orient himself in the environment are successful with inanimate objects. Because of their stability and constancy, and because he can explore them at his own speed, he can make them a part of his own experience. He is able to categorize them as to good or bad. . . . Unlike himself, inanimate objects do not change rapidly in an unpredictable way and thus serve as a frame of reference to the child struggling to control in a chaotic world.
>
> Aro's attempt at orientation by means of questioning succeed [sic] less happily. The answer provoked by his question is not predictable, either in terms of its final form, its ultimate meaning or its effect on him [pp. 205-206].

In this case the inanimate environment, while it is not as important as the human one, clearly takes the lead as a means of reality testing. Because it is less ambiguous and more reliable, its properties can be more easily learned.

In more auspicious cases the human environment will not be so disadvantageous. Piaget (1937) points out that in the child's world people are more lively centers of action than inanimate objects. Even during play hours, when major needs are satisfied, they give more pleasure and awaken more laughter, and this advantage soon shows in the child's attitude of expectant waiting to see what they will do. They thus serve admirably to educate him with respect to causality independent of himself. But it is still possible that the mother in her need-gratifying roles promotes this education less effectively than others who simply play with the child in his spare time. In any event, the objectification of the mother is accomplished slowly. According to Mahler and Gosliner, whose position on this point is very far from Melanie Klein's, the synthesis of good and bad images into someone who can be responded to as a "whole mother" does not take place until the age of three or three and a half. If this is true, it forms an interesting comparison with Piaget's finding that inanimate objects are recognized as independent wholes early in the second year.

Admittedly this whole subject needs a great deal more detailed observation. With so many uncertainties about chronology it is impossible to form a satisfactory theory about these developments. Perhaps enough has been said, however, to suggest the value of treating discrimination of self and not-self in terms of action and differential consequences, and to make a case for effectance as the motive for part of this learning. Playful exploration plays a distinct part in the discovery of what is and what is not a portion of one's own body, what is and what is not a product of one's own activity, and the many other discriminations by which the mature distinction is cumulatively achieved. Perhaps enough has been said also to show that the whole process must be presumed to take place partially, gradually, and at different rates for different aspects of experience. It seems to me that the resulting problem for concepts of instinctual-energy distribution, externalization, introjection, and incorporation must be considered very grave. These concepts were developed with a badly foreshortened view of what constituted the discrimination between self and not-self. We can see now that the achievement of this distinction in anything like adult form is not a single or simple accomplishment. It is a complex part of the whole slow process of constructing a knowledge of reality.

CONSTRUCTION OF A STABLE OBJECTIVE WORLD

A theory that derives the energies of behavior entirely from instincts runs into two difficult problems concerning our knowledge of reality. One of these, which we can call the *cathexis problem,* springs from the axiom that the world becomes real to the infant only to the extent that it receives an investment of instinctual cathexis. The difficulty here is that instinctual cathexes are periodic, being withdrawn once the tension is reduced, whereas objects come to be conceived of as existing constantly. The second problem, which we can call the *organization problem,* arises from the deduction that since objects enter our experience wholly in connection with the satisfaction or frustration of drives, they will become organized in memory according to their relation to drives. The difficulty here is that in the end they become organized according to the real relations that prevail among them, which have very little to do with our drives. How does a creature of instinct come to recognize that the world is there all the time, whether he likes it or not, and that it follows laws of its own, whether he likes them or not?

Concerning the *cathexis problem,* it will be recalled that Fenichel (1937), taking Freud's earlier thoughts on the subject quite literally, located the first externalization of cathectic energy at the point at which the infant can realize the necessity for an external object in the relief of his hunger. The infant can then long for the object, but only when he is hungry; once the need is satisfied, cathexis is withdrawn and the object no longer exists. Fenichel drew the logical conclusion that "the first 'affirmation' of the world is an intermediate aim on the way to its 'negation' " (p. 29). Clearly something has to happen in the course of development to get us out of this trap. One way to deal with the difficulty is to suppose that the instinctual energies themselves undergo a change. In 1952 Anna Freud cast a reviewing eye over this problem and mentioned several possibilities. For herself she preferred the hypothesis of a "decrease in the urgency of the drives themselves" (p. 44), at least in relation to ego organization: needs must lessen their imperiousness before unsatisfying objects can retain enduring cathexis. But she pointed out another solution, espoused particularly by Hartmann. According to this view, the shift from the merely need-satisfying object to the constant object is mediated by a change from instinctual to neutralized energy cathexes. Neutralized energy, since it no longer serves instinctual aims, can be conceived to have freed itself also from instinctual periodicity. Thus it can maintain a constant outflow and cathect a constant world.

These attempts at explanation in terms of energy have little to recommend them unless it is possible to specify the circumstances and mechanisms of change. How does it come about that energies lessen their strength or that instincts alter their aims? Rapaport (1951) undertook to deal with this subject in connection with the *organization problem*. Both problems, he believed, required structural concepts as well as dynamic ones, for it was only through the mediation of structures that instinctual energies could be neutralized.

Rapaport formulated the organization problem as a development from a "drive organization" of memories, guided by wish fulfillment, to a "conceptual organization" guided by the real connections among objects.

> In this new organization of memory, the transition from one idea to another was no longer determined by a belongingness to the same drive, but rather by a *connectedness along the pathways in reality* toward the need-satisfying object. The connections began to take on the form of reality connections: space, time, contiguity, similarity. . . .
>
> Thus the drive-organization of memories yielded to a conceptual-organization, even though the latter was still primitive. This yielding occurred not in the form of replacement but in that of a controlling system being superimposed. . . .
>
> The cathexes operating within this new memory-organization, limited in displaceability and amount and not striving toward direct and complete discharge, were conceptualized as *bound cathexes*. As we shall see, this concept of binding is not as unequivocal as it may seem at first [1951, p. 697].

It would have been possible for Rapaport to introduce at this point, following Hartmann's suggestions, the idea of preformed structures in the ego apparatus—"something in the individual that speaks out for reality" (Hartmann, 1956b, p. 32). While he did not reject this possibility, he believed that it was more in keeping with Freud's fundamental assumptions to interpret development as far as possible in terms of instinctual energies. His account therefore continued in the following way. When drive tension mounts to an intolerable degree in the absence of a satisfying object, drive cathexes can either be repressed or "their freely mobile character may change to a '*bound*' form" (p. 694). Either fate implies that "an energy-charge is pitted against the drive-cathexis. This charge is conceptualized as *countercathexis*. . . . What are the sources of these countercathexes? The analogy of a river, which where it is slowed down builds up sand bars to slow it further, may help us to visualize what the evidence seems to suggest: the countercathexes seem to be derived from the drive which they repress" (1951, p. 695). The restraints imposed by countercathexes—in other words, the defenses —are at first specific to a single drive impulse, but they soon become generalized and formed into a system that functions with respect to the id as a whole. Confronted by this system of restraints, drive cathexes become differentiated and begin to make their appearance in the form of *drive derivatives*. These are drive energies "altered in their rhythm, discharge-conditions, and discharge-form. The so altered drive is more attuned to reality-demands, being on the one hand more amenable to delay, and on the other more flexible as to the conditions of discharge, in that a greater variety of objects and activities will serve as its gratifiers" (1951, pp. 700-701).

In this way we arrive at an extensive differentiation of motives. Drive derivatives shade off eventually into those motives called *ego interests,* in which the ego seems to be concerned with its own affairs, so to speak, without any immediate reference to erotic or aggressive goals. Furthermore, defenses likewise yield new motives, typified in the kindness that is interpreted as a reaction formation against aggression. Rapaport pointed out the implication that both ego interests and defensive motives represent sources of energy that have become more or less autonomous from the original instinctual reservoirs and that are freely disposable toward different goals shaped in realistic terms. Ego interests, however, could still be conceived of as sophisticated drive derivatives operating with instinctual cathexis, and defensive motives could draw their energy from the same source by way of anticathexis. In terms of energy, this signified increased binding and neutralization. ". . . the process here described," he said, "repeats itself in a hierarchic series, controlling organizations thus being layered over each other" (p. 701). Only through extensive layering could the energies be fully neutralized.

Rapaport's exposition of these developments throws into bold relief the inherent difficulties of a scheme that seeks an explanation mainly in terms of instinctual energies. Limiting himself in this way, he could not, it seems to me, deal successfully with the question of structure, and even in terms of energy he was obliged to leave one problem unsolved. The weak spot with respect to energy is the assumption that instinctual energies can be split and thrown into an opposition of cathexis and anticathexis when circumstances present an obstacle to the original cathexis. If we take this literally, we have to imagine that "wanting food" and "wanting food" can stand in conflict so that one "wanting food" inhibits the other and causes it to send out a more realistic derivative. Such a feat on the part of energies is not made more plausible by the analogy of sand bars in a river unless one is prepared to suppose that instinctual energy contains silt which is deposited when the flow is made slower. Of course, Rapaport did not intend any of this to be taken quite literally. He was aware of dangers in the metaphors he employed, but he did not attempt a more explicit solution for the mysterious splitting of one stream of energy into two opposing forces.

It is worth noticing that Fenichel (1937) had struggled with the same problem and had solved it by invoking the occasional traumatic consequences of drive expressions and the threats and prohibitions directed against them. While these are humanly plausible, Fenichel's explanation in terms of energy was hardly more explicit. He assumed that pain and anxiety could deflect part of the instinctual energy back upon the other part, but he did not assign them any force of their own for this purpose, nor did he explain why they divided the energic stream rather than inhibiting it as a whole.

The difficulty with respect to structure in Rapaport's account lies in his invoking it as an unexplained consequence of the activity of energies. The collision of cathexis and anticathexis leaves a structural deposit that can duly become organized into a defensive system. Drive derivatives become attuned to reality because they are kept in line by this defensive system. As more layers are laid on, the realistic channeling of motives becomes more complete. Thus reality has stolen into the account and is strongly entrenched in the defensive system, but how did it get there? How have the impersonal relations that prevail among objects intruded themselves into this drama of energies?

Rapaport was dissatisfied with his formulation of these points. He returned to the problem in his paper presented at the Nebraska Symposium in 1960, giving a much more explicit place to structure. He approached the problem in two ways: through Freud's theory of attention, as given in *The Interpretation of Dreams* (1900) and in "Repression" (1915b) and "The Unconscious" (1915c), and through Piaget's work on the development of the sense of reality in early childhood (1936, 1937).

Freud had handled the problem of attention by postulating a modest reservoir of mental energy called *attention cathexis*. The derivation of this energy from instinctual sources was probably implied, but it had become a property, so to speak, of the system *Cs.-Pcs.;* it corresponds to what was later called the hypercathexes of the ego. This energy is attracted by excitations from within and without, giving rise to conscious experience.

> (12) Attention cathexis attracted by an excitation in a sufficient amount and for a sufficient duration gives rise to a structure (e.g., memory trace).
> (13) Structures so built retain only a small quantity of the attention cathexes that were needed to give rise to them. The condition of these cathexes is termed *bound,* and the process itself *binding.*
> (14) Once structure building is completed, the attention cathexes used in the process—except for those which have become bound in the structure—become available to other excitations [Rapaport, 1960, p. 229].

To my mind, these derivations from Freud's theory of attention do not help at all. To be sure, reality is explicitly admitted in the form of memory traces, and the endurance of these traces is guaranteed by assigning them a small allowance of bound cathexis. But this solution does not avoid the old difficulty. Energy is still involved in an unexplained way in the formation and perpetuation of structures, and attention cathexes have been arbitrarily split, as instinctual energies were before, into portions that become bound and portions that remain free. More serious is a fallacy in the fundamental assumption about attention cathexis. It is interpreted as an equilibrium system in which stimuli destroy the state of rest and there is an urge to return to rest. Every fact brought forward in the last chapter concerning exploration and manipulation testifies to the difficulty of using this type of equilibrium model. If attending and responding to stimulation is cast as a dreary chore from which surcease is desired, surely we would all quickly learn to close our eyes and bury our heads in defense of undisturbed equilibrium.

Rapaport's venture into Piaget's work seemed destined to provide him with happier solutions to the problem of structure. He was impressed by the part played by external stimulation in developing and maintaining cognitive structure, and he assigned importance to "stimulus hunger" which, however, he distinguished entirely from true motivational energies. In his Nebraska Symposium paper, one of the last things he wrote, this direction of inquiry was given only the briefest sketch, and Rapaport's exposition thus regrettably remained incomplete.

From the time when Freud abandoned the ego instincts and set up the ego as a structure of personality, psychoanalysis has been committed to fashioning a structural psychology to go with its dynamic one. Nowhere is this more essential than in dealing with the developmental problem of constructing a stable objective world. But the intention to be structural has not been supported by good ideas about the formation of psychic structure. Rapaport's careful exposition still reflected the historic preoccupation with instinctual energies and thus did not really explain the progression from a "drive organization" of memories to a "conceptual organization" that represents the real connections of things in the external world. This incompleteness can best be made good, it seems to me, by continuing to apply a theory that recognizes the close relation between knowledge and action.

Action and Its Consequences in Reality Testing

The introduction of independent ego energies (effectance) as a serious force in development puts the whole problem in a somewhat different light and opens it for systematic direct observation. Effectance is a neutral energy in the psychoanalytic sense. It is not tied to specific somatic sources, it does not have specific consummatory aims, and it is periodic only in the sense that the sleep-waking cycle is periodic. It is thus a neutral energy present from the start of life and expending itself in a relatively constant fashion. This assumption frees us somewhat from two awkward deductions from instinct theory: the deduction that objects can be real only when their representations are invested with instinctual cathexis, and the deduction that objects must first be organized through their connection with drives. There is a "neutral" interest in objects besides longing, loving, and hating; it arises from their part in action and their contribution to the feeling of efficacy. The concept of effectance brings with it quite naturally a series of ideas about structure. If effectance is conceived to be the energy inherent in the sensorimotor system, we have at our disposal all that has been discovered about learning, memory, concept formation, and the acquisition of skills, together with the still modest amount that is known about the central nervous system as a structure. In short, my main hypothesis equips the infant from the start with a kind of energy and with a kind of structure that dispose him to construct a stable, objective, real world.

This is not to say that the problems posed by psychoanalytic theory are solved at a stroke. Centering a theory on action and summoning the aid of independent ego energies do not do away with developmental problems in the construction of reality. It is still necessary to understand how the objective world comes to be separated from earlier formations in which object, action, feeling, and self are undifferentiated. It is still necessary to explain how objects come to be assigned permanent existence apart from action, and how the relations among them come to be conceived of as impersonal laws apart from our feelings of efficacy. The old problems are not solved; they are merely restated. But the restatement has important consequences. Movements of instinctual energies cannot be directly observed; when they are considered central, the most appropriate method of study is reconstruction from later fantasy, play, or free association. Action and its consequences, on the other hand, can be observed at the very time the crucial learnings are taking place. This gives us an additional means of scientific study, one that may be more accurate and more penetrating for these problems of ego development.

To illustrate this advantage we can take the situation of a child confronted by a somewhat novel object. We know that the object is likely to be explored and eventually put aside. Describing this transaction in terms borrowed from Freud's theory of attention, we can say that an external excitation has drawn attention cathexis sufficiently to form a structured memory image, binding a modicum of cathexis and releasing the rest. Such an account does scant justice to what we can see happening when a child is actually exploring an object. The exploration proceeds through a series of actions, starting with visual focusing and continuing with reaching, touching, grasping, tasting, smelling, turning, shaking, passing from hand to hand, dropping, throwing—whatever acts lie within the child's current repertory. The nature of the process is revealed most vividly when the child's repertory is still crude so that he tries to affect objects by such inappropriate measures as arching his back or rubbing the side of the crib. At any rate, he runs through his repertory, and the exploration ceases only when there is nothing more that he can do. What the child has learned about this new object can now be put in terms of the consequences of his several actions. His memory image, his "knowing what it is," means that he has tested the feedback from his repertory of acts; he knows what effects he can have and what effects he cannot have. The observer can deduce what he has learned by watching his behavior in future encounters with the object. Prior to concept formation and naming, the concrete consequences of action are the real meaning of his knowledge, and when conceptual and verbal aids begin to be available they do no more than introduce efficient short cuts into this learning process.

This view of the matter is again in general harmony with Piaget's ideas, and we stand to gain from his studies of the construction of reality in his own three children during the first eighteen months of life (1937). The sensorimotor learning of this period receives little help from language and is probably somewhat analogous to the playful and exploratory learning of young animals. It will suffice for our present purpose to look at two aspects of the process, the development of the object concept and the growth of the idea of causality. These two themes should give us clues to the establishment of stable, permanent objects and to the transition from an "action organization" of memories to a "conceptual organization" in which the real relations among objects are understood.

As we have seen, the infant's behavior in the beginning shows no differentiation of object, self, action, and cause. All are embraced in a single scheme. As evidence for this picture Piaget presents extensive observations to show (1) that up to seven or eight months his children made no effort to look for an object once it was out of view, and (2) that up to eight months they never used an object in such a way as to imply recognition of any force outside their own activity. The observations concerning vanished objects are eloquent: the still hungry child cries for the half-empty bottle while it is in sight but quiets immediately when it is put behind a small screen; the happy child reaches for an entertaining toy wherever it may lie, but stops short when a cloth is laid over it, although it is still within reach. The observations concerning action upon objects show that the child uses exactly the same repertory on animate and inanimate objects and has no sense of an agency outside his own acts: "he brings the activities of others into the cluster of phenomena subject to control by the efficacy of his own movements" (1937, p. 253). Thus Laurent, enchanted by his father's shaking a rattle or swinging a metal bird, attempts to get these acts repeated by arching himself, shaking his head, and waving his hands, all the time gazing at the object and ignoring the hint of his father's hands resting very close to it. If he responds at all to his father's hands, it is to shake them but not to move them toward the object.

The child passes beyond these limitations through further action and through increasing discrimination of consequences. With respect to vanishing objects, the first step forward consists of a persistence of the action that had been going on before the object was removed from sight. Piaget reports that his daughter Jacqueline during the tenth month would still often stop searching when an object in her lap was covered by a screen, but would continue to search if she had already begun movements of reaching and grasping. The first hint of permanence is thus connected with the prolonging of action. Observations on Lucienne at the same age display more fully the still dubious character of this permanence.

1. Lucienne is seated on a cloth. I place under its edge a familiar rubber doll which she likes to suck and nibble. Lucienne watches me (I work slowly and visibly), but she does not react.
Second attempt: This time I let the doll's feet emerge: Lucienne grabs them at once and pulls the doll out from under the blanket.
Third attempt: I again hide the object completely. Lucienne pulls the cloth about and raises it as though she were discovering this new

procedure in the very course of her groping, and perceives an extremity of the doll; she leans forward to see better and looks at it, much surprised. She does not grasp it [1937, p. 48].

[Two more trials are made with the doll completely hidden; the little girl takes no action to recover it.]

Sixth attempt: Lucienne again pulls the cloth about and makes half the object appear. This time she again looks at it with great interest and at length, as though she did not recognize it. Then she grasps and sucks it. . . .

Eighth attempt: She raises the cloth right away but still leans forward in order to have a close view of the doll before grasping it, as though she were not sure of its identity [pp. 48-49].

From this point onwards Lucienne has no trouble with this particular problem, but a small variation in the experiment brings to light a momentous new difficulty.

II. *First attempt:* I now place the doll under a coverlet 10 centimeters from the original place. I raise the coverlet, put the doll on the floor, and cover it slowly and visibly. As soon as the doll is hidden Lucienne manifests her anger, although it is just as easy for her to find the doll as it was before. She whimpers for a moment but does not search anywhere.

Second attempt: I again place the doll under the original cloth; Lucienne immediately searches for it and finds it.

Third attempt: I again place the doll under the coverlet. A strange thing happens. Lucienne not only makes no attempt to raise the coverlet but again pulls the cloth about and ends by raising it! [p. 49].

The object has not yet achieved permanence in the adult sense. Passive observation of its placement under a different covering does not yet suggest to the child that it has left its original place. Object is still bound up with action, and action is still bound up with a particular location. The child acts almost as if the doll under the coverlet were a different doll from the one under the original cloth.

Further experience, requiring two or three more months, will gradually set this matter straight. Search under the original cloth will go unrewarded, and the doll will be secured only when exploration is extended to the place where it last disappeared. When the child has learned to go straight to this second location he has made a forward stride in his concept of the object. As Piaget puts it, he "takes account of all the visible displacements he has observed and dissociates the object from its practical context" (p. 68). In such fashion the consequences of exploratory action lead the child by slow degrees to the concept of stable, substantial objects.

Progress in constructing a world of independent causality is likewise a result of increasing differentiation of actions and their consequences. As actions become more varied and skillful—less global and blundering—objects will be experienced as behaving in ways that are not quite part of the intended act. The ball will slip out of the hand unexpectedly and travel a great distance while the child watches helplessly. Piaget's daughter Jacqueline demonstrated this progress over a month's time in playing with her father's watch. At eight months she tried at once to catch hold of the watch when it began to slip from her hand. At nine months, in the same situation, she gazed at the slipping watch with signs of interest and surprise. ". . . the child now clearly reveals by his attitude that he locates in the moving object an autonomous center of forces, whereas up to this point he seemed to see in the movements of things only events in which he himself participated" (1937, p. 269). Laurent on his first birthday gave a mature expression of this achievement.

> . . . he takes possession of a new ball which he has just received for his birthday and places it on top of a sloping cushion to let it go and roll by itself. He even tries to make it go by merely placing it on the floor, and, as no movement is produced, he limits himself to a gentle push [1937, pp. 274-275].

On the basis of this insight, the child's active experimentation with objects soon begins to show him not only what single objects will do by themselves but also what effects objects have on one another.

A similar sequence appears in the child's interaction with human beings. At eight months and a half Jacqueline begins to discover that her parents act under their own power.

> . . . Jacqueline and her mother imitate each other in singing the same chant. At a certain moment Jacqueline stops, then, instead of making her mother continue by using the procedures characteristic of causality through efficacy (arching, waving her hands, etc.), she delicately touches her mother's lower lip with her right finger. Her mother then begins to sing again. New interruption; Jacqueline once more touches the lip. . . .
> . . . Jacqueline watches me as I alternately spread my index finger and thumb apart and bring them together again. When I pause she

lightly pushes either the finger or the thumb to make me continue. Her movement is brisk and rapid; it is simply a starting impulse and not a continuous pressure [p. 260].

At eleven months the little girl shows increased confidence in what father can do.

... Jacqueline takes my hand, places it against a singing doll which she is unable to activate herself, and exerts pressure on my index finger to make me do what is necessary. This last observation reveals to what extent, to Jacqueline, my hand has become an independent source of action by contact [p. 260].

Finally, just past her first birthday, she seems to recognize her father as an entirely autonomous source of actions.

... Jacqueline is before me and I blow into her hair. When she wants the game to continue she does not try to act through efficacious gestures nor even, as formerly, to push my arms or lips; she merely places herself in position, head tilted, sure that I will do the rest by myself [p. 275].

The child's construction of reality can thus be interpreted as a development based upon action and the differential consequences of action. Embedded at first in a global scheme of action, objects come to be discriminated and assigned stable, permanent existence because of the characteristic patterns of their occurrence in the course of action. Objects and people, once part of an unanalyzed global feeling of efficacy, come to be regarded as independent centers of force acting upon one another because of their wayward departures from intended and expected schemes of action. Piaget's examples. although they often consist of experimental situations artificially created, are close to the things children constantly do spontaneously. and they point to the importance of playful exploration and manipulation in the persistent testing process whereby the child constructs the properties of the real world.

The linkage of knowledge and action is by no means confined to the first eighteen months of life. From that time onward the child becomes increasingly adept at substituting mental operations for overt action. But it is clear that even at much later ages the world we know is the world in which we know how to act. The objective reality of the scientist and philosopher, itself the product of a highly specialized set of actions, is not the milieu that we know in our daily lives. Heinz Werner (1926) describes as follows the general character of the child's world.

> The child's world is above all a *world of action,* a behavioral sphere in which everything is framed in terms of handiness and unhandiness, of efficaciousness and inefficaciousness. Katz says that children approach nearly all objects with the questions, "What can I do with it?" "For what can I use it?" "Furniture which cannot be used for gymnastic exercises and houses in which no well-known acquaintances live hardly exist in the child's consciousness" [Katz, 1928]. At the same time it is natural that this world of action, to whatever degree it may differ from the world of the adult, is continually changing at different age levels in accordance with a change in the basic attitude governing it. The Scupin boy at the age of eight no longer recognizes the sea which he knew at the age of four. At that time the sea was determined by different things-of-action. Such small objects as mussels and little stones, butterflies, and the wet sand ready to be molded into simple forms—these made up the world of the seashore for the four-year-old, whereas the eight-year-old conceives this same region as an arena for sports and swimming, and no doubt thinks of the tremendous flat surface of the water as an invitation to adventure [pp. 382-383].

In further illustration of this principle Werner cites experiments made by Martha Muchow (1935) with children in the city of Hamburg. One of these dealt with what an adult would perceive as a canal dock approached by a steep fenced path from the street. Early school-age children paid little attention to these elements. They responded to, and remembered afterwards, the fences and the steep grassy banks, objects suitable for climbing, jumping, rolling, and sliding. Another study compared the meaning of a big department store for children of different ages. The younger children (six to nine) saw the store as an inviting field for action and games, remembering particularly the stairs, elevators, and escalators. Children from nine to twelve discovered the goods, but treated them as treasures to be collected and usually emerged with quantities of samples, rubber bands, and advertising matter. At thirteen or fourteen the store became a part of the adult world; the girls particularly roamed from counter to counter pricing the goods, discussing their qualities with the salespeople, and promising to return later for a purchase.

Hartmann (1956b) has recently made a similar point with respect to the child's social environment. Pointing out that when Freud spoke of reality he usually meant the scientist's objective reality, Hartmann reminds us that the reality to which the child is expected to adapt is a socially conventional reality. It is a world of practical, unsophisticated common sense, and it is also a world of attitudes which may lead to rewards for restricting one's insight and accepting biased versions of the nature of things. Adapting to the world of people with whom the child principally interacts is thus not the same thing as adapting to the objective world of the scientist, but it is bound to be more important for the child.

Going much further in the same direction, Erikson (1962) proposes that a systematic distinction should be made between reality and actuality. Problems of development and of identity, he believes, cannot be understood without a differentiation between reality and actuality, that is, between the mind's relation to phenomenal reality and the ego's relation to the world of action. If we think only in terms of reality conceived in the usual sophisticated way, we are led into the mistake of taking undistorted perception as the criterion of the ego's strength, growth, and health. We also become subtly committed to the idea of an unchanging reality to which the child must gradually accommodate himself. These rationalistic preconceptions need to be counterbalanced by recognizing the importance of interaction, especially with the human environment, and by realizing that the child's changing developmental needs are met at each stage to the extent that he can activate appropriate behavior from the people around him. The child's *actuality,* then, is a world of participation and mutual activation, changing in time as both the child's needs and the adults' responses change. The actuality of his parents evolves from feeding, caring, and cuddling, to helping, encouraging, and teaching, just as the actuality of the department store evolves from gymnasium to treasure hunt to adult shoppers' world.

The importance of the distinction is perhaps most dramatic in the earliest stage of life. Discussing ego strength, Erikson says:

. . . the infant, while weak in our reality, is competent in his actuality. Nobody is ever stronger; . . . Ego strength at any level is relative to a number of necessities: previous stages must not have left a paralyzing deficit; the stage itself must occur under conditions favorable to its potentials; and maturing capacities must evoke in others cooperative responses necessary for joint (ego) survival. This, then, is *developmental actuality* [1962, p. 466].

Erikson points out, furthermore, that actuality is an important consideration in the treatment of adolescents and young adults, who may still have personal demands to make upon the world before they are ready to view it with detached, undistorted perception. He offers Freud's unsuccessful treatment of the eighteen-year-old patient Dora as a case in point. Freud was disappointed in Dora because she confronted her mother, her father, her father's mistress, and her would-be seducer (husband of the mistress) with their sordid infidelities and deceptions. This was "acting out," an expression of her revenge, a bad failure to follow her doctor's teaching of complete honesty about one's emotions when dealing with the world as it is. But what about the adolescent Dora's actuality?

> . . . it is probable that Dora needed to act as she did . . . in order to set straight the historical past so that she could envisage a sexual and social future of her choice; call infidelities by their name before she could commit herself to her own kind of fidelity; and establish the coordinates of her identity as a young woman of her class and time, before she could utilize more insight into her inner realities [1962, p. 460].

Erikson's thoughts on actuality show the far-reaching appropriateness of treating the growth of the ego in terms of action and its consequences. Some of our knowledge about reality, such as the permanence of objects and their action upon one another, can be constructed rather early in life through manipulation and playful exploration. Other aspects of this knowledge must be more slowly acquired in the course of interaction with the human environment. For our present theme the main thing is to realize the constant connection between knowledge and action. We learn about the environment because we go out to it, seek response from it, and find out what kind of responses it can give.

CONCLUSIONS

The central problem of psychoanalytic ego psychology has always been to understand the child's learning about reality and adapting to it. At the beginning of this chapter the question was put in this way: how does behavior come to be guided by realities, so that even strong instinctual impulses are expressed in accord with existing conditions?

We have seen that the explication of this problem offered grave difficulties so long as psychoanalytic theory tried to cope with it almost wholly in terms of instinctual energies. There is of course a very important energic side to the problem which was badly neglected in those older theories of knowledge based on metaphors of the mind as sealing wax, a blank slate, or a photographic film. Yet psychoanalytic theory, swinging to the opposite extreme, had its worst trouble with precisely this aspect, the manner in which reality leaves some record of itself to influence outflows of energy. This has been expressed as the problem of structure, and it is impossible to derive a theory of structure simply from the activities of energies.

The thesis of this essay is that the objective stable world is a construction based upon action. The knowledge that we gain of the environment is a knowledge of the probable consequences of action. It is a knowledge of potentialities for action, of what one surely can do, probably can do, may be able to do, probably cannot do, and surely cannot do with objects and situations that arise. Perhaps it is permissible for some purposes to call this a network or to use some other figure of speech drawn from material structures, but such metaphors must not obscure the real nature of what is learned through experience. It is a system of readinesses for action, and it seems to me quite proper to conceive of it as patterns of facilitation and inhibition in the central nervous system. Reality leaves its record, then, in the form of action possibilities learned through action and its consequences.

The learning of this system of potentialities takes place partly because of the pressure of instinctual drives. Part of our exploration of the world occurs in the course of seeking instinctual gratification. But psychoanalytic theory has not been able to deal with all the problems without assuming neutralized drive energies, and the findings we have examined from research on child development seem to require an abundance of such energy from the very beginning. The hypothesis of independent ego energies (effectance) is helpful at this point in understanding the extensiveness and persistence of the child's exploratory and manipulative activities. The corollary that there exists an interest in the environment apart from instinctual gratifications makes it possible to avoid certain difficulties about the cathexis of external objects.

This way of thinking allows us to reach what I believe to be an improved conception of the governing of instinctual drives by reality. If drives are to issue in action of any kind, they have to operate with the aid of the central nervous system. They have to take it as it is, so to speak, using it with all its acquired facilitations and inhibitions. To the extent that facilitations and inhibitions (knowledge of reality) have been acquired, instinctual energy will necessarily appear in action in the form of drive derivatives more amenable to realistic restrictions. This indicates the manner in which drive cathexes become bound. We know from a variety of experiments (e.g., Solomon and Wynne, 1954) that inhibitions can be established quickly and durably when pain or anxiety are aroused. Perhaps the first inhibitory "structures" are set up in this way, but the building on this basis of a flexible system of controls over instinctual expression is the result of more discriminating learnings occurring in less drastic circumstances. This way of conceiving of the process allows us to put aside altogether the dubious notion that an instinctual drive can be split so that part of its energies oppose the other part.

Because of the prestige of instincts in psychoanalytic theory, a prestige well earned through Freud's revolutionary discoveries, it may seem for a moment that this account allows them to be tamed a little too easily. Can our playfully acquired knowledge of how wide a brook we can jump and how high a wall we can climb be expected to block or deflect an aroused instinct? Unquestionably it can. The lover in search of his lady may act more forcefully and recklessly than is his wont, but he does not forget what he knows about the width of the moat to be crossed or the height of the castle wall to be scaled. I believe that the thesis proposed here will help to represent this kind of control in psychoanalytic theory.

5

EARLY DEVIATIONS IN
EGO DEVELOPMENT

The early triumphs of the psychoanalytic method were achieved with psychoneurotic patients and pertained mainly to the sexual instincts. In "Instincts and Their Vicissitudes," Freud noted this fact and ventured a bit of prophecy: "With the extension of psychoanalysis to the other neurotic affections, we shall no doubt find a basis for our knowledge of the ego-instincts as well, though it would be rash to expect equally favourable conditions for observation in this further field of research" (1915a, p. 125). Since then it has been an article of faith, so to speak, that the study of the psychoses would open the door upon ego psychology. Early contributions, such as those of Abraham, Freud, and Melanie Klein, seem in retrospect to have dealt more fully with the id and its fantasies than with the ego and its growth. Psychotic patients, in whom the id is often so little covered, may be said to have verified many of the things that psychoanalysis uncovered in neurotics. The study of psychotics does, however, reveal certain aspects of ego activity that are different from neurotic defense mechanisms. This is especially true now that clinical interest has turned so strongly to disturbances of a psychotic sort in young children. These disturbances are being earnestly searched for the light they can shed on early ego development.

As Freud predicted, the conditions for observation are not entirely favorable. Everything about earliest infancy still has to be reconstructed, and much reliance has to be placed on the proposition, about which one perhaps never feels perfectly secure, that psychotic manifestations faithfully repeat the states of mind of an earlier stage. But there have undoubtedly been great gains in under-

71

standing and treating children with psychosislike disturbances, and each clinical case provides certain opportunities for direct observation as well as reconstruction. In this chapter we shall consider the psychoanalytic interpretations that have been placed upon disorders representing early deviations in ego development. Is this an area in which the concept of independent ego energies, as developed in the last two chapters, can improve our understanding?

PSYCHOANALYTIC VIEWS OF EARLY EGO DISORDERS

For some time there was great reluctance to speak of childhood psychosis, with its discouraging implications, in the absence of a clearly demonstrated relationship between later psychosis and the ego disturbances of the early years. This caution happily prevented a hasty application of familiar diagnostic categories. Three patterns have been described and have proved to be clinically useful, though no one claims that they cover all forms of early ego deviation. Spitz (1946) introduced the term *anaclitic depression* for a depressed and lethargic condition appearing abruptly in infants at six months or so upon separation from the mother. Perhaps we can say that his *hospitalism,* described in 1945, represents a chronic form of this acute disturbance. Kanner (1943) proposed the term *early infantile autism* to describe a pattern of traits consisting of serious lack of response to the human environment, backwardness in the use of communicative language, and a rigid demand for sameness in the surroundings. Mahler (1952) suggested *symbiotic infantile psychosis* as the name for a condition in which the child displays a tremendously strong dependent attachment to the mother and seems unable to take any autonomous steps of his own.

The autistic and symbiotic disorders, which more and more appear to be forerunners of later schizophrenic tendencies, have a good many underlying features in common. Psychoanalytic theory conceptualizes these features as deviations or delays in the several functions of the ego. These can be summarized as follows:

1. *Failure of social responsiveness.* Autistic children are singularly unresponsive to other human beings. As described by Weil (1956), they are deficient very early in smiling and in responding when picked up and cuddled. Children with symbiotic disturbances, though intensely dependent, are socially not much more advanced.

Like the autistic children, they may be deficient in imitation, in back-and-forth play, in gestural communication, and later in verbal communication. These signs indicate difficulties and delays in the early growth of social object relationships, and it is often noticed that the child falls seriously behind in distinguishing self and not-self.

2. *Failure to achieve stable defenses.* Such defense mechanisms as are used are primitive and not very effective, so that a stable defensive system is not formed. As a consequence, sexual and aggressive interests are openly manifested, often in bizarre forms. Ross (1955) describes a six-year-old boy who rummaged through women's purses whenever he got a chance, entered rest rooms to examine the pipes under bathroom fixtures, got on his hands and knees to look at women's legs, hit other children on the head, was deeply preoccupied with the daily mail delivery, crawled under parked trucks to examine fender aprons, and generally made of himself a veritable showcase of id impulses and symbolizations. Such children experience anxiety, often in acute form, but they have not succeeded in elaborating an effective system of controls over impulse.

3. *Inadequate growth of reality testing and active mastery.* The autistic child, with his interest in preserving sameness, and the symbiotic child, with his consuming dependence on the mother, are alike in making very little investigation of their surroundings. Some children who exhibit early ego deviations are hyperactive, but passivity and a limited repertory of action patterns are more characteristic. When a strong interest develops it may be pursued with a repetitive intensity that suggests heavy symbolic significance and a weak capacity to maintain a realistic sense of proportion. There is a persistence of magical thinking, and reality does not exert the expected amount of control over behavior.

Psychoanalytic theory thus enables us to see a kind of order in behavior that superficially could hardly be more disordered. The guiding theme is deficiency and delay in the growth of ego functions. How is this weakness of the ego to be explained? Are we dealing with an innate deficiency or with one that can be understood on a developmental basis?

The first attempts to deal with this problem proceeded from the hypothesis that early ego development is largely determined by the behavior of the mother. Various maternal shortcomings such as coldness, preoccupation, rejection, anxious overprotection, and engulfment came to light in clinical work and eventually added up to the composite image of the "schizophrenogenic" mother. Kanner's studies of autistic children emphasized a cold mechanical quality in the mother's relation to the child; later, Eisenberg (1957) showed that the fathers had a high incidence of similar traits. Rank (1949) attributed the child's difficulties to severe, chronic, overwhelming deprivation of mothering, which made deep instinctual gratification a rare experience and thus fragmented the growth of the ego. In cases of symbiotic psychosis the mother was seen as having a tremendous need for the child, as being dependent upon him for the emotional rewards and meaning of her life, and as feeling empty and incomplete if she could not be with him all the time. Hill (1955), who saw such mothers as themselves disordered personalities, emphasized the capricious character of their mothering and the frequent communication to the infant of their own tensions and anxieties. "This train of experience is one of uncertainty and discouragement," he wrote; "It contributes to a sense of futility in that the child does not have expectation of regular success in the simple business of being nourished and staying alive" (p. 141). Questionnaire studies such as that of Mark (1953) added to the picture by showing in the mothers of schizophrenic patients a leaning toward statements that emphasized devotion, sacrifice, restriction, and decided invasions of the child's privacy.

It is implied in these studies that the mother's effect on ego development can be disastrous. Growth depends upon adequate, affectionate mothering with reliable instinctual gratification, it is held; when this is not present, the functions of the ego cannot flourish. The work of Spitz seemed to clinch this argument. Deprivation, either in the chronic form of a cool hospital nursing regime or in the acute form of sudden separation from the mother, produced a generalized slowing down in ego development. This extended to the use of toys and other inanimate objects so that motor and perceptual development were impaired. But objects themselves belonged in the province of the mother. "In the normal child the toy is given by the adult and becomes important (gains its investment) in large part because it comes from the mother" (Ritvo and Provence, 1953, p. 159). According to this view, the normal child will be interested in nothing except the mother and the things she gives. When she is short of goodness and does not give, the whole path to ego development is effectively blocked.

This picture of maternal omnipotence, with its one-way causality —the mother's behavior as cause and the child's behavior as effect —was satisfactory neither to those who consider that human behavior is transactional nor to those who attach importance to constitutional predisposition. Could there be something about the child that influenced the mother and set up an unfortunate cycle of interactions? Erikson has this to say about the problem: "I think one should consider that these children may very early and subtly fail to return the mother's glance, smile, and touch; an initial reserve which makes the mother, in turn, unwittingly withdraw. . . . In those cases of infantile schizophrenia which I have seen, the primary deficiency in 'sending power' was in the child" (1950, p. 181). Mahler and Gosliner express themselves more strongly: "The children suffering from symbiotic child psychoses . . . are not to be thought of as normal children in whom a psychotic process is induced by an emotionally disturbed mother. These children are constitutionally vulnerable and predisposed toward the development of a psychosis" (1955, p. 201).

The nature of the possible predisposition has been studied by Bender (1953), whose findings point toward a general lag and irregularity of maturation starting during the embryonic period. Physiological immaturity is expressed in poorly maintained balance in the vegetative system, belated establishment of regular sleep patterns, and poor integration of muscular patterns. These and other irregularities interfere with the orderly organization of early experience and thus constitute the basis for a lag in ego development. Research on the physiology and biochemistry of schizophrenia is obviously not a finished topic, but a good many psychoanalytically oriented workers tend to accept the general idea of a constitutional predisposition.

INTERPRETATION OF EARLY EGO DISORDERS IN TERMS OF EFFICACY AND COMPETENCE

Hartmann (1953) has translated early ego deviations into the language of energies by postulating an impaired capacity for neutralizing sexual and aggressive instinctual energies. Weakness in ego development should certainly imply some degree of failure on the part of those energies that contribute to defense, control, and reality testing. The central hypothesis of this essay differs from Hartmann's in that I assume independent ego energies which contribute importantly to these "neutral" developments and which are not conceptualized as transformed sexual and aggressive energies. This changes the nature of the questions to be asked. The focus of attention shifts from something that goes wrong with a hypothetical energy transformation to something that goes wrong with effectance and competence, which means with the playful exploratory and manipulative activity through which the normal child establishes so much of his relation to reality. As we have seen, reality testing, the discrimination of self and not-self, learning about the autonomous nature of objects, and the building of a sense of competence or incompetence with respect to the human environment, all depend upon active tendencies to explore and try out one's efficacy. Our major question must be: *what happens to obstruct the infant's tendencies to explore and interact with his environment?*

Putting the question in this way, and using the already-described conceptions of feeling of efficacy and sense of competence, make it possible, I believe, to improve our understanding of the following points. (1) We can examine in more detail the relation of the mother to the infant's activity. This will enable us to clarify the growth of independence and to assess the proposition that all objects derive their initial interest from their connection with the mother. (2) We can form a sharper idea of the origins and maintenance of the mother's attitude toward the schizoid child. This will help us with the clinical paradox that some of the mothers have been reported to be severely disordered, while others have been described as devoted and capable. (3) We can focus more accurately on the precise ways in which effectance and competence are injured in pathological cases. This may serve to tighten the loose connections involved in propositions such as the one that deprivation and lack of instinctual gratification prevent the growth of ego functions.

Implications of Effectance as Independent Energy

The child's interest in efficacy is independent of hunger, love, and hate. Obviously this independence is not total in a living system in which each part tends to influence all other parts. Effectance is independent in the sense that it constitutes a push toward growth without any necessary collaboration by the instinctual drives, though it may be importantly influenced by them. The mother, considered as gratifier or frustrator of instinctual drives, is thus not the only force to be reckoned with in ego development. As Anna Freud puts it, "There are many among us who find it difficult to believe that failure in the early object relationships (i.e., 'rejection by the mother') should be powerful enough as an agent to suppress the innate possibilities of orientation in reality, speech and motor development in a child whose sensory and motor apparatus is intact" (1952, pp. 47-48).

Effectance, leading as it does to increased competence in dealing with the environment, can be conceived of as inherently an urge away from the necessity for being mothered. When a child undertakes to be independent, to do something in his own way or to achieve some goal without adult help, he is acting in opposition to mothering impulses. Independence being highly valued in our society, the child may be encouraged in just such actions, once he has taken them. This has led to a further flowering of the delusion of maternal omnipotence, according to which the child becomes independent only because the mother encourages him to become independent. She rewards him with love for feeding and dressing himself, for standing, toddling, and talking; otherwise he would continue indefinitely to prefer the delightful equilibrium of being fed, carried, and wheeled in his carriage. Neither academic reinforcement theory nor psychoanalytic instinct theory offers sufficient protection against this curious distortion of what actually happens.

No honest insightful mother who has enjoyed her maternal role would be willing, I suspect, to subscribe to such a theory. Those mothers who frankly yearn for another helpless baby as soon as their youngest child begins to take care of himself would particularly admit that any encouragement they had given to independence was done with a divided heart. Few mothers would say that encouraging self-feeding and self-dressing was a happy experience for them or that their child's exploration of the house and neighborhood found them always in the role of applauding audience. If a mother greeted her child upon his safe return from a forbidden adventure by praising his display of independence, we could only suppose that books on psychology had unhinged her reason. Perhaps the only mothers who can give single-minded encouragement to independence are the ones who dislike the nurturing role and are glad to be rid of their burdensome young. But these are the rejecting mothers whose effect on early ego development is generally supposed to be harmful.

This whole question of independence has been examined very carefully by David Levy (1955) in a paper on *oppositional behavior*. Levy uses this term to describe the familiar self-assertion and negativism of the second year of life, as well as phenomena both earlier and later, including the infant's refusal to suck when awakened too quickly and the generalized negativism found in adult catatonic schizophrenics. He makes it clear that behavior of this kind is not initially aggressive or destructive. Its adaptive significance lies in counteracting the pressures of the environment so that one's own inclinations and intentions can prevail. "Now we can see the oppositional behavior of the second year of life," Levy writes, "as a general movement towards the autonomy of the whole person, as the first flowering of self-determination, of which the budding had long been in evidence" (p. 214). Seen in this light, there is intrinsic opposition between child and mother in such episodes as "the battle of the spoon"—the occasion when the child seizes the spoon and crudely undertakes to feed himself. No matter how quickly the psychologically sophisticated mother realizes that this is something she ought to encourage, at whatever cost to her time and patience, it is to the child an experiment in autonomy. If he can do it himself, even at the price of less food successfully eaten, he is rewarded; and he is frustrated to the extent that his mother obstructs this intention by insistent ministrations. Levy's ideas imply that oppositional behavior carries intrinsic rewards, something akin to a feeling of efficacy. The mother can take away this reward by interfering, and she can sometimes add at appropriate points the further reward of appreciation, but the feeling of efficacy is not primarily in her power to bestow.

A similar situation prevails in connection with separation-individuation, which Mahler and Gosliner (1955) consider to be the central theme of development from eighteen to thirty-six months. They contend that

... this separation-individuation phase is a crucial one in regard to the ego and the development of object relationships . . . we need to study the strong impetus which drives toward separation, coupled with the fear of separation, if we hope to understand the severe psychopathology of childhood which ever so often begins or reveals itself insidiously or acutely from this second part of the second year onward [p. 196].

For purposes of understanding our points, we propose focusing on the position of defense of the eighteen- to thirty-six-month infant, to defend his own evolving, enjoyable and jealously guarded self-image from infringement by mother and other important figures [p. 200].

The process of separation-individuation can be conceived of as one which the mother can allow to happen or which she can largely prevent from happening. It cannot be conceived as one which derives its whole impetus from her gifts of love and praise.

The point is worth laboring because current psychological theory has beclouded it. Learning theories in which reinforcement is provided only by drive reduction have led to the idea that the mother, as supplier of nourishment and comfort, possesses a fund of reward which she can dispense in the form of love and praise. She expends her capital at such times as the child must be pushed over some developmental hurdle such as weaning, self-feeding, or learning to walk. The same idea, it must be admitted, has also cropped up in psychoanalytic theory, and with the same strange, though probably unwitting, implication that the infant has no desire to grow up and must be seduced into doing so. Not only does the theory misrepresent the nature of the active living organism, but it also fatally falsifies the meaning of independence. The child who requires maternal reward for doing things on his own is not independent at all. He is, in fact, rather like a child with a symbiotic psychosis, whose every step must have maternal ratification. Independence begins when the child can briefly dispense with his mother's approval, finding sufficient reward in his own sense of competence.

I have not quoted the foregoing authorities in order to claim their support for my view of independent ego energies. But I believe that their observations can be most adequately dealt with by a theory that gives real importance to concepts such as efficacy and competence. This is to say that there exists in every child an independent urge to explore and interact with his surroundings, as a consequence of which he draws the lines of his own autonomy and establishes his competence in dealing with things and other people. I would call this "oppositional" only in the sense that it is engineered, so to speak, from within, cannot always be in harmony with what other people want at each moment, and carries its own reward in a feeling of efficacy. How the mother responds to it is always an important consideration, but not because she generates it, not because she can always stop it, not because it always needs her reinforcement.

To complete this exposition it would be necessary for me to work out a chronological scheme for the relative importance of the mother. We know that in the course of time the mother progressively shares her position with the father, siblings, playmates, and teachers, and that children range ever more widely outside the sphere of maternal influence. We know that a child well short of his third birthday can manage considerable opposition to parental commands and can assert his right to do things himself. The assertive self-feeder need not be much beyond his first birthday. But when we get back to the first year, the seedtime of the more serious ego deviations, does the situation approximate more closely to one of maternal omnipotence? Do the findings of Spitz require us to admit that up to six months, at all events, ego development is just about what the mother makes it? This will require careful consideration, and I shall return to it after taking up the second topic on my agenda.

Challenge to Maternal Competence

Psychoanalytic theory leads to an interpretation of behavior largely in terms of love, hate, and anxiety. This has led to great advances in understanding both children and parents. The mothers of children with ego deviations, like the children themselves, show various patterns of love, hate, and anxiety, all of which must be grasped by the clinical worker. We have seen, however, that the children's behavior could be further illuminated by the concept of independent ego energies with their structural consequences. The mothers, too, deserve consideration in this light.

Most relevant to the mothers as adults is the idea of *sense of competence*, a highly developed product of a person's whole experience of efficacy and inefficacy. The adult sense of competence may be well differentiated. Many skills and excellencies which have been found unattainable or which are not important in the main life pattern will have been put aside so that they count for little in self-esteem. Other abilities will remain central, and failures will reverberate in such a way as to produce feelings of inferiority and humiliation. Concern about one's more central abilities is represented in academic psychology by the concept of ego involvement (Allport, 1943).

While we know that some mothers, consciously or unconsciously, have a personal distaste for the maternal role, it is, at least in our society, very difficult to admit that one is a failure as a mother. This is all the more true in view of the popular idea that simple, untutored, "bovine" women perform the task quite well, and in view of the recent more sophisticated idea that failure represents a far-reaching weakness in the capacity to love. Society expects parents to bring up their children: to nourish, protect, train, and discipline them so that they are reasonably socialized beings. To be unable to bring up children properly is just about certain to be a grave blow to one's sense of competence.

The nature and force of social expectation in this realm is thrown into relief by comparing the parental role with that of grandparents or of maiden aunts. We are familiar with the perennial complaint that grandparents spoil their grandchildren, thus stealing their love away from their parents and undoing the effects of carefully wrought discipline. How often it has sprung to a mother's lips to say: "You never let me get away with things like that." There are, of course, instances of the opposite sort in which grandparents try to impose the stricter standards of their own day on the lively products of permissive child rearing. But the role of grandparent in our society inherently permits greater spoiling. It allows an outflow of tenderness uninhibited by considerations of socialization. Grandparents, if so inclined, can be like callers who spoil a charming puppy, to the distress of its master who has got to develop a housebroken, socialized dog. Those who, a generation ago, spoke hopefully about spontaneity in mothering have perhaps now realized their ideal in the role of grandparents. Parents can hardly take it so lightly. They have to try to be competent in socializing their young. For this they are responsible, as grandparents and maiden aunts are not.

The ground is thus laid for a distressing sense of incompetence whenever the mother has to deal with a child who does not behave in the average expectable fashion. This is clearly visible in mothers of hyperactive children at whatever age. Even if the mother knows that she is in no way responsible for an attack of encephalitis, she can hardly avoid frustration over her daily failures to produce calmness, control, an attention span more than fleeting, and the internalization of necessary restraints. The business of "treating the mother" in such circumstances contains generous elements of advice designed to increase her competence in coping with unusual difficulties. Catharsis of her feelings of frustration may put her in a mood to heed the advice, but catharsis alone cannot do much for her feelings of incompetence. She will be "better" on those days when she can report that she has managed some situation with the child successfully.

Most of the children with early ego deviations are passive and unresponsive rather than overactive. As we have seen, there is a tendency now to think of these qualities as being constitutionally determined in the infant. If dealing with an overactive child is frustrating, dealing with a passive and unresponsive child is possibly even worse. How can one deal with an infant who doesn't do anything? He puts a block in the transactional process, obstructs maternal exploration, and thus remains impervious to both influence and understanding. The mother of the autistic child, whatever her shortcomings of affectionate interest, must forego most of the rewards of caring for a baby, which come from his responsiveness and smiles, and we can well expect her to feel desperately incompetent at her inability to evoke these expectable behaviors. The mother of the symbiotic child, however powerful her need to possess and engulf him, must in the end endure dire frustration when his development obviously halts because he will do nothing without her. Passivity and imperviousness to influence can be a grave challenge to maternal competence. A case reported by Rochlin illustrates this point dramatically. The mother "felt guilty, inadequate, frustrated—she could influence him so little that she was furious" (1953, p. 291).

It could be supposed that mothers of mentally retarded children would experience the same difficulty. The mental tester's rule that the mother be out of the room, lest she start answering for the child and giving him hints, points to a more or less universal problem of motherhood that will be all the more severe when experience has shown that the child will probably not respond well. We can predict about the mothers of retarded children that, not only out of love but also in defense of their sense of maternal competence, they will be concerned about having responses come from the child, and that they will hint and prod and virtually make the response themselves rather than admit that it is not forthcoming. Here, because we are confident that mental retardation is innately determined, we easily interpret maternal behavior as a response to the child's handicap. The situation may well be somewhat similar when the retardation is in the sphere of affect and initiative. This is strongly suggested in a study of maternal attitudes by Klebanoff (1959). Three groups were compared, mothers of a mentally retarded child, mothers of a schizophrenic child, and mothers all of whose children were normal. The most differentiating factor was a cluster of items labeled "overpossessiveness" which included covert control of the child by keeping him dependent and a perception of the mother's role as one of sacrifice and suffering. Both "abnormal" groups were much higher than the "normal," but the mothers of retarded children scored a little higher than the mothers of schizophrenic children.

It is my contention, then, that the concept of sense of competence yields us a gain in understanding the interaction between children with early ego deviations and their mothers. Both the omnipotence of hereditary constitution and the omnipotence of the "schizophrenogenic" mother must be rejected in favor of an interactive interpretation. Initial abnormality in the infant and initial pathology in the mother must be treated as variables neither of which is likely to be at a negligible value. In the interaction that ensues it is profitable to see that threat to the maternal sense of competence is one of the things to be weighed. Love thwarted and buried, hate threatening to gain the upper hand, anxiety undermining intelligent action may all be parts of the picture, but they can all be understood better if we look at the mother's activity as well as her affects and realize that she is experiencing a series of frustrations in her intended acts of mothering, frustrations which signify to her that she must be an inferior, incompetent woman. Treatment extended to the mother can be improved by the realization that she needs an increase of competence as well as release from tangled emotions.

We can now complete the symmetry of our interactive presentation by turning back to the infant and considering the consequences of his acts for his budding feelings of efficacy and competence.

Early Inhibition of Effectance

According to the conceptualization advanced in this monograph, effectance will give rise to active exploration, manipulation, and experimentation unless it is in some way inhibited. If it proceeds naturally, reality will be tested, self will be distinguished from not-self, a stable world of objects and people will be constructed, a sense of competence will be achieved, and there will be movement toward independence. Early ego deviations represent a serious obstruction of these processes.

To the extent that *constitution* may be involved as an obstructing agent, the incapacity might be presumed to lie in difficulty in achieving feelings of efficacy. This could be the case if activity level were low and effort uncomfortable, or if coordination were poor so that the effects produced upon the environment were not regular and repeatable. The cumulative developmental effects of initial low activity are well described by Weil in the case of Sandra, a little girl of five who had shown slowness, unresponsiveness, and lack of spontaneity practically from birth (Alpert, Neubauer, and Weil, 1956). In hyperactive children who cannot consolidate any modulated patterns for dealing with things, it is also probable that feelings of efficacy are elusive. The case of Tony, described by Neubauer in the same paper, is that of an overactive child with a history of even intrauterine hypermotility who "had no capacity for adequate control. . . . would fall repeatedly, injure himself, would not learn by experience" (p. 142), and who generally failed to produce advantageous effects on his surroundings.

The *mother's behavior* as an inhibiting agent has been conceived of in several different ways. Her interference, as we have seen, has been described as a deprivation of instinctual gratification, as a cold mechanical regime of nurture, as an engulfing obstruction of the infant's activity, and as a capricious unreliability that communicates and generates anxiety. These patterns are partly, though not entirely, inconsistent with one another, and it is suggested from time to time that different "kinds" of ego deviation, such as the autistic or symbiotic, are correlated with different maternal patterns. I believe that these ideas can be clarified by focusing attention more directly on effectance and the ways in which it can become inhibited.

Generalized obstruction by swamping. Earlier in this essay effectance was described as an energy that operates freely in the infant during the spare time that is not occupied by aroused instinctual urges or by sleep. When instinctual drives are aroused, the activity of the nervous system—the "ego apparatus"—is directed toward instinctual aims. Only when drives are quiet does the system operate in the pure service of feelings of efficacy, and with the breadth and nonspecificity that is most conducive to the growth of varied competencies. In the newborn infant there is very little of this spare time, though exploratory activity can be detected virtually from the start. By the end of the first year, however, playtime may amount to as much as six hours of the child's day, manipulation occupies great stretches of his time, and exploration has become a very obvious part of his behavior.

One way to conceive of the inhibition of effectance, then, is to say that the mother prevents the use of this spare time. This does not imply that she literally stops the infant from playing; rather, it means that spare time is squeezed out because instinctual drives are in a continual state of arousal. The easiest way to picture this possibility is to suppose that anxiety and a longing for satisfaction —two things that are closely related during the early months—tend to be active all the time the infant is awake. Needs for security and satisfaction dominate his waking time so completely that nothing is left over for the more "neutral" exploration of the environment. This is a situation that might come about through circumstances beyond the mother's control, such as a severe physical illness with chronic discomfort and pain. If it is created by the mother's behavior, it must be through a pretty severe early deprivation, probably including the whole group of needs that ordinarily finds satisfaction in the total feeding situation. This is the sense in which it seems to me legitimate to speak of instinctual deprivation as obstructing ego development. The ego does not gain its strength just through instinctual gratification; it must have enough time to itself, free from need tension, to explore its own way toward full development.

Spitz's cases of anaclitic depression can probably be interpreted as traumatic forms of this type of all-inclusive inhibition. Loss of the mother, coming at a time when she is still the predominant feature of the infant's world, when his spare time is still rather limited, and when even his manipulative mastery is incomplete, can produce a swamping of effectance by longing and anxiety. The time range during which this can happen is a limited one. If the infant can respond trustingly to people besides the mother, or if he has gone far enough in elaborating spheres of play that yield feelings of efficacy, he will have alternatives and the devastation will not be so complete. But the perpetuation through anxiety of an intense dependence on the mother can have a restrictive influence on effectance. This often seems to be the case in the severe symbiotic psychoses. A dramatic illustration is a boy described by Maenchen (1953) whose consuming demands on his mother literally prevented his growing up. At the age of nine, after five years of treatment, he still insisted on having his mother help him to dress, and although his incessant questions drove everyone to distraction he refused to learn to read and thus acquire power to provide his own answers. Another illustration is the boy Aro, already mentioned (Mahler and Gosliner, 1955), whose relation to his mother had frozen into the form that she must never be right at his side (because he hated her interference) but must never be more than a little way away (because of his anxiety at separation). It is easy to see that the energy expended in constantly maintaining this state of affairs would leave little spare time for relaxed and happy exploration.

If we take it as our task to understand the inhibition of effectance we do not have to confine ourselves to the generalized "swamping" pattern just discussed. The obstruction of effectance may be more direct and somewhat more focused. It may occur specifically in the realm of human interaction and leave relatively intact the dealing with inanimate objects. There is also the opposite possibility of a direct inhibition of play with inanimate objects, though this will not often occur in an otherwise benign human setting.

Specific obstruction of social efficacy. During the first year of life the infant's experience of efficacy in dealing with human objects is heavily concentrated on the mother. The reward of feeling of efficacy can be obstructed by a mother who is not responsive to the infant's efforts. If she does not permit herself to be influenced, if she does not bend to his whims, if she is out of tune to the extent of not sensing his impulses, he will be repeatedly unsuccessful in producing any effect upon her. This seems to be the approximate situation of the child with a cold, mechanical, obsessive mother— the autistic child as described by Kanner (1943). Mothers of this type, following a routine, manage to provide quite reliably some of the most essential needs like food and cleanliness. The deprivation therefore lies mainly in the absence of affective exchanges of warm mothering and of responsiveness to the child's signals of desire at other than scheduled times. In these circumstances we might expect a less generalized spread of injury to ego functions, a concentration of the difficulty in the sphere of social interaction. In point of fact Kanner has reported that autistic children are often not particularly retarded in dealing with inanimate objects. What does seem to be characteristic is a strong desire for sameness in the environment. We can guess that this partly reflects the regularity of the regime of gratification. The infant has found no ways to influence what comes to him, and he can hope only that the environment and its signals will remain the same. For him, change disrupts gratification, whereas sameness guarantees his usual pittance. Unfortunately, the interest in sameness will if anything discourage explorations of the inanimate environment directed toward novelties.

This conception of a somewhat less wholesale inhibition of effectance in the autistic child can be illustrated from a study by Ritvo and Provence (1953). They report upon six children of twenty-two to thirty-nine months who showed marked retardation in imitative behavior and language development but approximate normality in form perception, as measured by form-board tests. During the testing sessions the children almost never looked the examiner in the face, even more rarely smiled at her, and dealt with her hands as if they were inanimate objects. The young patients could not be induced to play ball or pat-a-cake or any other truly interactive game. This agreed with the mothers' reports such as, "he shuts me out," "he seems in a world of his own." Nevertheless, performance on the form-perception tests was at the normal level.

It is noted that the children's approach to playthings was at a primitive younger level with a tendency to intense repetitive play with one or two favored objects. In the case of these objects, however, manipulative skill was undergoing development; in fact, one boy became quite adept at building and fitting blocks together. There was progress, too, in the sphere of motility, though on the whole the children were stiff, uncertain, and poorly coordinated. ". . . none of the children impressed the observers as being especially agile or graceful at this age but they did appear to be working hard on the development of motor skills" (1953, p. 157). One boy practiced with great absorption the feat of going upstairs without using the banister, smiling to himself when he was successful.

These findings suggest to me a strong focal inhibition on human interaction, from which inhibition the play with inanimate objects and the attempts at motor mastery are partially exempt. The child has given up trying to influence the human environment, except to keep it out, but can still find a certain scope for effectance in the inanimate sphere. Some competence has thus been developed in dealing with things like form boards, but none in dealing with people.

This explanation, based upon independent ego energies and their selective obstruction, seems to me simpler and more direct than the one adopted by Ritvo and Provence. They see evidence in the lack of imitative behavior that object relationships are tenuous and that self and not-self are insufficiently differentiated. Reasoning as if this basic step in ego development has to be accomplished once and for all with the mother before it can exist for any other object, they do not accept the form-board achievement as a normal one and attribute it to a quite special process with unusual cathectic investments. The child, they believe, senses a difficulty in establishing ego boundaries, in cathecting the periphery of the body, and in establishing certain proprioceptive patterns. He thus concentrates on edges and boundaries, and overcompensates in the sphere of form perception. To me this is an awkward bit of speculation, and I believe that it is wholly superfluous. If we recognize that ego development is not entirely a matter of interaction between mother and child, there is no difficulty in supposing that the discrimination of self and not-self can be accomplished in exploratory play with inanimate objects while it is still not made with the human ones at whom the child will not even look. There is also no difficulty in interpreting the form perception as a consequence of such dealing with objects as has taken place, especially in the case of the young builder with blocks.

Specific obstruction of exploratory play. Turning now to the conceivable opposite pattern, that in which the playful exploration of the inanimate environment is directly inhibited, we shall certainly not expect to find pure cases in conjunction with intact human interactions. A case reported by Mahler and Elkisch (1953), however, involves serious early obstruction of play by a cause that does not necessarily imply an unusual maternal attitude. The boy Stanley, seen at six years of age, had been a feeding problem with vomiting and refusals for the first six months of his life. For the second six months he suffered from inguinal hernia, as a result of which he had abrupt attacks of intense pain. His parents, told that prolonged crying might worsen the hernia, tried their best to comfort and quiet him, usually by feeding; obviously they could not always be successful. At six, Stanley's behavior showed two characteristic states. One of these was a very active but bizarre state, likened by the authors to catatonic excitement, which was completely dominated by the earlier traumatic situation of crying in pain and being fed. It was set off by anything that reminded him of babies, and while it sometimes entailed acts of feeding a pictured baby there was no evidence that this had anything to do with stopping the baby's crying. The whole scene was redintegrated like a battle dream in primary-process terms. The other state was one of complete listlessness—"semistupor"—in which the child would fumble with things in a dazed way, finger them or drop them without any aim or continuity, or wander about with no sign of a focus of interest. It was believed that he sought the excited state as relief from the listless one.

Stanley's ego development was plainly much arrested. Mahler and Elkisch point out the lack of causal relation in the scene of the crying baby being fed, the lack of selective repression that would permit a differentiated recall of early happenings, the failure to decathect the significant early experiences, and the lack of differentiation between self and not-self, especially during the listless periods when he seemed to be "a quasi part of the environment, . . . in a state of cohesion with it" (1953, p. 255). Freud (1915b) is quoted to the effect that an intense stimulus like strong hunger or pain makes repression impossible. The authors attach great importance to the failure of repression. "In normal repression, different objects, although perceived simultaneously, are handled as separate entities and may be disconnected from each other and from the affect by which they had been accompanied. In Stanley's case, a trigger stimulus caused total recall of the stored syncretic engram" (1953, p. 260). This ego defect constituted a "grave disability of learning" which impaired reality testing and prevented differentiation of self and not-self.

It seems to me that this conceptualization can be improved by bringing in the ideas of effectance and competence. It is unfortunate, I think, to make the differentiation of experience depend upon repression, which means, according to Freud's views after 1926, that it is produced by anxiety, commonly considered to have the very opposite effect. As we saw in the last chapter, the differentiation of objects, including the discrimination of self from other objects, occurs as a result of exploratory and manipulative activity which proves to have different effects on different parts of the environment. Considering Stanley's listless attitude toward toys, we might wonder what has happened to effectance in this sphere, and the authors supply an answer in one detail the importance of which they do not develop: ". . . from the age of six months on he had suffered intense pain which came on suddenly while the child was 'happily' and quietly playing. 'All of a sudden Stanley would break into violent crying'" (p. 257). Here we have a sequence of events, repeated many times, that must have been quite sufficient to load happy and quiet play with unbearable anxiety. For Stanley, feelings of efficacy could be blotted out by sudden intrusions of sharp pain; small wonder that he gave up exploratory play and thus abandoned a whole sphere of reality testing and differentiation. The crucial sequence began at six months, when manipulative activity is the major outlet for effectance. Stanley's dazed, uninterested fumbling with objects bears testimony to the fatal obstruction of this phase of exploratory play.

This case is certainly not one in which human relations were unimpaired. Even if there were no other evidence, the feeding difficulties would arouse our suspicion, and the inability of the parents to assuage the child's intense pain would go far to injure his trust in them. The case reported by Maenchen (1953) involves the maternal attitude even more clearly, but contains this detail: "When Robert was one and a half, his play pen was placed in the back yard behind bushes. There the child cried most of the time" (p. 265). When seen at four, he "refused to play with toys as if he were afraid of them" (p. 266), and we can well understand why. Maenchen sees very clearly the importance of the isolated play pen.

> The path for the mastery of the motor apparatus, so essential for the growth of the ego, was at least partially blocked. Prevented from moving around, from conquering more and more reality by testing it, prevented from approaching it—in the literal sense of the word— the child was thrown back into primitive modes of discharge (temper tantrums). Even at the age of four the boy gave an impression of carrying his pen with him, with his hands still between the rails [pp. 266-267].

But she maintains that this kind of thing is not decisive unless there is an acute difficulty in the maternal relation. The difficulty specified in this case is the mother's withdrawnness and poor sense of reality. "I would think that introjecting such a vague, emotionally withdrawn person, as Robert's mother was, would be bound to produce a reality-shy ego" (p. 267). And might it not be, she speculates, that the blocked aggression becomes destructively directed at budding ego functions?

There can be no disagreement that the mother-child relation was the central difficulty in Maenchen's case. But it seems to me legitimate to protest a little when she makes introjection of a reality-shy mother the critical agent of pathology, and when she evokes unexternalized aggression as the inhibitor of ego functions. Her report contains mountains of evidence for the blocking of independent ego energies. All the patterns we have been discussing appear to be represented. The swamping of spare-time exploratory play by the constant pressure of needs for gratification and security is strongly suggested by the material. Specific inhibition of effectance in the manipulative and motor spheres can be deduced from the play-pen incident. Specific obstruction of social efficacy is clearly implied in the descriptions of the mother's autistic tendencies. The intense symbiotic relation in which the patient became entangled would still further obstruct explorations away from his mother's side. With this immense accumulation of circumstances tending to block the child's exploratory interactions with his environment, both inanimate and social—with all these obstacles in the normal path to reality testing—we certainly need not assign to aggression the feat of directly inhibiting ego functions, whatever else it may have done, and it seems to me equally superfluous to suppose that a child so obviously destined for reality shyness can fulfill this destiny only by introjecting a reality-shy mother. If these two processes are of critical importance, they should be demonstrated in a case that is not already sufficiently explained.

Concluding Comments

I should here indicate my awareness of the perils that lie in reinterpreting other people's case material from published reports. What I have said is in no sense intended as a commentary on what was done to understand and help the disturbed children. My concern in this essay is with theory, and what I am trying to bring forward in commenting on these cases is the kind of interpretation one arrives at through the use of a theory of independent ego energies. My argument is that psychoanalytic theory has failed to provide sufficient specific concepts to account for the ego's relation to reality. It has not drawn attention to the actions and learning processes whereby the child tests reality, adapts to it, and learns to exert some influence on his surroundings. I believe that this lack in psychoanalytic theory has been a very real handicap to workers who are trying to understand early deviations in ego development, and that it continually forces them into a kind of improvisation with concepts not ideally suited to the task. The conceptualizations I have criticized—compensatory cathexis of boundaries, repression as the mechanism of differentiation, introjection of a reality-shy mother, aggression directed against ego functions—all strike me as having this improvised character. It would be difficult to make the implicit assumptions underlying these conceptualizations consistent with one another or with psychoanalytic theory as a whole.

It is my hope that the concepts of effectance, feeling of efficacy, competence, and sense of competence will be experienced by clinical workers as helpful, as tools which will enable them to form a clearer and more consistent picture of just what it is that goes wrong in early ego deviation. The chief service rendered by these concepts is their serving as reminders that the child is intrinsically active, tending to explore, manipulate, and produce effects upon the environment beyond the call of instinctual gratification. He has an intrinsic interest in how to deal with things, a push toward mastery and independence that does not borrow its energy from instinctual pressures or from rewards administered by the mother. It is through this activity that a substantial part of ego development is achieved, particularly the testing of reality and the learning of flexible controls. Children with early ego deviations are weak in these achievements. Constitutional factors may contribute to this weakness if they are of the sort, like passivity or overactivity, that make the experience of efficacy difficult and rare. The human environment makes its contribution by obstructing and inhibiting effectance. This may amount to a generalized swamping because the infant is rarely free from instinctual tension or anxiety; it may be a more specific obstruction of social efficacy by unresponsiveness to the infant's initiative; and it may include specific inhibitions of exploratory play through association with anxiety or pain. Such an account is not intended to eliminate familiar and valuable concepts like deprivation, rejection, overprotection, and aggression, which are surely essential in understanding why parents behave as they do. It is intended to make theory more complete by specifying how these attitudes become translated into actual obstructions of those processes that make for ego development.

The tactics used by therapists in their endeavors to assist their young patients seem to me to fit well into this sort of conceptualization. The work is usually described in terms of giving the child the gratifications he has missed, restoring his security and trust, and gradually coaxing him into a real human relation. But when we look at a detailed clinical report to see how these things are actually done, it is surprising to observe how much of the procedure can be interpreted as giving the child opportunities to experience efficacy in dealing with the play objects and especially in dealing with the therapist. After spending long hours excluded from his patient's confidence, the therapist must often put in a heroic period when he lets the child dictate every word that he utters and every move that he makes. Here we see the child's first crude attempts to establish some feeling of control over his human partner, to assure himself that he can do something without being swamped by unexpected communications and unwelcome interferences, and the therapist must go through this ordeal of proving himself controllable before he will be admitted to a less one-sided participation. Sometimes this treatment is described as strengthening the ego, and this is certainly correct provided we remain aware that it is the child who strengthens his ego, actively exploring and testing a world in which, by happy design, a child's initiative and intentions are often enough efficacious. A growing sense of competence does not necessarily lead to love, but love cannot dare to exist until there is some minimum sense of efficacy in human interaction.

6

IDENTIFICATION AS A
PROCESS OF DEVELOPMENT

The idea of identification has long been a part of everyday thinking about the development of personality. The child growing up in a world of other human beings does not have to construct all his patterns of conduct by piecemeal trial and error. A large array of patterns constantly surrounds him, and a substantial part of his behavior shows in one way or another the influence of these models. Long before developmental psychology took a technical interest in the subject, the process of identification was implied in ethical injunctions that parents should set a good example to their children and should keep them away from the kind of company that might offer bad examples. If a child brought up among intended good examples behaved badly, the natural suspicion was that he had strayed from his proper surroundings and fallen under the influence of evil companions. Identification was thus assumed to be a powerful thing in the shaping of character.

During the last century the concepts of imitation and suggestion emerged as important tools in understanding social behavior. Tarde in 1890 pronounced imitation to be the main law of society and likened the involuntary imitative process to hypnotic somnambulism, an idea which influenced Le Bon in his theory of crowds and thus Freud in his group psychology. J. M. Baldwin (1895) gave imitation an important place in the "dialectic of personal growth," showing that the child's behavior as a self and his conception of himself depend upon interaction with those around him. This line of thought was further developed by C. H. Cooley (1902), whose phrase, "the looking-glass self," serves as a constant reminder of the social origins of self-awareness. Cooley's influence helped bring into prom-

95

inence the idea of social roles which are learned by individuals through role-playing or role-taking, and which may be copied to a large extent from appropriate role models. Around the turn of the century, students of child development began to direct systematic observation at imitative processes. The learning of language clearly involves much copying of models (Preyer, 1888; Sully, 1896; Stern, 1914) as does the dramatic play that seems to be so much enjoyed by children (Groos, 1901). It was presently seen that identification figures, either adults or slightly older children, played a significant part in growth during the early school years and on through adolescence.

When psychoanalysis brings under scrutiny a topic of this kind, about which a fair amount is already known, we expect an illumination in the direction of depth. This implies on the one hand revealing the unconscious aspects of the process, and on the other hand tracing it back through childhood to its earliest manifestations in infancy. We may hope that depth analysis will also lead to a clarification of concepts through seeing things in their simplest forms. Freud's thinking on identification rewards us, as usual, with much fresh insight into what lies beneath the surface, but it cannot be claimed that he achieved a conceptual clarification. Knight (1940), Tolman (1943), Nevitt Sanford (1955), Kagan (1958), and many others have pointed out the varied and inconsistent ways in which the idea has been used. Sanford even suggests that if we cannot agree upon a restricted meaning, it would be better to abandon identification altogether. This heroic renunciation might well help to sharpen observation and clarify theory.

We already have the term *imitation* to describe behavior or fantasies in one person that have been modeled upon some other person. When *identification* is used for such phenomena, the intention nowadays is not merely to describe but to explain. For most people the term signifies a mechanism or learning process, one that Freud declared to be highly important for the growth of the ego; more than that, it is likely to imply an affective tie with the person whose behavior has been reproduced. The real danger in the present use of identification is that it leads us to take these things for granted and to feel that we are offering an explanation, when in fact the processes included under the term have never been properly elucidated. For a time Freud's use of identification steered our eyes toward important new facts. Now it seems likely to prevent us from getting any closer to the facts.

The first task of this chapter will be to see what Freud made of identification and how it has been handled in subsequent psychoanalytic ego psychology. Since the concept has more or less run riot through recent clinical literature, something useful may be accomplished by trying to find for it a consistent definition based on essential properties. I believe that this step can be taken successfully by using an action theory in which the ideas of efficacy and competence are given an important place.

FREUD'S VIEWS OF IDENTIFICATION

Freud's ideas of identification first took a definite shape in "Mourning and Melancholia" (1917). The similarity between mourning and melancholia led him to deduce that the melancholic has suffered the loss of a loved object psychologically just as the bereaved person has done in reality. It then became necessary to explain the melancholic's characteristic self-reproaches and loss of self-esteem, experienced by the patient as a loss in himself rather than the loss of an object. Close listening showed that the self-reproaches often fitted the patient poorly but applied readily to someone else. "So we find the key to the clinical picture: we perceive that the self-reproaches are reproaches against a loved object which have been shifted away from it on to the patient's own ego" (p. 248). Then followed the celebrated deduction that abandoning an object cathexis might serve to "establish an *identification* of the ego with the abandoned object" (p. 249). If this happened, the ego began to receive the reproaches originally directed at the object: ". . . the conflict between the ego and the loved person [was transformed] into a cleavage between the critical activity of the ego and the ego as altered by identification" (p. 249).

At this point Freud was speaking about an unconscious process occurring under stress in quite special conditions. Loss of a loved object by no means necessarily initiated just this series of events. Indeed the "normal" outcome would be a withdrawal of libido from the object and its transference to a new one. Identification happened only (1) when there was strong fixation on the object, and (2) when the object choice was on a narcissistic basis, permitting an easy regression to narcissism. In this essay identification thus seemed to play a part analogous to that of the defense mechanisms, with which it is sometimes listed in subsequent psychoanalytic literature. While the dynamic and economic conditions for its occurrence were specified, there was no attempt to describe the manner in which the ego is altered by an identification, except through the analogy of devouring.

Freud took up identification again in *Group Psychology and the Analysis of the Ego* (1921). He developed an earlier idea that identification is the most primitive form of object relation, coming before true object cathexis. It is "the earliest expression of an emotional tie with another person," and its most significant manifestation in childhood is the little boy's interest in being like his father, taking his father "as his ideal" (p. 105). The child will soon add an anaclitic object cathexis toward the mother, and the two "psychologically distinct ties" will exist side by side until the oedipal situation brings to the fore the hostility that is always implicit. Freud wrote:

> Identification, in fact, is ambivalent from the very first; it can turn into an expression of tenderness as easily as into a wish for someone's removal. It behaves like a derivative of the first, *oral* phase of the organization of the libido, in which the object that we long for and prize is assimilated by eating and is in that way annihilated as such [p. 105].
> [The next step in Freud's exposition is to establish the basic difference between the two kinds of tie.]
> It is easy to state in a formula the distinction between an identification with the father and the choice of the father as an object. In the first case one's father is what one would like to *be,* and in the second he is what one would like to *have.* The distinction, that is, depends upon whether the tie attaches to the subject or to the object of the ego. The former kind of tie is therefore already possible before any sexual object-choice has been made. It is much more difficult to give a clear metapsychological representation of the distinction. We can only see that identification endeavours to mould a person's own ego after the fashion of the one that has been taken as a model [p. 106].

We can agree, I believe, that Freud's formula is clear, but can we say that he was able to stick to it? One can see what he had in mind when he called identification a form of object relation. The object is clearly an essential part of the transaction, even if sexual object choice has not taken place. But confusion creeps in the moment identification is further described as an emotional tie. It is at one and the same time "the earliest expression of an emotional tie with another person" and a tie that "attaches to the subject . . . of the ego," not its object. Furthermore, it is derived from the early oral libidinal stage in which there are objects "that we long for and prize"—and devour—an imagery that fits wanting to *have* more closely than wanting to *be*.

What happened, I think, was that Freud mingled two definitions which are not strictly compatible. If identification is to be defined in terms of copying, as the endeavor "to mould a person's own ego after the fashion of the one that has been taken as a model," then it cannot also be defined as a particular kind of emotional tie. We know that the emotional relations involved in imitation can be numerous, ranging all the way from the unambivalent worship of the little boy for his father, as Freud pictured it, to the anxiety and desperation involved in identification with an aggressor, as Anna Freud (1936) was presently to point out and as Bettelheim (1943) observed in concentration camps. The only constant feature is the need to be like the model. The object can be loved and his agreeable traits admired, he can be feared and his competence admired, he can be hated and his powers envied. The emotional tie in identification is a variable feature rather than a defining constant.

These variations did not escape Freud's astute clinical ear. In hysterical symptoms, such as Dora's famous cough, when *"object-choice has regressed to identification"* (p. 107), he used the idea of partial identification (copying of a single trait) and noticed that either a loved or an unloved person might be imitated. But as he proceeded in *Group Psychology* with his interpretation of social behavior he was again drawn into the question of emotional ties. Having shown to his satisfaction that groups are held together by aim-inhibited libidinal ties, he presented identification in the light of a mechanism for producing such ties. The earliest experience of group formation takes place in the family circle. Among the children there is initially only envy, but because this does not work out successfully the child

> . . . is forced into identifying himself with the other children. So there grows up in the troop of children a communal or group feeling, which is then further developed at school. The first demand

made by this reaction-formation is for justice, for equal treatment for all. . . .

Thus social feeling is based upon the reversal of what was first a hostile feeling into a positively-toned tie in the nature of an identification. So far as we have hitherto been able to follow the course of events, this reversal seems to occur under the influence of a common affectionate tie with a person outside the group [pp. 120, 121].

Is identification, then, a mechanism that prepares the way for an emotional tie, or is it itself the tie? In this particular connection it is apparently the latter, for the essential dynamic process is effected by another mechanism, reaction formation. But when Freud noted that "A path leads from identification by way of imitation to empathy" (p. 110, footnote 2), he seemed to have in mind something more like a mechanism. Meanwhile the meaning of identification as "what one would like to *be*" (p. 106) had expanded to include the unwilling recognition of a common plight, forced upon the child by his need to retain his share of parental love. This is a case of what one *has* to be rather than what one would *like* to be.

It is noteworthy that in *Group Psychology* Freud brought identification out of psychopathology and turned it into a general developmental process. What he had described in 1917 as an unconscious regressive process occurring in special circumstances was now seen on a larger developmental canvas as a regular feature of preoedipal growth, sibling relations, and adult group life. This trend was continued in *The Ego and the Id* (1923), where, curiously enough, Freud went back to the special mechanism of melancholia, the substitution of an identification for a lost object cathexis, and discovered it to be "common," even "typical," having "a great share in determining the form taken by the ego," and contributing essentially "towards building up what is called its 'character' " (1923, p. 28). "At any rate the process, especially in the early phases of development, is a very frequent one, and it makes it possible to suppose that the character of the ego is a precipitate of abandoned object-cathexes and that it contains the history of those object-choices" (p. 29).

Freud was heading, of course, toward an explanation of the origins of the superego through resolution of the oedipus complex, but if we stop at this point it is hard to see the force of his new idea. One cannot help wondering what he had in mind as the succession of object cathexes abandoned by the child "in the early phases," and no help is given by the proffered example of women who have had many love affairs—obviously not in the early phases. But if Freud's generalization of the melancholic mechanism seems not very helpful for preoedipal ego development, it becomes a downright incubus when applied to the oedipal drama. Freud himself pointed out the inconsistency: the boy must give up the object cathexis of the mother, but instead of a regressive identification with her he strengthens his identification with the father. Giving rein to his clinical wisdom, Freud called attention to bisexuality and the full oedipus complex, but the situation could be retrieved only by postulating that the inherent strength of the child's masculinity or femininity decided the course of identification.

This is a real snarl, but worse is to follow. The identification with the father turns out to be not an identification at all, in any previous meaning of the term.

> The super-ego is, however, not simply a residue of the earliest object-choices of the id; it also represents an energetic reaction-formation against those choices. Its relation to the ego is not exhausted by the precept: 'You *ought to be* like this (like your father).' It also comprises the prohibition: 'You *may not be* like this (like your father)—that is, you may not do all that he does; some things are his prerogative' [p. 34].

With respect to what Freud considered to be the emotional heart of the oedipal situation, the boy's wish to take his father's place in his mother's bed, it would be more correct to say that the boy has to renounce his identification with his father and accept aim-inhibited status with his mother. Sanford (1955) points out that internalizing the parents' code of precepts and prohibitions fits the concept of introjection but not that of identification. Freud never made a real distinction between the two.

When we consider Freud's theme in the third chapter of *The Ego and the Id,* it is not hard to see why he tolerated so much confusion about identification. He was developing one of his most important concepts, that of the superego, and he used identification simply for the help it might offer in understanding the origins of this major institution in the mind. He was struck by a certain analogy between the hypothetical events in melancholia and those of oedipal renunciation and internalization, but he was not diverted from his main theme when it turned out that the analogy held scarcely at all. Unfortunately he did not return to identification as such and attempt any clearing up of the confusion he had created. Thus the concept was left with a variety of meanings. It had been used (1) for melancholia, where it occurred as a regression when a cathected object was lost; (2) for the little boy's admiring imitation of his father, where it was a primitive type of object relation; (3) for the internalizing of parental values during resolution of the oedipus complex; (4) for relations among siblings, where it developed as a reaction formation against envy and rivalry; and (5) for the aim-inhibited tender tie among the members of an adult group who have substituted a leader for their ego ideals. Some of these usages fit the idea of wanting to *be,* but others involve the additional element of an emotional tie. Some of them depend upon a love object being lost or renounced, but others do not. Some point to a lasting change in the character of the ego, but others deal with superficial and temporary change. The concept had obviously come to mean too much too easily.

FURTHER PSYCHOANALYTIC VIEWS OF IDENTIFICATION

It is easy to see that a concept launched with Freud's blessing and equipped with such an abundance of meanings would have a prodigious career in psychological theory. I shall here make a small selection from a large literature, concentrating on some applications that were not strictly implied in Freud's own writing.

Identification with the Aggressor

As already mentioned, Anna Freud (1936) developed the idea of identification with the aggressor. This was conceived of as a defense mechanism, hence as a means of mastering anxiety, and as "one of the most natural and widespread modes of behaviour on the part of the primitive ego" (p. 119). The examples she gives range from imitating the gestures and mannerisms of a threatening authority figure to copying the aggressiveness and masculinity shown by such figures. In the case of a child whose diffusely aggressive play followed a painful visit to the dentist she points out that there was "no actual impersonation of the dentist. The child was identifying himself not with the person of the aggressor but with his aggression" (p. 120).

The example of visiting the dentist suggests Freud's formulation of a certain kind of play in *Beyond the Pleasure Principle* (1920). Anna Freud develops the idea of shifting from the passive to the active role, with its consequence of visiting the unpleasant experience on some other object or person and thus obtaining a kind of revenge. She mentions also the situation in which a child tries to cope with anticipated punishment and aggression by displaying fierce aggressiveness beforehand—a "reversal of the rôles of attacker and attacked" (p. 123). But in these examples she makes it clear that identification with the aggressor involves two mechanisms: identification (introjection) and projection. This may lead to a complete reversal of roles, as in the case of the boy who "assumed his mother's indignation and, in exchange, ascribed to her his own curiosity" (p. 126). Together the two mechanisms represent a preliminary phase of superego development and are conceived of as "normal activities of the ego," although in special circumstances they may lead toward paranoia.

Anna Freud's account deals entirely with anxiety and aggression, thus effectively separating this form of identification from the tender emotional tie that crept so insistently into her father's thinking. It is clear that she is describing a process that involves identification (introjection, copying) without being fully explained by it. Her felicitous insight has put all clinicians so greatly in her debt that the concept of identification with the aggressor has been swallowed perhaps a bit hastily, to the neglect of the other element she intended it to contain. It was never offered as a pure example or as a variety of identification; rather, it was a process in which the mechanisms of introjection and projection played complementary parts.

Identification and Ego Identity

In his work on ego identity Erikson (1950) gives a prominent place to identification. After describing a dramatic instance of a boy's identification with his father ("Son of a Bombardier," pp. 210-213) he states: "The ego identity develops out of a gradual integration of all identifications" (p. 213). This suggests, perhaps, Freud's sweeping idea that the ego's character is a "precipitate of abandoned object-cathexes" (1923, p. 29), but we must notice the important differences. In the first place, Erikson does not assume that identification usually takes place through abandoning an object cathexis. The concept is not hobbled by linking it to a sequence of events first hypothesized as taking place in special circumstances in melancholia. In the second place, Erikson does not use identifications to account for the whole character of the ego, but only for that particular characteristic which he calls a *sense of ego identity*. In the third place, he makes clearer than Freud did the active synthesis that is a normal part of the whole process.

> ... none of the identifications of childhood (which in our patients stand out in such morbid elaboration and mutual contradiction) could, if merely added up, result in a functioning personality. . . . The fact is that identification as a mechanism is of limited usefulness. Children, at different stages of their development, identify with those *part aspects* of people by which they themselves are most immediately affected. . . . Their identifications with parents, for example, center in certain overvalued and ill-understood body parts, capacities, and role appearances. . . . The final identity, then, as fixed at the end of adolescence is superordinated to any single identification with individuals of the past: it includes all significant identifications, but it also alters them in order to make a unique and a reasonably coherent whole of them [1946-1956, pp. 112-113].

Thus in his use of identification Erikson recognizes that limits must be placed upon the concept if it is to mean anything specific, and that it cannot be used at all as a self-explanatory process apart from the child's learning and synthesizing activities. At the same time he gives it a significance in development that extends beyond that of a mechanism of defense.

Identification with the Mother and Reality Testing

Freud's glowing picture of the little boy who identifies admiringly with his father, while reserving for his mother a dependent love, did not at first do justice to the mother's potentialities as an identification figure. It was implied, however, that she served in this capacity for the little girl and indeed to some extent for the boy in the complete oedipus complex. One of the moves made by subsequent workers, encouraged by Freud's derivation of identification from the incorporative urges of the early oral stage, was to carry the concept backward to a time when the mother is the predominant person in the infant's life. Here it has been put to a variety of uses. Among them is the idea that identification with the mother is crucial to the growth of reality testing and the synthesis of functions.

Two extracts from clinical reports will illustrate this idea. Beata Rank (1949), describing the part played by mothers in the early lives of "children with atypical development," finds the emotional climate "not favorable for the development of a clear-cut distinction between the self and the outside world, thus crippling the capacity for identification with the mother and her attitudes and thereby interfering with the development of both a unified personality and the reality principle" (1949, pp. 135-136). In a later report, Rank and MacNaughton (1950) amplify the statement as follows: "When the ego recognizes only fragments of reality (part-objects), it develops single functions; but without the central core built from the introjection of a stable maternal image, conceived as a whole, it does not acquire the synthetic function capable of controlling instinctual drives" (p. 56).

It is important to notice what is implied here. Both reality testing and the synthetic function of the ego are pictured as results of an act of introjecting a whole mother figure. Before this is done, the ego has a fragmentary, stimulus-response quality, but by identifying with a stable whole mother image it acquires the power to pull things together and respond to the rest of reality as a whole. This theory, it seems to me, illustrates the trouble that besets psychoanalytic ego psychology through lack of a sufficient concept of activity in the child, and of the part played by this activity in testing reality, including the reality of the mother. Benedek (1938) has described the infant's relatively early advance from responding to gratifying objects such as the bottle to searching the mother's face and treating her as a whole person. There is surely a more satisfactory way of understanding this progress than by using the metaphor that the infant has gulped the mother down. Indeed the hypothesized introjection of a whole person implies that the child has already conceived of the mother as a whole person; he already possesses the capacity which the act of introjection is supposed to confer on him. We get a less jumbled sequence of events if we suppose that the infant, through active exploration and manipulation, and with the probable assistance of maturation, discovers progressively the boundaries of and relations among things. Just as he learns to bring together his visual and tactile impressions of material objects, achieving a hand-eye coordination not present at the start, so he learns to gather up the discrete sensations of the total nursing situation and of the human object who is present on such occasions. In my opinion we do not need the concepts of introjection and identification at all to account for the achievements Beata Rank derived from them.

A similar line of thought applies to the idea that the child starts trying to feed himself because he has identified with his mother. This explanation is as superfluous as the one which makes self-feeding dependent upon rewards of love. A child who has achieved some degree of manipulative competence, who has mouthed the spoon, banged it, thrown it on the floor, and stuck it in the cereal, can take things a step further without any special act that would have to be described as an identification.

Identification and Introjection

Finally we must take notice of what has been done to distinguish between identification and introjection. Freud did not separate the two in any systematic way. He preferred to speak of identification and used Ferenczi's term, "introjection," as an occasional synonym. Melanie Klein, following Abraham, may be said to have reversed this preference. Introjection and projection became central processes in her theory of early development, and identification tagged along as a natural consequence of these mechanisms (1955, pp. 309-313). But others have not been satisfied to have two words for the same process, or to make one concept stand for what goes on in the infant at the breast and what goes on at five or six years during the resolution of the oedipus complex.

Nevitt Sanford (1955) proposes a sharp distinction between the two concepts. The most useful conception of introjection, he believes, is Melanie Klein's, which corresponds to Freud's idea of identification in melancholia.

> Here we find the conception of a psychological taking in that is modelled after oral incorporation. When the object of love or imperious desire is withdrawn, or lost, or when its withdrawal or loss seems imminent, the subject may set it up imaginatively inside his personality, where he may, so to speak, have it for good. In infancy, when the boundaries between inside and outside are not yet clearly

drawn and when the danger of losing objects upon which there is total dependence is subjectively acute, introjection is probably very common if not universal [1955, p. 115].

Sanford goes on to point out a clinically observed connection between introjection and oral character traits. The mechanism can be understood as one that occurs in an early stage of ego development, and it is not without significance that it manifests itself most clearly in psychotic regressions.

Identification, according to the usage proposed by Sanford, is a different process occurring under different conditions.

> In identification . . . the individual may be observed to respond to the behavior of other people or objects by initiating in fantasy or in reality the same behavior himself. This is identification of the self with the object; it is different from empathy, fellow feeling, vicarious living, and the like—those phenomena which Knight has properly called identification of the object with the self [p. 109].

Examples of this mechanism resemble the simpler ones given by Anna Freud, such as copying the gestures and mannerisms of a threatening authority figure. In psychotherapy it often appears in the form of copying the therapist's role, becoming the psychologist and studying oneself at moments when true self-revelation entails an unbearable threat. The typical situations that evoke identification are those that carry a threat to self-esteem, and the function of the maneuver is "to acquire a sense of power and hence to feel equal to the threat" (p. 110). While it is possible to describe introjection in the same language—acquiring power to hold the desired object by incorporating it—the mechanism of identification points clearly to a more developed condition of the ego in which imitation can be employed, objects are more firmly external, and self-esteem is sufficiently organized to be threatened.

The distinction drawn by Sanford is approached in somewhat different terms in a paper by Jacobson (1954). She follows Freud's practice of using identification for everything, but then makes a distinction between "primitive preoedipal identifications" and "ego identifications" (p. 97). The preoedipal identifications, "founded on primitive mechanisms of introjection or projection" (p. 102), correspond to what Sanford calls introjection.

> Thus the hungry infant's longing for oral gratification is the origin of the first, primitive type of identification, an identification achieved by refusion [*sic*] of self- and object-images and founded on wishful fantasies of oral incorporation of the love object [p. 99].
> ... the earliest wishful fantasies of merging and being one with the mother (breast) are the foundation on which all future types of identification are built [p. 98].

Jacobson then calls attention to motor imitation as a "more active type of primitive identification" (p. 99), but this is only a transition to true ego identifications.

> In fact, we must not speak of ego identification before the child begins to develop lasting ego attitudes and character traits taken over from the parents, and before he manifests true ego interests and practices meaningful ego functions guided by their example and their demands.
> This presupposes a transition from desires for a complete union with the mother to strivings to become only "like" her [p. 100].
> The main progress manifests itself in the child's growing desire to achieve this goal no longer only by way of oral gratification from the love object, but also by activity of his own [p. 101].
> The processes leading to ego identifications set in with the transition from the stage of infantile dependency to ego independence [p. 104].

Jacobson's distinction is not an absolute one. It is based essentially on the degree of maturing of the child's ego. She implies some continuity by using "identification" for both stages and by referring to ego identifications as "partial introjection" or "partial incorporation." But she clearly places the preoedipal identifications with wanting to *have* (oral gratification) and the ego identifications with wanting to *be like,* and she makes this difference turn on the child's own activity in producing the behavior inspired by the model. Her further use of ego identification is not, like Sanford's, restricted to a particular kind of unconscious mechanism of defense. It becomes an important general developmental process having something of the breadth attributed to it by Freud and by Erikson.

The distinctions drawn by Sanford and by Jacobson are different in several respects. What they have in common is a recognition that Freud's concept of identification cannot be used consistently to describe events at different levels of ego development. The early oral model, with its desire for merging and incorporation, does not adequately represent the identifications of three years or five years, when the ego has developed a varied repertory for imitating the behavior of others. Questions are also raised, as they were by Erikson, about the range of events that can properly be brought under the heading of identification. How much of the learning process during formation of the superego, for example, can be appropriately described by this term? Clearly the path of progress lies in the direction of increasingly refined analysis.

IDENTIFICATION IN TERMS OF ACTION AND COMPETENCE

The first step in applying the notion of independent ego energies to the problem of identification is to consider what is known about *imitation*. Identification, which involves producing in oneself the behavior of a model, must be classed as a form of imitation. The genesis and development of imitative processes in young children have been the object of considerable study, and the findings may thrown light on those copyings that have been called identification.

The Nature of Imitation

The first point to notice is that the child in his earliest manifestations of overt imitation is able to copy only those acts that he has already performed by himself. This is conspicuously true with vocal imitation, which gets under way during the fourth or fifth month and may occupy considerable stretches of time at six months. For some time the infant shows no interest in unfamiliar sounds but will imitate sounds like those he has already produced, achieving greater accuracy in successive attempts. This fact was pointed out some time ago by F. H. Allport (1924) in his work on the acquisition of language. Imitation can happen only when the child has put in an apprenticeship of playful babbling, during which he has discovered what kinds of vocal effort and action produce what kinds of audible result. When these "circular responses" begin to be established, similar sounds made by someone else can cut into the circle, so to speak, and stimulate the actions that previously produced those sounds. Piaget (1945) makes the same point in his own terms, saying that the child must already have formed through his own action a sensorimotor schema into which the stimulus to be copied can insert itself. Piaget adds the observation that for a time a child can imitate the bodily movements of others only when his own corresponding movements are within his visual field; in other words, when his own exploration has already taught him something about the relation between active effort and visually perceived consequence.

These initial limitations on the mechanism of imitation, characteristic well into the second year, are transcended by further experience, and the whole process becomes less overt as the child interiorizes images and imitates the internal representations of models. "Now," says Piaget, ". . . the image acquires a life of its own, and the child who imitates is often unaware that he is doing so. His response to the model seems to him to come from within himself" (1945, p. 75). This step in development allows us to understand how identifications can occur with no conscious sense of copying, but it does not alter the fundamental process. Even when the child's imitations show flexibility and creativeness, they are formed by experimental variation from a repertory of acts he has already learned to perform.

Language is one of the things we say the child acquires through imitation. The human child can ordinarily learn any language that is in the air around him. Yet a close study of the acquisition of language makes it necessary to say that the child constructs his language rather than literally copying it. As we have already noticed in connection with reality testing, the child constructs reality through acting upon it and discovering the differential consequences of his actions. He thus sorts out the things that can be done—the effects that can be produced—from among all the possible variations of action. The parallel process with respect to language was pointed out by Wilhelm Stern (1914), who showed that children try out all kinds of grammatical combinations and learn only through experience to limit themselves to those that are customary. This is most evident when a child produces a seemingly legitimate but actually "incorrect" extension of grammar or vocabulary. Thus by analogy with other past participles he may insist on saying "drinked" even when quite familiar with the word "drunk." To this example I add one produced by my son when quite young: his dog, he said one morning, seemed to be very "barkative" today, and when we could detect no cause for her excitement he concluded that she was "barking through her hat." These particular extensions became part of the family idiom, but it is the general fate of "wrong" linguistic ventures to be rejected by the environment. The child proposes, the adult disposes, and it is thus that each child through his own active participation constructs for himself the traditional language that surrounds him.

Imitation, then, even in its simplest forms cannot be conceived of as an abrupt act of copying another's behavior. Imitation can occur only in an organism that has already elaborated a sufficent matrix of actions so that it can produce something resembling the act to be copied. The child can imitate when he is, so to speak, already almost there, when manageable variations of his existing repertory will produce behavior similar to the model. In other words, imitation is an active process of changing one's established behavior to make it more like that of a model.

Identification as a Form of Imitation

What distinguishes identification from other kinds of imitation? In a sense the distinction is an arbitrary one. We do not usually think of the imitation of sounds or gestures by themselves as identifications. We do not conclude that the child playing pat-a-cake is identified with the other player in any usual meaning of the word. We do use this expression, however, for the little boy who admires his father and wants to be like him, and for the scared child who acts like the playground bully, even though the outward manifestations may consist largely of an imitation of sounds and gestures. I believe that the distinction has to turn on something internal, and that it can be indicated by contrasting the two phrases, "wanting to do something that someone else has done" and "wanting to be like someone else." The first phrase is illustrated in the situation of having the salesman show you how to work the gadget you are buying. You want to know how to run it, and you gladly copy the salesman's acts, but you would as willingly accept the same instruction from anyone, and if necessary you would use the diagrams in a book of instructions rather than a living teacher. In such situations nobody speaks of identification because the model has no personal importance. Anyone, anything will do, provided we become able to perform the desired act.

Wanting to be like another person implies something more. We speak of identification when the model *does* have personal importance, when we want to be like someone in a way that transcends any single act. Thus the boy who watches the operator of a power shovel or a big crane wants to be like that man who can do so many different things with such assured competence. The boy who identifies with his father wants to be like that person on whose pleasure the household turns during the evening, who can drive the car, run the power lawn mower, and generally display such effectiveness in dealing with the environment. The university student, it is to be hoped, wants not just to take away knowledge like so much booty but to become more generally like the seekers after knowledge who have captured his imagination. Identification, then, is a particular form of imitation in which copying a model is generalized beyond specific acts and has the character of wanting to be, and trying to be, competent like the model.

In this way, I believe, we can make identification a consistent concept. But we shall then have to abandon several other meanings that have been heaped indiscriminately upon the word. If we define it in terms of wanting and trying to be competent like the model, we cannot also have it mean a particular kind of emotional tie, libidinal or aggressive, and we cannot also have it mean a primitive mechanism or a primitive form of object relation.

We saw that Freud often used the term loosely so that it implied an emotional tie, particularly the warm tie that bound together the members of a group. This was not consistent, however, with the later idea of identification with the aggresssor, where fear and even hate for the model left no room for tenderness. It is also hard to reconcile with his idea of the melancholic mechanism, where an object cathexis, tender but ambivalent, turned regressively into an identification with only the hostile elements remaining prominent. All of this trouble is dissolved by a stricter usage of identification in which it is recognized that various combinations of love, tenderness, fear, and hate can exist in relation to the model whose competence one wants to emulate. The one invariant affect is admiration of the model's competence. We may think him conceited and thoroughly dislike that side of him, yet admire and try to copy his poise and assurance in situations that would upset us. Or we may love him and admire and try to copy his lovable characteristics. Identification can go with several types of emotional relationship provided they permit admiration.

Our definition implies that identifications will not occur until a certain level of ego development has been reached. This is consistent with deriving identification from imitation, in which the imitated acts must be already approximately formed in the child's repertory. To admire another person and want to be like him in a somewhat general way probably implies that the child has begun to take himself in a somewhat general way—in other words, that he has developed some sense of unified selfhood, and probably some sense of competence beyond specific efficacies. Our concept thus corresponds fairly well to Jacobson's "ego identifications," but it excludes the "primitive preoedipal identifications" based on introjection and projection that she treats as direct forerunners, a point to which we shall return in a moment. Our definition takes a different tack from the one recommended by Sanford, who recognized identification as a more mature and developed process than introjection but still wanted to limit it to being a rigid, unrealistic defense mechanism employed to cope with serious threats to self-esteem. This seems to me to exclude arbitrarily identifications that occur under happier circumstances, more as an attempt to build up self-esteem than to save it, and I would attribute the rigidities of the clinically observed mechanism to the restrictive primitivizing effects of acute anxiety. Our usage permits us to see the developmental significance of identification in much the way that Erikson sees it.

When and how does identification begin to assume its importance in development? No doubt it emerges sporadically during the second and third years, though on the whole not a great deal has been made of it during the anal stage, dominated by anal interests, motility, retentive and eliminative modes, crises of negativism, and the assertion and testing of autonomy. Spitz (1958) attaches developmental importance to role-playing games as early as fifteen months, such as using a toy telephone or walking with father's cane, and to a kind of identification with the aggressor implied in adopting the head-shaking "No" and turning it on oneself and others. These copyings are rather transient, and it may be more appropriate to consider them as imitation without much element of imaginative identification, especially as Spitz finds little evidence for empathy at this age. But it is surely out of such beginnings that identification grows. It seems to come into its own at whatever point we are ready to say that the phallic stage has supervened. The child's capacities, ripening through practice, now permit him to produce a much

larger repertory of behavior that resembles an adult's, and his interactions with adults take on a more equal character. Erikson (1946-
1956) calls attention to the importance of gains in locomotion,
language, and imagination. Locomotion moves from being a difficult stunt to a serviceable tool, its utility often much extended by a
tricycle. The child walks like an adult, begins to explore the neighborhood somewhat like an adult, and achieves such coordinated actions as sawing and cutting, throwing overhand, and dressing himself without assistance. These accomplishments will presently be
recognized by giving him an adult-sized bed and allowing him to
take some of his meals at the family table. He also talks more like
an adult, with rapid gains in sentence structure and grammar, so
that his conversations have much more the character of exchanges.
Imagination likewise matures so that it becomes possible to invest
plain objects like blocks with the attributes of vehicles, airplanes,
animals, and people. For the first time it may become possible to
sustain the continuous fantasy of an imaginary companion.

It is in the setting of these other achievements that we see unmistakable evidences of identification. The child seems to reach a point
of understanding at which for the first time he can contemplate his
place in the family and his relation to other people in general. He
can compare himself as a self with grownups, noting differences in
size and capacity and thus generating desires for more grown-up
competence. So we find children indulging in make-believe, dressing up in adult clothes, and imitating dramatic instances of competence by pretending to drive the car, telephone orders to the mar-
ket, or be the host and hostess. The child, in short, reaches a point
in his repertory of behavior and comprehension which permits him
to act a little like an adult, and he then begins to use identification
as a means of becoming more like one.

Seen in this light, identification can be said to serve as an
imaginative short cut to the mastery of complex adult patterns of
behavior. The child imagines these patterns as wholes with their
associated feelings. What he imagines may be very different from
the experience of the model. The operator of a bulldozer may be
grumpily turning over in his mind an unfairness in work assignment
or a rumor of his wife's unfaithfulness rather than enjoying the
magnificent mastery that fills the fancy of his youthful sidewalk
superintendent. But identification permits the child to try out vari-

ous roles more rapidly and effectively than he could do if he had to discover them bit by bit. It is in this way that he uses identifications in the formation of his own sense of identity. Some are tried and discarded because they prove unworkable or are punished. Others are retained as part of his own repertory, suitably modified and integrated in the course of time into a workable identity of his own.

Difficulty with the Oral Model

It will be observed that in this account I have derived identification from the imitative behavior that begins to be prominent around six months, but have not otherwise related it to events in the oral stage. This is at variance with the genetic connection postulated by Freud between identification and the incorporative activity of the first oral phase. We are faced here, I believe, with the necessity for making a radical choice between two of Freud's ideas which cannot be reconciled. One of these, the one I have preferred, makes identification turn on wanting to be like an object in contrast to wanting to have the object. The other is that identification is the same as introjection and that it is derived from the model of oral incorporation. I am convinced that it cannot be both. The resemblance between the two ideas seems to me quite superficial. I even suggest that as psychological processes and experiences they are about as different as any two things can be in a system as full of internal relations as is the human personality.

This is true, I think, no matter what version we accept of the introjective process. Freud emphasized the oral core of the infant's experience, the act of feeding, in which "the object that we long for and prize is assimilated by eating and is in that way annihilated as such" (1921, p. 105). This way of expressing it runs a risk of being more sophisticated than anything that is likely to be happening in an infant's mind. It just skirts the danger into which Melanie Klein (1955) fell so disastrously when she assumed "aggressive impulses and phantasies arising in the earliest relation to the mother's breast, such as sucking the breast dry and scooping it out," soon followed by ideas "of entering the mother and robbing her of the contents of her body" (p. 310)—all of this at ages when the bright and well-stimulated Piaget children were still months short of discriminating self from others or grasping the stable existence of

objects. Question could be raised concerning the hypothetical experience of assimilation if mother, breast, self, and milk are as yet
undifferentiated; still more so concerning the alleged annihilation
of the prized object, if no objects as yet have permanent existence.
These questions could be avoided by assuming that the fantasies
of assimilation and annihilation are gradually added as the infant's
comprehension matures up to the middle of the second year, but
this would seriously weaken the genetic importance of the incorporative experiences.

Such difficulties have encouraged the development of a somewhat
different version of the introjective happenings. This version puts
the emphasis on the total feeding situation, with what an adult
would describe as its several different kinds of satisfaction—sucking, swallowing, being held cozily, being patted and gently stimu-
lated and made comfortable—but which an infant would experience
in more global and undifferentiated fashion. Sanford (1955), in his
charitably moderate statement of Mrs. Klein's meaning, speaks of a
psychological taking in of loved objects in order to keep them from
being lost. Jacobson (1954) points toward a feeling of union with
the mother, a "refusion [sic] of self- and object-images" (p. 99),
based on "the earliest wishful fantasies of merging and being one
with the mother (breast)" (p. 98). In a recent paper, Sandler
(1960) speaks of feeling "at one with the object and close to it"
(p. 151), wherein "the earliest state of being at one with his mother
is temporarily regained" (p. 154).

We have, then, two versions of the situation that is supposed to
serve as the genetic model for identification. One emphasizes oral
incorporation in a rather literal way; the other accents the global
feeling of blissful unity and gratification that occurs during nursing.
One can question the legitimacy of continuing to call the second
version "oral incorporation," as Jacobson does, but that is not
germane to the present issue. Sandler puts the case for continuity
persuasively when he says that "Identification is a means of feeling
the same as the admired and idealized object, and therefore at one
with it" (1960, p. 150). Yet I think he is wrong. Identification is a
means of feeling the same as the admired object, but not necessarily at one with it. The child who pretends that he is the operator
of a bulldozer is not trying to feel at one with the surly real operator
in any sense that is analogous to restoring the unity of the nursing

situation. He is trying to be effective and move things powerfully around, as he has seen the model moving them.

It is here that I think the concepts of feeling of efficacy and sense of competence can produce a clear distinction where one has long been wanting. They allow us to describe identification consistently in terms of wanting to be like someone, without any confusing implication of wanting to have someone, even in the sense of feelings of merging and union. Our concepts are helpful because they call attention to a form of satisfaction that is related to independent ego energies rather than to instinctual drives. Psychoanalytic ego psychology has by no means overlooked the importance of "mastery." Spitz (1958), for example, sees in the young child's "identificatory imitations . . . one quality in common, that of mastery," and notes that such actions "originate from the child's insurgence against his infantile helplessness" (p. 391). But in traditional theory, where everything has to be derived ultimately from libidinal or aggressive drive energies, calling something "mastery" does not protect it from being blurred into something else. Thus Spitz wonders whether "the boy who dons father's hat, the girl who preens herself before the mirror, the child who plays 'nurse,' handing out diapers" (pp. 390-391) are not in some sense identifying with the aggressor, and thus expressing aggression by inflicting on others what has been done to them. And we can likewise wonder, leaping in the quite different direction suggested by Jacobson and Sandler, whether the children are not in some sense incorporating their objects or seeking to restore the union of infantile nursing. Does it not lead to better understanding if we say that identifiers are always trying to strengthen their sense of competence by copying competent models—that the mechanism and its motives shall be defined in terms of competence? Then if sometimes aggressive satisfactions, sometimes libidinal ones, and sometimes regressive longings for union appear in the pattern, we can simply say that something is present besides identification—for no one will claim that identification has to occur always in pure form.

If we picture a boy proudly going fishing with his father, copying his movements with the fishing rod and perhaps as well his gestures and tone of voice, we must certainly allow that affection and the desire for a warm man-to-man relation may be importantly involved. The child handing out diapers may be moved by sibling jealousy and a need to recapture an alliance with the mother by being helpfully grown up. The child playing dentist on a compliant companion may be working off the hostility engendered by his own session in the dental chair. The boy who imitates the operator of the bulldozer may have unconscious fantasies that he is exerting his father's sexual power. It is no intention of mine to challenge such possibilities or to question the fluid spread of unconscious associations that psychoanalysis so constantly reveals. But if we are to find a common denominator in the phenomena of identification, if we are to use this term as a systematic concept rather than as a loose designation for a lot of things only vaguely similar, then the central meaning is best found in the adaptive process of copying the competence of others in an attempt to improve one's own competence. Copying, as we have seen, means modifying through action, often with much help from fantasy, the behavior of which one is already capable—modifying it in directions suggested by the model. The central affect is for the single act a feeling of efficacy, for the sustained series of acts a growth of the sense of competence.

This means, of course, that identification is separated entirely from the concepts of incorporation and introjection. Copying for the sake of competence is not *psychologically* a "taking in" at all. Its essence is action, with associated feelings of efficacy. The focus of the experience is upon the producing of effects through effort. No implication need be present that the model who is being copied does anything more than remain there; the goal of the action would not be better served by swallowing him, annihilating him, or feeling merged in union with him. The process of identification modifies the ego in a way that can be clearly described because it is consistent with all other modifications brought about by actions put forth and consequences produced. Previous experiences of incorporation are not likely to be reanimated by later happenings in which action is the central event.

These remarks lead to the conclusion, furthermore, that incorporation and introjection are not the appropriate concepts for the internalizing of parental prohibitions during the resolution of the oedipus complex. Again we must beware of being taken in by the words "taken in." It may be correct linguistically to say that a precept is taken in when a child begins to act upon it without an external reminder, but it is not correct psychologically to consider that this is experienced as an intaking. It is a learning process not so far removed from a conditioned response in which a painful consequence has come to inhibit an impulse to act. The trouble with calling this kind of learning "introjection" is that we then cannot escape calling almost all learning by the same name. We are forced to speak of introjecting the rules of grammar or of incorporating the multiplication table—and, must we add, annihilating it, or, according to another version, becoming like it? Learning the multiplication table is certainly experienced as action, efficacy, and mastery of a task. Learning parental precepts is a good deal more like this than it is like setting up in oneself the image of the mother and her ministrations.

It is best, it seems to me, to restrict the concept of introjection to the fantasies of the early oral stage, when the child wishes for reinstatement of the total nursing situation but cannot do much to produce that result. As fantasy this may recur repeatedly and have an influence on development, and it may reappear portentously in regressed states. But it can lead only to confusion if we try to extend this concept into realms of learning where action and efficacy have become prominent features.

Identification and the Superego

The foregoing considerations permit us what seems to me to be a clearer understanding of the events that make up the oedipus complex and the formation of the superego. Identification is present in these events, but it is only one of several processes, and we shall have to renounce the custom of saying that the superego is formed by identification with the parents and their precepts. What takes place is actually a whole series of adaptive efforts in a situation that is complex and difficult for the child.

Taking Freud's lead with regard to the full oedipus complex, we can assume that the child has ambivalent feelings toward both parents and has to some extent identified with both. The parents are too prominent in his world to be the objects of uncomplicated feelings and attitudes. In usual circumstances the child is not prepared to forego their support and their love, yet they are also agents of restraint and frustration. The situation is then further complicated by a stronger emergence of erotic feeling which, now that the child has gained some understanding of positions and privileges in the family, exposes him to the startling emotions of the eternal triangle. To all this the child must try to adapt through some sort of compromise between parental support on the one hand and his own urges toward love, hate, initiative, and independence on the other.

The child enters this situation with important preconceptions about sexual roles. Freud was obliged to lean heavily on the constitutional strength of masculinity or femininity in order to explain the course of events. These variables need not be rejected out of hand, and the anatomical difference between boys and girls certainly plays its part, but we now know from studies inspired as much by sociologists as by psychologists that training in sex roles gets under way quite early and has already achieved no small effectiveness at the beginning of the phallic stage (Watson, 1959, pp. 441-445). The sexual urges of boys and girls at this stage may not be very different, but sexual differentiation of behavior has gone forward through the agency of parental role definition. Girls and boys alike may play with dolls until the boys find out that "boys don't do that"; alike they climb trees, hit each other, and roar around like racing cars until the girls find out that "girls don't do that." The spontaneous activities of children become selectively molded into masculine and feminine roles through their differential consequences with respect to adult approval. This has an important influence on the choice of objects for identification. It serves to define for boys and girls the kinds of competence that are most appropriate for them.

Sex roles have an important bearing on one of the difficulties that Freud himself pointed out in his discussion of the resolution of the oedipus complex: the fact that identification seemed to be strengthened not with the relinquished love object, as in melancholia, but with the parent of the same sex. Freud got himself into this trap by generalizing the melancholic mechanism. In 1917 he saw regression from object cathexis to identification as a process that occurred only under quite special conditions, but by 1923 it had become a general law of development that ought to apply to the oedipal events. What Freud saw in melancholia, however, was not identification at all in the meaning we have developed here; it corresponds to a primitive introjective process that is most likely to occur under pathological stress. Once we clear up this point, it is no mystery that the little boy continues an identification with his father rather than shifting to the mother whom he is relinquishing as a love object. He is sticking to the choice dictated by his learned sex role.

The other outstanding difficulty in Freud's account came from his use of identification to cover not only a striving to be like the model but also the internalizing of the model's prohibitions, even when this meant behaving differently from the model. Recent psychoanalytic theorists such as Jacobson (1954) and Sandler (1960) have recognized the trouble with such an interpretation. It strains to the breaking point the meaning of being like someone to say that you are being like him when you accept his prohibition against acting the way he does. The child may accept a parental prohibition and incorporate it in his own behavior because he wants to preserve a good relation, but in this particular case the price of a good relation is to stop trying to behave like the parents. This difficulty is resolved by giving identification a consistent restricted definition and by allowing that there is more in the resolution of the oedipus complex than just this one psychological process.

Understanding can be substantially improved, it seems to me, by scrutinizing the events in more detail and by thinking of them as a somewhat extended learning process rather than as a dramatic crisis. Freud probably did not think of these events as necessarily happening with dramatic abruptness, but his favorite type of conceptualization in terms of transformations and redistributions of instinctual energy did not seem to imply much extension in time, and he certainly left the impression that the whole business was resolved one way or another by the end of the fifth year, after which the main outlines of personality remained fixed for life. If we recognize that at the outset the child's level of ego development is far from sufficient to deal with the oedipal situation, we can agree that his first whacks at the problem are likely to be impassioned, indiscriminate, full of global defense mechanisms and faulty testings of reality. His first struggles may have the character of crisis behavior, and it is this that the clinician can most easily reconstruct or observe. But Freud's description of the *"normal" resolution* of the oedipus complex—and this applies to any tolerably mature solution—is of a process that is much better conceptualized as an extended series of trials and testings, in the course of which the child gradually learns the more mature relation to his parents that circumstances now require.

When the boy arrives at the "normal" solution, his mother cannot be correctly described as "given up." She is retained as the anaclitic love object Freud postulated her to be, and the only thing that is renounced is the more recently experienced sexual desire for her, with its associated bedroom privileges. This renunciation is not incompatible with a continuing aim-inhibited tenderness which constitutes an enrichment of the preoedipal dependent tie. There can be, in short, a highly selective renunciation with respect to the mother that does not in the end undermine her as a source of security and affection or as an object of affection. Objectively considered, the situation does not call for the dramatic and total renunciation of the love object, through disappointment in it, that Freud postulated for melancholia. It requires the learning of a compromise, or, to put it another way, a discovery of the terms upon which the boy is permitted to love his mother—terms somewhat less inclusive than his urges tend to dictate.

With respect to the father, close inspection may lead us to question the customary statement that the identification is strengthened. The boy's identification may be supposed to build up to maximum strength when in fantasy he copies the father's sexual behavior with the mother, or in reality tries to do so. In a "normal" solution of the oedipus complex this part of the identification has to be renounced. Just as with the mother there has to be a selective renunciation of certain aspects of the affectionate relation, other aspects being retained, so with the father certain aspects of the identification have to be given up while others can be kept. Discriminations of this kind cannot be accomplished through any conceivable conglomeration of primitive processes and irrational defenses. At the outset the child may use such processes in abundance, and he may get stuck in them so that the oedipus complex becomes nuclear for a neurosis. The "normal" resolution can start only when he somewhat gets over the furies and panics that may first have gripped him and becomes able to test reality in a more discriminating fashion. To the extent that he can do this, resuming varied and observant interactions with his parents, he will discover that all is not lost: he can continue to have an affectionate, dependent relation with his mother, provided it is sexually aim inhibited, and an admiring identification with his father, provided it excludes bedroom privileges. The "normal" solution, after all, is not such a bad compromise for a child who still very much needs his parents and who is not sexually mature. Indeed, it is likely that the aggressions are harder to control than the genital urges.

Our grasp of the solving of the oedipus problem is made easier if we take the view that it occurs over a relatively extended period of time. Here we should remember Anna Freud's caution, in her monograph on child analysis (1926), against treating the young patient as if his parents were a thing of the past instead of an active part of his daily life. A continuing interaction with the real parents goes on through the latency period and beyond. Their supporting presence continues for some time to be a needed basis while the child learns to find satisfactions and comforts, and to avoid anxieties, in the company of his contemporaries. We thus have a situation in which it is not necessary to suppose that the mastery of the oedipal triangle and the formation of the superego take place with finality at a particular time. This point has been increasingly recognized in psychoanalytic ego psychology, especially by Hartmann, Kris, and Loewenstein (1949) and by Bornstein (1951). Certainly up to eight years, if not beyond, it is possible to observe behavior that can be described as an evolution of the superego, which at the start is harsh, rigid, yet erratic, like a person unfamiliar with newly acquired authority, but which advances toward flexibility and a better working relation with the ego. The internalizing of prohibitions and of positive values is a gradual process which allows time to arrive at better solutions through effort expended and experience received.

It can be said, in short, that the establishment of the superego is a fairly complex learning process arising out of the necessity to work out a compromise among instinctual urges, parental frustrations, and need for parental support. Probably the first and most critical step, that of accepting prohibitions and coming to act upon them without direct external reminders, does not depend at all upon identification. The essential element is anxiety, which may be sufficient to produce a defense mechanism such as repression or reaction formation. Identification does play a part, however, in that aspect of the superego which reflects ideal ways of behaving. Defining identification as a form of imitation in which copying occurs in order for the copier to become competent like the model, we expect to find it playing a crucial part in connection with ideals of conduct.

7

SELF-ESTEEM, SENSE OF
COMPETENCE, AND EGO STRENGTH

If we were to ask any reasonably reflective person to tell us what kinds of experience would seriously threaten his self-esteem, he would be likely to describe some combination of failure in his own actions and fall in the esteem of other people. It might be an interesting test of personality to see which he mentioned first and to which he attributed greater importance. The balance between these two sources of self-esteem undoubtedly varies from person to person. To some extent it is affected by the conditions of everyday life and by cultural evaluations of what is important. Fromm (1947) has pointed out in his account of the "marketing orientation" that economic conditions characterized by vast impersonal markets, machine production, and large business organizations tend to shift the basis of self-esteem away from what one accomplishes objectively and toward how well one sells oneself in the estimation of others. Riesman's account (1950) of "inner-directed" and "other-directed" people suggests that the latter's self-esteem may depend more heavily than the former's on the social response to what they have done. Thus we would be prepared for variation in the replies to our question, but we would not expect informants to reject one source altogether, trying to persuade us that their self-esteem depends wholly on what people think of them or that it depends wholly on their own judgment of their achievement regardless of social response. At the level of common sense a dualistic—or, more accurately, an interactive—theory of self-esteem seems inevitable.

Psychoanalytic investigation serves as usual to illuminate the topic by uncovering unconscious fantasies and tracing them to early origins. Psychoanalytic theory, however, has had a good deal of trouble with self-esteem. As with reality testing and identification, it has worked with infantile fantasies and instinctual energies, but it has not had ready for use a sufficient concept of ego development through action. This has resultéd in schemes that make self-esteem turn too much on infantile fantasies assumed to be still active, too little on a developing sense of competence that tends to displace these fantasies.

PSYCHOANALYTIC VIEWS OF SELF-ESTEEM

Freud was still using the idea of ego instincts, though he was in the act of destroying it, when he wrote "On Narcissism" (1914). What he had to say there about the "self-regarding attitude" (p. 98) seems rather more colored by the rising idea of narcissistic libido than by the declining one of ego instincts. To be sure, the following paragraph sounds as if he saw things in terms of mastery or competence.

> In the first place self-regard appears to us to be an expression of the size of the ego; what the various elements are which go to determine that size is irrelevant. Everything a person possesses or achieves, every remnant of the primitive feeling of omnipotence which his experience has confirmed, helps to increase his self-regard [p. 98].

But Freud was headed in the opposite direction. What interested him was the possibility of a new triumph for libido theory at the expense of the ego instincts. His theme was that "self-regard has a specially intimate dependence on narcissistic libido" (p. 98). By 1922 he had decided that "the instincts of self-preservation were also of a libidinal nature: they were sexual instincts which, instead of external objects, had taken the subject's own ego as an object" (1922, p. 257).

The history of Freud's thoughts on narcissism has recently been traced in detail by Bing, McLaughlin, and Marburg (1959). It suffices for our purpose here to note that in his final formulation of instinct theory, self-regard or self-esteem could no longer be distinguished from self-love. The "everything a person . . . achieves" of 1914 has been assimilated to the image of Narcissus gazing fondly at his reflection in the clear pool—or, less pictorially, to the image of the infant securing various forms of autoerotic satisfaction. Freud did not conceive of externalized aggression as an independent source of self-esteem, and he thought of externalized libido as definitely antithetical:

> ... it is easy to observe that libidinal object-cathexis does not raise self-regard. The effect of dependence upon the loved object is to lower that feeling: a person in love is humble. A person who loves has, so to speak, forfeited a part of his narcissism, and it can only be replaced by his being loved. In all these respects self-regard seems to remain related to the narcissistic element in love [1914, p. 98].

Self-esteem, then, is a function of narcissistic libido, and it is supported either by one's own self-love or by the achievement of the goal of narcissistic libido with respect to others: namely, to be loved by them as one loves oneself.

Within this conceptual pattern it became possible to develop a further equation between instinctual gratification and sense of omnipotence. Ferenczi attributed unlimited omnipotence to the child in the womb. He saw omnipotence as meeting its first restriction when excitations could not be immediately removed. Working on this basis, Fenichel proposed the following definition of self-esteem: "The individual's experiences connected with omnipotence lead to a most significant need of the human mind. The longing for the oceanic feeling of primary narcissism can be called the 'narcissistic need.' 'Self-esteem' is the awareness of how close the individual is to the original omnipotence" (1945, p. 40). In the earliest experiences of frustration, omnipotence is restored when unwelcome excitations are removed. It is from this premise that Fenichel came to his conclusion that "The first supply of satisfaction from the external world, the supply of nourishment, is simultaneously the first regulator of self-esteem" (p. 40). And later regulation follows the same principle, except that literal nourishment is replaced by tokens of love: "The small child loses self-esteem when he loses love and attains it when he regains love" (p. 41). This is the basis of the idea that self-esteem is determined by one's income of narcissistic supplies.

Going back as it does in this fashion to the very earliest experiences, even into the womb in Ferenczi's theory, the formulation was, not surprisingly, one of complete passivity. Conceptualization

reached back to a time when whatever happened to the infant was
not of his own doing, permitting one to suppose that his state was
wholly regulated from the outside. Both Ferenczi and Fenichel, it
seems to me, moved from this point one short chronological step
ahead and then let the subject drop, as if what they had said about
origins were the whole metapsychological truth. Ferenczi (1913)
allowed omnipotence to be associated progressively with magical
gestures and magical words. These were magical because they entailed no testing of the intervening steps, but in themselves they
represented forms of activity on the part of the infant. Fenichel
(1945) stated that the stage of primary narcissism was succeeded
by "a period of passive-receptive mastery in which difficulties are
overcome by influencing powerful external objects to give what is
needed" (p. 41). This stage, as we have seen, may be pathologically extended in the symbiotic psychoses when the mother continues to be utilized as an external ego. When Fenichel's account
advanced beyond this stage, however, to that of motility and active
mastery, he saw something of the relation of these to reality testing but made no further mention of self-esteem.

The formula that has most often guided psychoanalytic theory
in describing the later vicissitudes of self-esteem is based on the
relation between ego and ego ideal. This presupposes that ego ideal
and superego are at least partly separate institutions of the mind.
The ego ideal becomes the repository of the original narcissistic
omnipotence, and the ego enjoys self-esteem to the extent that it
matches its ideal in actuality. But the adult ego ideal contains more
than this. Piers and Singer (1953) attribute to it the sum of positive
identifications with parental images and parental ideas, together
with layers of later identifications with siblings, contemporaries,
and admired adults, and they also picture it as being constantly
affected by ego potentialities. This view of the ego ideal entails
considerably more cumulative development than is implied in Fenichel's account, and it also suggests that an important part is played
by activity. Thus the concept of tension between ego and ego ideal
tends to supersede the formulation that applied in early childhood.

One psychoanalyst, at least, stands firmly opposed to any passive
and purely cathectic interpretation of self-esteem. Silverberg (1952)
has returned to the dual or interactive theory that sees self-esteem

as compounded of one's own activity and the recognition of it by others.

> Throughout life self-esteem has these two sources: an inner source, the degree of effectiveness of one's own aggression; and an external source, the opinions of others about oneself. Both are important, but the former is the steadier and more dependable one; the latter is always more uncertain. Unhappy and insecure is the man who, lacking an adequate inner source for self-esteem, must depend for this almost wholly upon external sources. It is the condition seen by the psychotherapist almost universally among his patients [p. 29].

The "effectiveness of one's own aggression" surely implies a very broad use of "aggression." In this context it could not mean a history of tantrums and successful destructions of the environment, and Silverberg makes it plain that what he has in mind is general activity leading to competence. If we admit general activity—independent ego energies—as something different from aggressive instinctual energy, Silverberg's picture of self-esteem is the one I shall now try to develop.

Self-Esteem and Sense of Competence

The primary difficulty that has hampered psychoanalytic theory in dealing with self-esteem is, it seems to me, the failure to distinguish between esteem and love. Esteem has more to do with respect than with love, and respect for oneself is essential for self-esteem. Freud lost the distinction between respect and love when he squeezed out the ego instincts and made self-regard a function of narcissistic libido, and he did not recover it through his conception of the death instinct. Self-respect should in some way have reappeared along with the structural ego, but the image of the ego as a mechanism that was put in action by instinctual energies did not encourage this way of reasoning. We saw in the last chapter that the concept of identification has been badly blurred by failure to isolate the central phenomenon of admiration and respect, and by attempts to read in an emotional or libidinal tie. The difficulty becomes all the greater when we turn directly to the psychological nature of self-esteem. A theory that finds the ultimate value and meaning of life in the discharge of libidinal and aggressive energies is clearly predisposed to transmute the phenomena of respect and self-esteem into manifestations of love and hate. If the theory can be enlarged to include independent ego energies, with recognition of the intrinsic value and meaning of feelings of efficacy and sense of competence, we shall come much closer, I believe, to an understanding of self-esteem.

It should first be noted that self-love and self-esteem, which I should like to treat conceptually as partly independent variables, may often manifest themselves in a close relation. A person may at once love himself for his beauty and respect himself for his competence, in which case the attitudes will reinforce one another and be difficult to separate. In similar fashion there may be a concurrence of sense of incompetence and feeble self-love, with each new manifestation of inefficacy tending to block any increase in narcissistic cathexis. I should suppose that self-love and self-esteem, both involving positive affects toward oneself, would go together more often than not, but correlation, unless it is perfect, does not signify identity. If we can point to types of personality in which self-esteem is definitely stronger than self-love, or the reverse, we are establishing at least a partial independence between the two variables.

As a first example of partial independence we can take a person who has attained high competence in the important areas of behavior. With the help of good physical and intellectual abilities he has met the several crises of childhood and adolescence with marked success, so that as a young adult he faces new experiences, whether objective problems or human relations, with a high level of confidence. This is a man of strong self-esteem; he trusts his competence and feels himself to be capable of dealing effectively with his environment. I am not making him up: one actual example will be found under the pseudonym of York in a monograph by Murray and Morgan (1945, pp. 133-138, 187-189, 227-230, 267-268), another in the case of Hartley Hale (White, 1952, pp. 26-91). Such a man may have a certain amount of self-love as well, but he is not conspicuous in this respect when compared with other young men of similar age and circumstances. His interests are well exteriorized, his concern is much less with himself than with other people and objective tasks, and his object libido must be rated relatively high as against his narcissistic libido. In this respect he contrasts sharply with the young man called Couch by Murray and Morgan (1945, pp. 76-80, 174-179, 208-213, 284-286) and even with the less striking example of Joseph Kidd (White, 1952, pp. 135-207). Couch is an almost perfect example of rampant self-love. In interviews he talked constantly about himself, confessed to "extreme egoism, extreme ambition, and self-interest" (p. 76), and portrayed dotingly his hope to become a sensitive, discriminating person insulated against the common concerns of the world. Yet there was no conspicuous self-esteem to go with this cherishing love of himself. "The artist or writer," he said, "isn't very important anyway, he doesn't effect anything" (p. 76); and he was not at all sure that he himself could be successful in either capacity. His daily life was constantly disturbed by worrisome doubts about health and general effectiveness.

The most dramatic instance of this second pattern is the deluded schizophrenic, whom Freud believed to have a maximum exaltation of self-regard. It is true that the hospital Napoleon exhibits a high degree of self-love and that in fantasy he thinks of himself as infinitely competent. But we must bear in mind that, quite unlike the real Napoleon, he fails to take arms against his plotting foes, may not even try to break his prison, and may do literally nothing in actuality to effectuate his status. Untested fantasies of vast power do not conceal the fact of his greatly injured sense of competence and of his painfully low self-esteem if he ventures outside the realm of his imagination. Indeed the hospital hero who quietly sweeps the floor perhaps represents the maximum divorce between self-love and self-esteem. The whole understanding of schizophrenia, as already indicated, turns on recognizing the pathologically low sense of interpersonal competence.

If we take as our starting point the child's overt behavior, disregarding for the moment the reconstructed infantile fantasies, it would appear that self-esteem has an important root in experiences of efficacy. Children chuckle and laugh when their efforts have effects on the environment—when one block can be balanced upon another, when the wobbly legs can be made to carry one across the room, when an act like hand-clapping can evoke an imitative response from the parent, when a bonnet can be attached to the patient family dog. Success in these ventures leads to greater confidence in further action, just as later on a success in schoolwork leads to more confidence in one's mental prowess, and a victory on the playground to more faith in one's physical skill. Just as esteem for another person is based upon what he can do, self-esteem is based on a sense of what I can do—a sense of competence.

If we think in such terms as these, it becomes necessary to examine carefully Ferenczi's idea about the original sense of omnipotence. Ferenczi attributed omnipotence to the child whose every need was satisfied the moment it arose—the fancied happy state of the child in the womb. With this initial assumption, the whole course of life could be seen as a progressive reduction of a delightful omnipotence through the cruel incursions of cold hard reality. Ruth Munroe (1955) urges us to be cautious about this hypothetical initial state. "Ferenczi's term," she says, "also connotes, for adults, a *gratifying* sense of personal power, and one may wonder whether the infant's emotional state is really correctly described" (pp. 179-180). She introduces an illustration from a later time, a boy of about four who, after being whirled around terrifyingly in the air by his father, began half-laughingly to pummel the father and said, " 'I can beat you up. . . . I am the biggest man in the world.' " Munroe speculates that the omnipotent fantasies of the child hark back not so much to "a golden age when he always felt powerful," but to a time "when complete power was at his command" when needed (p. 180). This would be a somewhat different experience. It would imply some knowledge of efficacy and inefficacy, some sense of being able to influence the course of events through effort expended, yet at the same time a very small experience of the real circumstances that separate a desire from its fulfillment. As earliest prototypes we can take the hungry infant's cry or even his early sucking efforts, but we cannot take a situation in which there is no experience of activity. Ferenczi's child in the womb may be able to have an oceanic feeling, but he cannot have an omnipotent one prior to the basic experiences of efficacy and inefficacy. Only much later is it legitimate to assume a gratifying sense of personal power.

This may seem a small point on which to quarrel, and I have brought it up only because I think Ferenczi's image of original omnipotence gets us off on the wrong foot for understanding self-esteem. Development cannot start from a passive fantasy, as if all later strivings for efficacy, mastery, power, and the building of empires sprang from an urge to restore the sleeplike state of the womb. The genesis must be in those events, whenever and however they occur, in which action and its concomitant effort can be experienced as bringing about the next state of perception and affect. If we base our thinking in this way on action and its consequences, we can hope eventually to trace the genetic history of sense of competence and to find the true origins of fantasies of omnipotence. Perhaps we can also dispel the apparent paradox that the child generates such fantasies when he is still actually rather helpless.

This genetic inquiry exceeds the scope of the present essay. Suffice it to say here that the course of development cannot be conceived of as a simple one from glowing omnipotence to cold objectivity. We must allow that the picture is more complex: two somewhat different sequences go on at the same time. These two lines of development originate in the paradoxical circumstance that the infant is both helpless and powerful. He is helpless in the sense that in objective reality he cannot take care of himself and satisfy his own needs; but, as Erikson (1962) has pointed out, he is indeed a power in the interactive actuality of the family, where he can make other people take care of him. With respect to part of the environment the infant starts out helpless, but through exploratory action discovers competence where none was before. He discovers that the rattle can be made to sound, that blocks can be piled, that other people can be induced to imitate and play, that he can feed himself, that he can stand up and walk and fetch things he wants. There is a steady growth from being *unable* to being *able* to affect the environment in desired ways. With respect to another part of the environment, especially the mother in her nurturing activities, he rather quickly reaches a peak in his capacity to command services. This form of efficacy will then go into a contractive phase as the mother becomes less willing to do everything, and renunciation of power will be necessary. But the two lines of development quickly become complementary: as the child progressively sacrifices his privileges of command over the household, he becomes less needful of these privileges through growing competence to deal with things by his own efforts.

Fantasies of omnipotence reflect, to my mind, these two aspects of infantile experience. They are perhaps typified, on the one hand, by the common tendency to set stories in surroundings of affluence and abundant service, where the principal characters, be they lovers, villains, or the cast of a murder mystery, deal at least with all their minor problems by ringing for the servants; on the other hand, by the oft-repeated themes of adventure, struggle with difficulties, and ultimate mastery of the most baffling obstacles, in the manner of Robinson Crusoe and his mechanized successors, Superman and the heroes of modern science fiction. Both types of fantasy hark back to experiences of efficacy, not to the free gratifications of the womb. The first reflects omnipotence in summoning the nurse, while the second represents omnipotence in doing things oneself.

Self-esteem, then, has its taproot in the experience of efficacy. It is not built merely on what others do or what the environment provides. From the very start it is based on what one can make the environment provide, even if it is only through more vigorous sucking or more loudly sustained cries. In the infant's actuality the feeling of efficacy is regulated by the success or failure of *his* efforts, for he has no knowledge of what else may be affecting the environment's response. From this point onward self-esteem is closely tied to feelings of efficacy and, as it develops, to the more general cumulative sense of competence. It is constantly undergoing modification as the child directs his efforts toward manipulative activity, locomotor accomplishments, mastery of language, and assertion of his desires with respect to others. It moves up or down as social roles are tried out and as identifications are attempted. In favorable circumstances it reappears when the libidinal and aggressive storms of the oedipus complex have somewhat subsided so that new patterns of relation to the parents can be explored and tested. During the latency period there are fresh vicissitudes connected with what Erikson calls the "sense of industry"—the child's attempts to use his powers in activities such as schoolwork that have significance for his later entrance into adulthood. There are also new tests of competence in competitive relations with contemporaries and in cooperative action and team play. Understanding self-esteem means understanding the history of action and its consequences.

The other source of self-esteem, the esteem in which we are held by others, begins to assume importance as soon as the child attains a clear enough conception of others to sense them as the source of attitudes. Starting perhaps from a vague discrimination between parents pleased and parents displeased, the child moves toward a more distinct awareness of the way he is being taken by others. His self-esteem is then influenced by the evaluations that proceed from others; through their acts and attitudes he learns how they perceive him and is influenced to perceive himself in the same way. We well know how a young child's self-esteem can be buoyed by parental praise and crushed by contempt. Stern (1914) pointed out with reference to the second and third years that the child "feels a craving not only for sympathy but for applause for his little accomplishments from those around him. No child really flourishes without the sunshine of this praise, with the encouragement it gives to ever-renewed effort" (p. 503). Gardner Murphy (1947) emphasizes the importance of the verbal labels that adults apply to children and that children apply to each other, labels which may have a moral tone like "naughty" and "good," but which may also refer to competence as in the case of "strong," "smart," "dope," "stupid." "Most of the trait names that are used," says Murphy, "represent general action tendencies; . . . the child lives up to the terms employed. . . . The child forms general ideas of himself" (p. 506).

It is a virtue of this point of view, I think, that we can recognize the formative importance of external sources of self-esteem without losing sight of the child's part in regulating their flow. For the oddly one-sided notion that self-esteem is regulated by the income of narcissistic supplies we can substitute the more realistic image of mutual regulation. On the whole, "supplies" are not bestowed whimsically; they represent a response to what the child has actually done. As Erikson (1950) puts it: ". . . children cannot be fooled by empty praise and condescending encouragement. They may have to accept artificial bolstering of their self-esteem in lieu of something better, but their ego identity gains real strength only from wholehearted and consistent recognition of real accomplishment" (p. 208). Why cannot they be fooled by empty praise? Because they have an internal criterion of the success and value of their actions to oppose to the external one. Praise will be experienced as empty if the act fell short of one's intention, brought no feeling of efficacy, added nothing to one's sense of competence. If we are to use the metaphor of an income of esteem, we must complete it by recognizing that coin can also be minted within the personality out of the bullion of efficacy and sense of competence.

This view of self-esteem is more serviceable to our understanding of development, it seems to me, than one that is stated in terms only of instinctual energies and infantile fantasies. By anchoring self-esteem to experiences of efficacy and competence it allows us to maintain the distinction between self-esteem and self-love. By directing attention to the actual history of the growth of competence through transactions with the environment it permits us to detect various stages in the child's fantasies of omnipotence, thus freeing us from the difficulty of referring all later interest in power to the earliest months of life when power could be experienced only dimly. It encourages us to continue the study of self-esteem through the latency period and beyond, making us open-minded on the question of how firmly the outlines of personality are set through resolution of the oedipus complex. And it further encourages us, since it is framed in terms of actions and their consequences, to see the whole process as one of transaction and mutual regulation between the child and his environment.

EGO STRENGTH

The concept of ego strength is recurrent in the psychoanalytic literature because of its practical importance in treatment. I first met it in Hendrick's (1934) account of the "analyzability" of patients: he referred to it alternatively as "ego potentiality" and "strength of character." In everyday language he described it as "a certain capacity for fighting difficulties, 'grit,' the ability to 'come back' and try again" (p. 240). More technically, it signified the capacity to endure frustration and emotional tension and to keep working toward the goals of treatment. Ego strength, however it comes to be defined, is an important diagnostic consideration in analytic work, and it has become a concept much resorted to in our efforts to understand different outcomes both of treatment and of development.

It is interesting to observe the emergence of a very similar concept in one of the most abstract corners of academic psychology: the factor analysis of traits of personality. Here the procedures of measurement, consisting of questionnaires and little experiments, seem to be of so superficial a kind that one would hardly expect a convergence with the findings of depth psychology. But it is noteworthy that Eysenck (1953), in his very extensive work on the measurement of traits, has repeatedly come out with a basic dimension characterized at one end as "neuroticism" and at the other as something like "will power." Furthermore, Kassebaum, Couch, and Slater (1959), submitting to factor analysis that widely used questionnaire, *The Minnesota Multiphasic Personality Inventory,* found what appeared to be the very same factor, which they chose to name "ego weakness vs. ego strength." Low scorers showed evidences of general maladjustment, anxiety, dependency, and tendencies toward psychological disorders, whereas high scorers were free from anxiety and psychopathology and showed tendencies toward leadership and effective intellectual ability. These findings indicate that ego strength is not an esoteric quality open only to the intuitive third ear. It manifests itself quite clearly at the surface as well as in the deeper layers of personality, a fact I suppose we all find congruent with our experience in dealing with people in everyday life.

In 1938 Fenichel undertook to put the concept on a technically sound basis by asking the question: "When is an ego strong?" The answer required an explicit statement of different functions in which it might be strong or weak. Fenichel enumerated the ability to tolerate tension or excitation; the ability to judge validly and to carry out intentions despite hindrances; strength in controlling and channeling the instincts; ability to modulate the more archaic manifestations of the superego; and power to reconcile conflicting elements within the ego itself. But he did not allow ego strength to fall apart into a list of separate abilities. Underlying everything was a more basic formula whereby ego weakness was related to the damming up of instinctual energy and the consequent curtailment of energies available to the ego. "The strongest ego is the ego which has developed the least in the way of defensive measures of the anti-cathectic type and has undergone least alterations leading to its own impoverishment" (1938, pp. 75-76). Only when it is in full possession of organismic energies, so to speak, not wasting itself on heavy internal armaments, can it tolerate tension, judge validly, and control inevitable conflicts in a flexible, efficient manner.

Fenichel's formulation is certainly valuable, but it is strictly from the point of view of the physician. It describes the psychopathology that can afflict the ego and take away its strength, but it leaves health unexplained. When there is no sickness the ego works as it is supposed to work. For an ego psychology and for a complete theory of personality we cannot take so much for granted. We must beware also of an almost inevitable consequence of a theory expressed so largely in terms of energies and their blocking: namely, the assumption that ego strength is a simple function of the amount of anxiety to which the person was exposed during early childhood. To see this function in its true complexity we must have a positive theory of how the ego is supposed to work, of how it manages the business of dealing with anxieties, tensions, frustrations, and conflicts when it is not reduced to using primitive anticathectic defenses. How does a person learn to deal with such things competently, so that anxiety can be kept within bounds and primitive defenses do not have to be summoned?

This problem can be clarified if we start from the idea that anxiety and competence stand in a reciprocal relation. The point has been sharply made by Goldstein (1940), who conceives of anxiety as the subjective aspect of a threat that ordered, adequate behavior will break down and turn into catastrophic behavior. Goldstein's extensive experience with brain-injured patients showed him in rather dramatic form the relation between environmental pressure and capacity to respond. The patients were often badly upset by a seemingly simple task that happened to involve some of the power of abstraction which they had lost through cerebral injury. Threat is not solely a quality of the stimulus; it lies rather in the relation between the stimulus and our ability to deal with it. Children are usually afraid of a ball thrown straight at them, but after they have learned to play baseball no sight is more welcome than a hard throw or a line drive that can be caught for an "out." This very American illustration would certainly not have occurred to Freud, but his theory involves the same implicit reciprocity. ". . . anxiety," he wrote, "is seen to be a product of the infant's mental helplessness. . . . The progress which the child makes in its development—its growing independence, the sharper division of its mental apparatus into several agencies, the advent of new needs—cannot fail to exert an influence upon the content of the danger-situation" (1926, pp. 138, 139).

Fenichel's formulation of ego strength can now be restated in what I believe is a more adequate and illuminating fashion. A strong ego, let us say, is one which has developed substantial competence in dealing with impulse and with environment. A weak ego is one which, lacking this development, has had to make heavy use of defensive measures of the anticathectic type, thus sacrificing further flexible learning. With respect to the specific functions mentioned by Fenichel, I noted in an earlier chapter that delay and the tolerating of tension were related to an acquired confidence in one's ability to influence the course of events. When ultimate gratification is not entirely a matter of luck, but lies at least somewhat within the sphere of one's own effort, it is easier to put up with a frustration and wait for the expedient future. Fenichel's second point, being able to make valid judgments and to carry out one's intentions, clearly relates to what has been accomplished through active exploration and the testing of reality. Intentions can be carried out to the extent that one has learned competence in dealing with the various exigencies that may obstruct them. The power to channel and modulate instinctual urges and superego demands, and the ability to reconcile conflicts within the ego, likewise depend upon how much progress has been made in manipulating the environment where channels must be found, where modulated expressions must take place, and where conflicting ego interests must be resolved. It is by developing competence that the ego betters its position in relation to future threats.

Hartmann (1939) has advanced the valuable idea that the ego does not make all of its gains in situations of stress. What it learns through dealing with the environment in conflict-free situations may prove to be useful knowledge in the next scene of conflict. It cannot be said, therefore, that the strength of the ego is purely a function of past performance in situations of crisis and stress. When a child learns at conflict-free times that his mother is an agreeable companion whose favor can be gained by a winning smile, he may well produce the winning smile the next time she descends in wrath —often to her·discomfiture. We have to know more than the history of crises in order to understand ego strength. The ideal thing would be to know the whole history of explorations in efficacy and of the sense of competence which is produced by the outcome of these explorations.

This conception of the growth of the ego and of the sources of its strength yields an altered view, it seems to me, of the psychosexual stages of development. Although they are cast in terms of libidinal energy and its transformations, the psychosexual stages at the same time revolve around certain crises in the relations between child and parents, crises which can have a "normal solution" as well as various pathological alternatives. I have dealt elsewhere (1960) with the widening of the theory of development that results when we introduce independent ego energies, efficacy, and competence into the story of growth. It is again a question of having to understand what happens outside the chief situations of instinctual conflict in order to grasp the full meaning of the ego's capacity to deal with conflict.

The idea of a reciprocal relation between competence and anxiety is of value in understanding different varieties of psychopathology. I have already noted this in my discussion of early ego deviations (Chapter 5), where I showed that autistic disorders could be considered to be the consequence of a highly generalized obstruction of strivings for efficacy, especially those directed toward other human beings, the obstruction occurring at a time when little progress had been made toward competent discrimination and action. Starting from this basis of a very general inhibition of ego functions, one can describe different levels of fixation in terms of the extensiveness of the inhibition or injury through anxiety. Thus the symbiotic disorders are one step beyond the autistic: the child has discovered the avenue to "passive-receptive mastery" and uses the mother as an external ego, but he does not dare to seek efficacy apart from rather primitive ways of influencing his mother. In the neuroses the area of inhibition is much smaller. Obstruction has happened to certain kinds of human relations, such as those that involve authority or competition or intimate love relations, but the patient is still free to explore and test his way toward competence in the material world and in less sensitive human areas. Development of a systematic theory of psychopathology requires a fairly precise knowledge of the chronology of competence. This would include a knowledge of what defense mechanisms become available at what times, as Hartmann (1939) has argued. It would also include knowledge of the growth of discrimination, which has a great deal to do with the child's power to limit the spread or generalization of anxiety, and knowledge of the development of sense of competence, which will be decisive in determining his susceptibility to feelings of helplessness.

Ego strength would seem to be favored by the presence of alternative sources of security, affection, and interest. The ego does well to observe the maxims that advise against putting all one's eggs in one basket and having only one string to one's bow. Development should be scanned with a view to understanding the differentiation of spheres of satisfaction. Losing the mother at six months may be cause for anaclitic depression with a retarding of ego development in virtually all its aspects. Losing her at five years may be bad enough, but the devastation is less complete: there are now many interesting aspects of life that do not depend upon her presence. At ten the bereavement may be counterbalanced by increased activity with contemporary friends, at fifteen by increased activity with the opposite sex. An important theme, then, in the growth of ego strength is the opening of alternative ways of being contented and efficacious, which put one less at the mercy of frustration in any particular sphere.

These considerations are helpful, it seems to me, in dealing with a problem that has persistently plagued psychodynamic theory. This is the problem of people whose histories seem to be crushingly loaded with situations conducive to psychopathology but who have come out healthy, effective, and happy. Well-studied cases of this kind have been reported especially by Macfarlane et al. (1954), and it is noteworthy that most attempts to predict future development have erred in the direction of pessimism. Rather than hastening to the conclusion that clinicians are orally frustrated types, I believe that this sort of thing reflects perfectly a lack of concepts for understanding the ego and its adaptive activities. We go wrong in our predictions because we are more skillful in detecting destructive psychodynamic situations than we are in discovering constructive replies to them. I believe that the concepts of efficacy and competence can do much to restore the balance, but rather than argue this any longer in general terms I should like to discuss a single case, hoping to satisfy my readers that these concepts make a helpful difference.

An Illustrative Case

The case I have chosen for this purpose was reported by Annie Reich (1958) under the title: "A Character Formation Representing the Integration of Unusual Conflict Solutions into the Ego

Structure." Reich herself, recognizing a gap in the psychoanalytic literature, chose to present the case for the light it might throw on successful character development. For the patient was "normal" and "healthy" by average standards: he was free from symptoms, functioned rather well in work and family life, and seemed well adjusted to love objects and to society. Indeed, he came to analysis with a single major complaint: he felt that he was not productive in his own work and was in this respect falling far short of his potentialities. Reich warns us that the history will reveal "an abundance of traumatic situations, difficult conflicts, and a preponderance of regressed pregenital and sadomasochistic strivings," but she hopes to be able to show how the highly unfavorable childhood situation issued in a result that was "amazingly positive" (p. 310). But at the end of the paper she admits to being still puzzled. ". . . in view of his history," she says, "it seems quite striking that Roger was not sicker." In spite of everything, "he succeeded singularly well in developing defenses the results of which could be used in such constructive form for ego purposes and could be integrated as character traits into the structure of the ego" (p. 322).

This last statement points to the very heart of the difficulty in bringing psychoanalytic theory to grips with normal development. The patient has had profound conflicts entailing great anxiety, and he has met them by defenses. So far, so good: we are in the realm upon which Freud turned the searchlight of his genius. But if defense is to be the central concept in explaining adaptation, it is indeed quite a mystery that the results should be "amazingly positive." Conceivably Reich might have found that the infantile problems were not very severe, which would justify the interpretation that defenses of the anticathectic type were used lightly and with small impounding of energies. She did not find this, and we are left with the paradox that major defenses were necessary and that a strong ego developed. Hartmann (1939) has tried to cover such outcomes with the idea that patterns of behavior first devised for defensive purposes may turn into autonomous adaptive maneuvers. This could hardly happen if they were originally of the anticathectic type with damming up of energy; in any event, we need to know what conditions must be present to permit this happy outcome rather than the dismal picture drawn by Fenichel. We must concentrate on defenses the results of which can be used in constructive forms for ego purposes. Current psychoanalytic ego psychology, it seems to me, gave Reich very little to work with at this point, leaving a soft spot in her otherwise illuminating interpretation.

The patient, Roger V., was a successful psychologist in an academic position, well established in his field, keenly intelligent, and unusually skilled in psychological observation. He was well liked by his friends, loved by his family, and generally regarded as a solid, reliable citizen. Much concerned with the welfare of others, he was constantly helpful to students and colleagues, devoted himself at home to the needs and interests of his wife and three children, walked the dog, and took on household chores and repairs which he liked to do wholly by himself without outside aid. He also spent much time trying to "straighten out" his parents, a contentious pair who seemed forever destined to reach a hostile impasse. One can see that this pattern of life permitted little time or energy for the incubation of ideas and the scholarly labor that might have issued in productive work, and that Roger, now in his forties, might be increasingly worried about his sluggishness in this aspect of his life.

By the world at large Roger was probably praised as an unselfish man. Reich describes him as "a little overconscientious, too well-intentioned—maybe one could best describe it as too 'virtuous' " (p. 310). This judgment is supported by evidence of real dissatisfaction: he was aware that his dutiful activities were not sufficiently spontaneous, that he "was always in a state of watchfulness with regard to himself" (p. 312) as if selfish and aggressive impulses were ready to spring out, and that in the end his services to others did not yield a deeply desired sense of closeness. He "lived in a lasting state of inner loneliness and isolation, which represented the antithesis to the deepest aims of his fantasies" (p. 313). And the mere fact that he sought the heroic remedy of psychoanalysis suggests that he suspected inhibition, not just a crowding out, of his "own" productive work.

Reich's paper includes, of course, a consideration of the psychodynamic determinants of these dissatisfactions, but the central theme is to understand the near success of Roger's character structure. In particular, it is important to explain (1) his considerable independence, seen among other places in his household "do-it-yourself" proclivities; (2) his excellent object relations, shown both in his family life and in his work; and (3) his professional success, particularly with respect to his marked psychological insight. Are we to find a history of early good object relations, of healthy encouragement of independence, of identification figures setting patterns of unselfish caring and sympathetic insight? Reich discovers none of these happy supports; the early situation seems to press in each case in the opposite direction. Roger's character begins to look like a striking creative achievement. Let us see what lay behind each quality.

Independence. Reich's analysis brought to light a deep fantasy of fusion with the mother. This dated from the oral stage, but it very soon came to be injured by the mother's overconcern and infantilizing tendencies and by her occasional cruelties and oral deprivations. The wish for fusion became dangerously associated with the fear of being devoured. Later the primal scene, witnessed and interpreted as violent aggression with injury, still further endangered the passive fantasy by connecting it with the castrated mother. But phallic-sadistic urges were also dangerous; neither passive nor active fantasies provided a safe recourse. The defensive solution of this dilemma consisted of surrendering the phallic-sadistic urges, shifting libido from objects to self, and developing the fantasy of producing babies anally and alone. "In this fantasy," Reich comments, "he was strong, active, *creative,* and quite on his own, completely independent of the dangerous love object. Thus, a new feature emerged here which was to become very important in his later makeup: for the first time, he was a 'do-it-yourself' person" (p. 316).

Not "for the first time," let me suggest. This fantasy may have been the child's first symbolization of his wishes about the mother in active, independent terms, but is it an adequate explanation to say that this happened all at once through a shift of libidinal energy? The implicit assumption reveals itself that independent strivings arise only as an anxiety-propelled expedient when object relations become overcharged with danger. I would interpret this differently, although quite in accord with Hartmann's (1939) idea that patterns developed in the conflict-free sphere may be drawn into service when conflict supervenes. The small Roger, it seems likely, had already enjoyed experiences of efficacy, probably with inanimate objects in situations that did not incite maternal devouring, and he had already found a parallel pleasure in controlling the excretory process. He already knew, in other words, the satisfaction of "do-it-yourself," which he had arrived at primarily through the promptings of independent ego energies. The creative achievement of his anal birth fantasy lay not in his having suddenly invented independence but in assimilating his tangled libidinal fantasies to another part of his experience which was satisfying in itself and free from human intrusion.

This is a difference that makes a difference when it comes to understanding the outcome. Reich's account implies that Roger's independence was motivated by a persisting unconscious fantasy representing a happy combination of libidinal and aggressive elements. Giving anal birth to babies could never be realized in actuality or turned into competent action, so that expression was always displaced to such things, ultimately, as repairing the house. This raises a difficult metapsychological question concerning the amount of satisfaction or tension reduction that can be presumed to accompany the enactment of a fantasy entirely in displaced or symbolic terms. The most likely deduction would be, I think, that the recurrent pressure of the never fully satisfied wishes would produce independence in a highly rigid, compulsive form, much like a neurotic symptom; the result could scarcely be "amazingly positive." What we need here is a way of explaining the generally satisfying and efficient character of Roger's independence, with only traces of compulsiveness, and this is exactly what our hypothesis can provide. By hooking the libidinal-aggressive fantasy onto already successful enterprises springing from effectance, the child could bring extra energy into his independent tendencies without taking from them the feelings of efficacy which were their intrinsic reward. The effect of this might even be to speed the natural growth of competence in the manipulation and mastery of inanimate objects; and if the unconscious fantasy was never satisfied, there was still the satisfaction of efficacy and growing competence. No doubt, as Freud always said, a subtle quantitative factor determines whether a linkage of this sort will foster competence or sour it with compulsiveness. But our hypothesis at least states what it is that will be fostered or soured, and shows how in the absence of serious souring this can grow in cumulative fashion into a realistic, satisfying skill.

Human Object Relations. Reich sees in Roger's unselfish behavior and concern about others a "curing-healing-giving compulsion" (p. 322) which she traces to reaction formation. An incident at the age of six may have precipitated this defensive maneuver. The parents quarreled more violently than usual and the mother threatened to leave the father, taking the boy with her. This let loose a storm of anxiety which led to repression of both passivity and phallic-sadistic wishes, reaction formation, and the establishment of a rigid superego "whose most pre-eminent demand was *not* to be like the aggressive, sexual parents" (p. 318). Now he began the pattern that was still prominent in his forties, that of reconciling and re-educating the parents, becoming their support, "straightening them out" and setting for them an example of reasonableness. "A reversal thus had set in," says Reich (p. 318); "We see that Roger has succeeded in *becoming active again,* but in a nonsexual, nonaggressive way. He now enjoyed building, improving, rescuing others, being rational and constructive. Here he was identified with the feeding mother, the strong and protective father" (p. 319).

Here we have a second and more significant turn to activity, one which determined a large part of his later behavior with colleagues and students, wife, children—and dog. We notice again the implicit assumption that such a revolution can be accomplished only under the influence of powerful anxiety and that the means of its happening is a redistribution of instinctual energies through defense mechanisms. Reich calls the curing-healing-giving behavior a reaction formation and a compulsion, but she also points out the paradox that no small libidinal energy escaped through it: Roger was really fond of people, helped them effectively, and for the most part enjoyed taking care of them. She calls attention also to the remarkable selectiveness in superego formation whereby the boy rejected and worked against the main characteristics of his parents and chose to copy aspects which must have displayed themselves far less often. As before, Reich's concepts seem well suited to describe a change of heart and of behavior, but they do not explain the "amazingly positive" outcome in Roger's adult life. Why did he not become a whining juvenile prig, nagging his parents to keep the peace and insinuating himself into the lives of others with unwanted exhortations? This is the behavior that would represent a compulsion.

What we have to allow here is that Roger's pattern of behavior, even if it sprang out of acute defensive necessities, underwent a progressive development that kept it in realistic tune with the needs of other people. In a way that the true compulsive neurotic does not, he must have kept responding to the individual and novel characteristics of people as he met them, so that his help and advice were more or less appropriate to the circumstances. To me this signifies that something was being satisfied, something more was being achieved than the denial of passive erotic and active erotic-aggressive urges. It has long been recognized that the defense mechanism of reaction formation often leads to new ego interests, but how this happens has not been made sufficiently clear. Roger is a good case in point. My formula for him is that he found in "straightening out" his parents not only relief from anxiety-arousing impulses but also a satisfying feeling of interpersonal efficacy. This motive continued and very likely gained on the original defensive ones, making possible a cumulative growth of social competence of the nurturing sort. As we saw in Chapter 3, effectance is a gentle motive without compulsive pressure. Its progressive satisfaction depends on the person's encountering novelties and adapting to them; reality must be correctly assessed in order to experience efficacy.

It would be easier, I think, to reach a full understanding of Roger's turn to activity if we assumed that he had already experienced some success, at least on occasion, in influencing his parents. There are perhaps hints in Reich's account that this was the case, but, unfortunately, psychoanalytic theory does not encourage the investigation and reporting of such facts. The metaphor of energies—changes in the distribution of instinctual forces—suggests something that happens all at once in a crisis; it does not invite a search for continuities between a new pattern of behavior and earlier ones. But let us go along with the possibility that before the acute crisis Roger had never had either kind or dominant impulses toward his parents and that they burst into being under the acute stress of threatened parental separation. What happened? They worked. Reich does not say so, but it is clear from the story that the parents did not separate, then or later, that they were not happy in their bickering existence, and that they really needed the help of a domestic peacemaker, even if at first it was only to use his evident distress as a means of controlling their own aggressions. The role of family trouble shooter is a difficult one for a child to achieve and an easy one for parents to suppress. Because his parents needed it, Roger was able to experience efficacy in this role as well as relief from anxiety. Just as his turn to fantasies of active erotic independence hooked onto a movement toward efficacy and competence with the inanimate environment, so now his urge to control his parents led to a growing satisfaction with interpersonal competence. And as he grew competent in dealing with people he found it increasingly safe to love them.

Psychological Insight. Reich finds the origin of Roger's rare capacity for psychological insight in an infantile urge to understand himself as his mother tried to understand him. It was thus part of the deep need for communion and fusion with the mother and could also be understood as a desexualized looking into and penetrating the self, a symbolic sadomasochistic gratification in which he was independent of objects. Later this preoccupation came to be directed toward others. Reich notes that "The libidinal undercurrents of Roger's interest in observing and understanding never interfered with the quality of his performance. . . . there was never an intrusion of one sphere into the other, never a lowering of the standard of his reality testing" (p. 321). She suggests that we may need to assume in Roger's ego a particular capacity for sublimation.

The reality testing is, of course, the critical point. Exactly the same libidinal undercurrents could be used to explain a rigid compulsive projecting of one's own fantasies upon others. But we have not accomplished much if in a search for the determinants of ego strength we end by finding only an innate capacity. We saw in Chapter 4 that reality testing goes on through investigative action, and that reality governs fantasy to the extent that discriminated and practiced actions have been acquired. If Roger's self-inspection had not already turned outward before the crisis at six years it would certainly have done so then, when understanding the parents and reaching their feelings became one of the guiding purposes of his life. Here there was a double premium on reality testing. It was necessary for efficacy, and efficacy was necessary if anxiety was to be controlled. Not because of its instinctual roots did Roger's psychological insight become flexible and realistic, but because he needed it in an early crisis where the understanding of others was requisite, and because, achieving some success with it here, he found that it yielded agreeable feelings of interpersonal competence and opened new channels for safe libidinal relations with others.

In summary, I hope it is clear that I have not tried to second-guess Reich with respect to Roger's fantasy life and infantile psychodynamics. I have made suggestions only on the point which Reich herself finds puzzling: the relatively strong character structure that emerged from so much early adversity. And the point is really the same one whether it is applied to the patient's independence, to his unselfish concern with helping people, or to his excellently developed psychological understanding. In no case does the pattern of instinctual energy and defense, stated alone, offer any ground for predicting a successful outcome rather than a rigid, compulsive, self-defeating one. The secret of success lies elsewhere: it lies in what happens after the defensive realignment of forces has taken place. Everything depends upon the extent to which the ensuing behavior is effective in influencing the environment, yielding a satisfying feeling of efficacy and producing cumulative contributions to a sense of competence. I do not mean to exclude from this formula the satisfactions that come from finding safer and better outlets for libidinal and aggressive energies, but I believe that the finding of such outlets is pretty much a function of the extent to which the new behavior can be exploratory and investigative, getting itself caught up with the interest in efficacy and with the consequent attention to reality testing. If we are to understand ego strength we must see not only how an alignment of instinctual forces solves an immediate psychodynamic problem but also how it fits into possible programs of testing and effecting, which are the means whereby an ego grows stronger.

In looking for these things it would be arbitrary to exclude altogether such likely constitutional factors as general level of activity. The vigor of the child's effort doubtless affects the outcome, usually, but perhaps not always, in a favorable direction. But we must also consider two other things: the inherent probability that a psychodynamic pattern can be translated into effective actions, and the responsiveness of the environment to such actions. Roger's solution of an acute psychodynamic crisis by a reaction formation against both phallic aggressiveness and passivity, leaving an urge toward kindly action, was inherently destined for greater success in human relations than would have been, let us say, a resentful passivity or an aggressive assertiveness displaced to the realm of speech. But it is also true that the parents responded favorably to their child's peacemaking efforts: they needed him and therefore let him have an effect upon them. We can easily imagine parents who would have nipped this in the bud, putting the child firmly in his place, defeating the intention of his reaction formation, and thereby forcing him into some different and less favorable psychodynamic solution.

In separating these aspects for discussion I surely do not do justice to the actual complexity of events. It would doubtless be more accurate to assume that in reaching his psychodynamic solution Roger was already responding to what he knew and felt about his parents; the situation influenced the solution. But this only emphasizes all the more the effort we must make to understand the strengthening of the ego in terms of action upon the environment, feelings of efficacy, and cumulative growth of a sense of competence. This means in terms that include independent ego energies.

8

FURTHER CONSIDERATIONS OF
ENERGY: ANXIETY, CATHEXIS,
NEUTRALIZATION

If we stand back for a moment from the details of the previous chapters and look at Freud's basic concepts in their historical perspective, it becomes evident that the libido theory had a special place in his heart. During his student days and early years in physiological research, he was constantly exposed to the idea of energy, which was perhaps the greatest conceptual achievement of nineteenth-century science. As a concept, energy had the great virtue of gathering into a single interpretation all ideas about force; and forces, in their turn, were considered to be the hallmark of the truly causal explanation (Holt, 1963). When Freud's interest turned to psychology he was naturally on the lookout for forces, and when his psychoanalytic work convinced him of the ubiquity of sexual urges he took the logical step of postulating libido as the basic energy underlying these widespread manifestations of force. The libido theory thus enshrined two of Freud's deepest convictions: that human emotional life could be captured in a scientific system, and that in perceiving the latent sexual theme he had exposed the real power behind human behavior.

We know that in the dramatic series of disagreements whereby members withdrew from further participation in Freud's intellectual circle the libido theory was almost always the central issue. This was conspicuously true in the two earliest defections. Adler explicitly rejected the theory in favor of his own ideas about aggression and the striving for superiority, while Jung removed the specific sexual element and equated libido with general energy. We

151

know also that the libido theory tended to absorb strivings which other workers had considered to be distinct and separate forces. At the start it managed to encompass aggression, which in the forms of sadism and masochism appeared as an appendage to basic erotic striving. It absorbed anxiety, which for years was presented as a direct transformation of impounded libido. In effect it stole hunger from the ego instincts by emphasizing the importance of oral erotism, and it later swallowed the ego instincts entirely by means of the concept of narcissism. With his conceptual preferences so clear, and with the triumph of libido so complete, it is the more remarkable that Freud did not bring his speculations to an end at this point. Setting a memorable example of intellectual integrity, he removed anxiety from its earlier bondage to libido, and he established aggression as an instinctual energy in its own right, though with a proviso that Thanatos usually operated in fusion with Eros. We should not cavil that an old and ailing man failed to work out the full implications of these changes, but it was perhaps his last homage to his favorite conceptualization that he did not set himself to see how he had clipped its wings.

These considerations are helpful in understanding certain of Freud's decisions with respect to energy. Two such decisions are particularly relevant to the theme of this essay. We must notice, first, how he handled the energy problem that arose when he separated anxiety from its earlier connection with libido. His solution, in which he treated anxiety as a danger signal and attributed defense to the operation of the pleasure-pain mechanism, is not the only possible one. It is not the one that has found favor in biology and academic psychology, either earlier when fear was considered an instinct or at the present time when avoidance of anxiety is interpreted as a powerful drive. Second, we must review the choice he made, once he had eliminated the ego instincts, to account for ego activities not obviously instinctual in character. Here he did not elect the alternative of independent ego energies, even though certain facts had led him occasionally to toy with this idea. He preferred to assume that instinctual energies became neutralized and could then operate in the service of aims which were not instinctual. This was a conception by no means easy to reconcile with prevailing ideas about energy and force in the physical world.

Why should one be dissatisfied with these solutions to problems of energy? Much can be said in their behalf. Freud's theories as he left them continued to give great importance to sexuality and aggression, the uncovering of which in all their ramifications will always stand as the major contribution of psychoanalysis to scientific knowledge. His conception of anxiety allowed him to consider anxiety the central problem of neurosis and gave it access to deep sources of power. The doctrine of neutralization has encouraged psychoanalytic ego psychology to take serious notice of ego interests and other processes unconnected with instinctual aims. Case reports using these concepts seem to indicate that the authors have found them useful, and therapeutic activity has not been forced to sacrifice its precious nonconceptual attributes of devotion, sensitivity, and common sense. Is this not a situation in which we should let well enough alone?

No, in the search for knowledge we can never let well enough alone. I rest the case for my grumblings about contemporary psychoanalytic theory on the following points. (1) It is short of concepts on which to build an adequate theory of the ego and of normal ego development. (2) It tends to draw attention away from the kind of observations that would be most useful for this purpose. (3) Its concepts depart more widely than is necessary from those that are steadily commending themselves in research on the physiology of instincts, on brain mechanisms, on human learning, and on the various aspects of child development. This tends to perpetuate a deadening atmosphere of cold war between different sides in the study of human behavior, thus obstructing the cross-fertilization of ideas that is so necessary today for scientific progress. On none of these grounds is it possible to be satisfied. But I am far from claiming that this essay will set everything right, even in my own mind. It aims to take but a single step, which consists of pressing the claim of exploratory actions and their consequences to a significant place in development, and proposing that they occupy the vacant conceptual niche of independent ego energies.

To this end I have reserved for this chapter a specific consideration of energy problems as such. Problems both of adequacy and of consistency seem to me to beset (1) the theory of anxiety, (2) the concept of cathexis, (3) the explanations of play, and (4) the idea of neutralization of instinctual-drive energies.

THE POWER OF ANXIETY

With respect to the first topic, the problem springs from the fact that in making his reformulation in 1926 Freud suddenly invested anxiety with enormous power. In his own words, "the affect of anxiety occupies a unique position in the economy of the mind" (p. 150); the ego "has only to give a *'signal of unpleasure'* in order to attain its object with the aid of that almost omnipotent institution, the pleasure principle" (p. 92). By initiating repression and other defense mechanisms, anxiety could enforce the most extensive restrictions on instinctual expression, including the abandonment of real outlets in favor of sublimated and symbolic ones. Whence came this unique position, this virtual omnipotence? The solution of such a problem had never seemed difficult to academic psychology. If one judged only by the importance of fear in overt animal and human behavior, knowing nothing of the subtleties of mental defense, it seemed obvious to postulate a fear instinct, or, in McDougall's more careful wording, "The Instinct of Flight and the Emotion of Fear" (1908, p. 51). Even in today's sophisticated drive theory, which makes a virtue of postulating the fewest possible number of drives, avoidance of anxiety has a prominent place in the select company, and experimenters often speak of conditions of high drive or low drive when referring to levels of aroused anxiety. Strictly speaking, avoidance of anxiety in this scheme of thought is a secondary drive, derived from the primary urge to avoid pain, but Mowrer (1950) has nominated it as the chief motive in ego development, while Solomon and Wynne (1954) testify to its unique position in animal conditioning by showing that its effects are extremely hard to undo, a finding that is wholly congruent with therapeutic experience. How did Freud avoid the conclusion that in making anxiety the force behind defense he was postulating a very powerful independent drive?

Examined closely, his solution was a curious one. Anxiety, he decided, was not an affair of the id, which "cannot have anxiety as the ego can" (1926, p. 140). It was an affect experienced by the ego, having its origin as part of a serviceable reaction to the crisis of birth, but serving thereafter as a signal of possibly impending danger. This description of anxiety, first as a reaction and then as a signal, denies it much significance as a source of energy and fails to explain its role in the defensive process. For this step Freud assumed that the ego took an active part by passing on the signal, so to speak, and thus arousing the power of the pleasure-pain mechanism. So it was here, through its activation of this virtually omnipotent principle of the id, that anxiety acquired its unique position in the mental economy. Did not Freud in this way invoke an independent source of power fully as strong as any instinct, but then fatally confuse the issue by calling it a principle and a mechanism rather than a drive?

Freud conceived of the pleasure-pain mechanism, so called, as an economic principle more general than any drive. He used it to represent the economic necessity to keep down tension, which is painful, and restore a pleasurable state of equilibrium. Instincts operated under the principle: their arousal produced unpleasant tension and their gratification a pleasant relief from tension. Freud believed, of course, that most danger situations were created by instinctual urges. The typical sequence was one in which an aroused libidinal impulse prompted a line of action that led to alarming consequences. According to the pleasure principle the impulse would press toward gratification and relief, but now the ego, perceiving the possible consequences, experiencing some degree of anxiety, and making this state of affairs known to the id, produces a new action under the principle which largely reverses things by clamping defenses upon the operation of the impulse. In this way Freud allowed the anxiety to function as an unpleasant tension so strong that it overruled the unpleasantness of hungering libidinal drive. In the end there was no way to avoid bringing the antagonists together in a battle of unpleasant tensions, from which libidinal drives often emerged badly warped.

Avoidance of pain and anxiety are different in nature from sexuality, and I certainly have no complaint against Freud for treating them differently. But I cannot escape the conclusion that it was his deep partiality for his instinct theory that led him to express himself as if anxiety were merely an affect used as a signal to put a mechanism into effect, when in fact he was interpreting it as a powerful force in the most profound psychodynamic sense. One might say that he let anxiety into the id by a back door so that on the brass plates at the front door Eros and Thanatos could announce themselves unchallenged as "the ultimate cause of all activity" (1940, p. 19). In fact, Freud attributed to the avoidance of anxiety everything that drive theorists have attributed to it, including great power to generate unpleasant tension and a strong inhibitory effect on actions and impulses leading toward danger. But he would not allow it the status of an instinctual drive.

It is not necessary to call avoidance of pain and avoidance of anxiety instinctual drives if one wants to reserve this term for erotic and aggressive urges. If this terminological limit is imposed, however, it can no longer be claimed that the two instinctual drives are the sole driving forces of behavior and the ultimate cause of activity. *Inhibitions, Symptoms and Anxiety* was a revolution which destroyed forever the psychodynamic special privileges of libido and aggression. Failure to recognize the passing of the old order can have only a hampering effect on the development of theory. In one conspicuous place it has already done so. As we have seen, the attempt to conceptualize the formation of a defensive organization ran into deep trouble over the question of energies. The proffered solution that the energies of the impulse were split into two streams, one of which turned back upon the other to check it, not only makes a highly dubious assumption about the nature of energy but also draws attention away from the significant facts needed for better understanding.

Recognition of the force of fear, particularly the inhibitory properties that have been so clearly demonstrated in research with animals, would have made it clear whence comes the force that checks and deflects instinctual impulses. It would have hastened the building of a consistent theory of neurosis and of psychotherapy on Freud's insight that anxiety is the central problem. Clinical acumen, to be sure, outran formal theory and acted upon an anxiety theory of neurosis in advance of conceptual ratification. But concepts are supposed to lead the way, not work like sand in the gears. An understanding of defensive organization needed two concepts that were not esteemed in psychoanalytic theory: avoidance of anxiety as a powerful motive force, to explain the power to thwart and distort instinctual urges, and effectance as independent ego energy, to explain the transformation of rigid into flexible defensive arrangements.

DIFFICULTIES WITH THE CONCEPT OF CATHEXIS

Cathexis ranks today as a central concept in psychoanalytic theory. The word stands for the German *Besetzung,* which Freud used to signify an investment or accumulation of psychic energy in the mental representations of objects. This concept appeared quite early in his thinking, when he was under the strong influence of the physical theory of energy and when his discoveries about sexuality were leading him to the libido theory. Cathexis is a remarkably apt concept for urges of an erotic character. It translates into terms of energy the striking fact of common experience, especially the experience of falling in love, that objects of erotic impulses acquire a powerful and lasting affective significance. Freud used the concept frequently throughout his writings; its final appearance was in his last *Outline,* where it again served to account for the disposition of libidinal energy—the changing of narcissistic into object libido (1940, p. 23). Although libido could sometimes become fixated, it was capable of great mobility, and the idea of cathexis was needed to account for its occupancy from time to time of different objects and different channels.

Can the concept of cathexis be used in the case of the death instinct? If the destructive instincts are conceived of as a fund of energy, and if cathexis is defined as the accumulation of energy in particular channels, there would seem to be no reason to avoid speaking of aggressive cathexis. Indeed this was often implied before 1920 in the term "negative cathexis," a quite illegitimate use because libidinal cathexis could only be present or absent, not negative. Freud, however, was content to leave the energy of aggression without any technical term, although others proposed words such as "mortido." He was content to leave unspecified the many questions that might have arisen with regard to "mortidinal cathexis," as it could have been called. It counts as evidence, I believe, for my remark about Freud's final homage to the libido theory that at no time between 1920 and his death did he attempt a thorough and systematic incorporation of the death instinct into his theory as a whole. He continued instead to write about cathexis as if it necessarily implied an investment of libidinal energy.

Perhaps Freud spared himself a good deal of trouble in refusing the challenge of theoretical symmetry. This challenge was taken up in 1949 by Hartmann, Kris, and Loewenstein, who undertook to make the needed systematic comparison between libidinal and aggressive instincts and who tried to introduce the latter into the psychoanalytic system on an equal basis with respect to defense, object relations, neutralization, and the formation of psychic structure. The three authors confess to difficulty in establishing the relation of pleasure to aggressive instinctual expression and in defining the real goals of aggression (1949). They are aware that a simple symmetrical approach is somehow uncomfortable. Yet in a way it is quite easy to set up symmetrical statements. The instinctual aim of aggression is "to destroy things" (Freud, 1940, p. 20), and the affects are those of anger and hate. To say that an object becomes invested with aggressive cathexis could mean that it is hated and that it will be approached with a view to injury and destruction. Aroused aggression could constitute unpleasant tension, and pleasure would result from reduction of this tension through effectively destructive action. Thus the concept of cathexis could apply equally well to libidinal and aggressive energies, even though aim and affect are virtually antithetical. In fact, aggressive cathexis has already been invoked to account for certain phenomena such as injury to internal functions in psychosomatic disorders.

What, then, is the source of discomfort in using the scheme? Simply, it seems to me, that it is so much at odds with the way Freud used cathexis and with the way it is still being used very widely in the psychoanalytic literature. Freud brought us all up to associate cathexis with libido, and we have done it. Cathexis of an object thus almost automatically means loving it, valuing it, cherishing it; the whole historical importance of the concept lies in its power to account for these positive attitudes, enduring beyond the immediate rise and fall of instinctual pressure. When cathexis begins to be directed toward external objects, this means that the infant develops a positive interest, not that he wants to destroy the objects. When the permanence of objects is explained as an enduring cathexis, this necessarily means a libidinal cathexis, not a destructive one. When functions are described as cathected, this almost always implies that they are loved and strengthened, not that they are hated and injured. This current common usage of cathexis is an anachronism dating perhaps from 1917, when the libido theory reached its systematic peak and when the whole relation to the surrounding world was based on the analogy of love. But it is an anachronism with which we have all become deeply imbued.

This is an example of a concept doing harm, obstructing the further growth of theory and observation. Freud's introduction of destructive instincts should have had more effect than he allowed it to have in breaking down the hegemony of libido. For even this step had the consequence of showing that the energies within us prompt us toward different kinds of relations with objects, as different as loving and hating, cherishing and destroying, binding together and pulling to pieces. His elevation of anxiety to a powerful force should have broadened the scope of these relations still more. We know that people form lasting avoidant tendencies in relation to objects that have caused anxiety, and that they develop strong positive feelings toward symbols of security. I suggest that the libido theory and its associated concept of cathexis has been a substantial hindrance to psychoanalytic ego psychology, obstructing understanding of the relations between ego and reality which need to be examined in all their breadth.

In this essay the claims of independent ego energies have been advanced, and this has suggested still another dimension to our relations with objects. Effectance prompts us to deal with things and to be interested in them. The relation depends upon the feeling of efficacy, and it therefore has to do with effects produced upon objects. Being interested in objects in the way prompted by effectance is not the same as investing them with a libidinal cathexis. There is much less attachment to the object as such, much more to what can be done with it, and objects may be set aside very coolly when their manipulative possibilities have been exhausted. When a child becomes greatly attached to a plaything beyond the possibility of doing anything new with it, so that it no longer yields feelings of efficacy, we are probably justified in supposing that the toy has acquired symbolic meaning and has become the object of true libidinal cathexis. Discarded objects, however, continue to form part of the child's knowledge of reality. They may cease to interest him for themselves, but if they should again enter the sphere of his interest as parts of a larger enterprise he will know what can be done with them and will use them appropriately. Finding a new use for an old toy is a common experience of childhood. The implied relation between ego and reality is well conceptualized in terms of action and efficacy; the addition of a fluid energy concept analogous to cathexis would be entirely redundant.

Cathexis and the instincts have created certain difficulties in psychoanalytic theory that seem to be born of the theory itself, not of any problems of fact. Instinctual energies have the status of concepts rather than measurable quantities, yet they became so concretely real to Freud that he was tempted to speculate about their disposition at the beginning of life. At the start, he reasoned, the infant had no knowledge of the external world; therefore libidinal and aggressive energies must be directed internally, and their externalization to objects would not come until later. Perhaps this reasoning is not compelling; since the infant also has no knowledge of self, we might do better to say that instinctual energies are directed at his whole undifferentiated experience, in which case they point as much outward as inward when that discrimination begins to be made. It has been argued by M. Balint (1937), C. Bühler (1954), and a good many others that mental life in its very earliest phases is directed toward objects. But the greatest difficulty lies in showing what these energic concepts can possibly mean in terms of concrete happenings. Jacobson (1954) rightly complains that they have no clear operational meaning, and because to her the most that they could imply would be discharge into visceral as against skeletal muscular channels, she suggests that the initial energy should be considered neutral, differentiating later into libidinal and aggressive forms. To me this only raises a fresh difficulty. Sucking is one of the earliest things that happens, and surely we cannot ask psychoanalytic theory to abandon the idea that this has an important libidinal aspect.

If the problem seems a little unreal for erotic and aggressive energies, it vanishes altogether for independent ego energies. There is no reason at all to assume that such energies, with their origin in nervous tissue, cannot be evoked directly after birth and, in line with the observations of Wolff (1959), that they cannot be responsive to the external environment. If we are content to start with observable manifestations in the infant, it seems clear that libidinal, aggressive, and "neutral" behavior all show themselves very early and in some kind of relation to external stimuli. It is along these lines of precise observation that we can hope to deduce the internal state of affairs in the newborn child.

DIFFICULTIES WITH THE ENERGIES OF PLAY

Earlier in this essay I pointed out the remarkable agreement that prevailed among psychoanalytic ego psychologists on the material needed for fuller understanding of the ego. The desired information has to do with the cumulative growth of adaptive behavior, including manipulation, locomotion, language, the mastery of motor skills, the growth of cognition, and the perfecting of higher thought processes. It is through such behavior that the ego establishes and refines its relation to reality, thus performing what Freud designated as its most characteristic function. Since these adaptive activities do not show any clear and regular relation to instinctual aims, it becomes necessary either to postulate other sources of energy or to hypothesize an underlying relation to the instincts that is not apparent on the surface. Those who favor the second alternative can proceed by using very broad definitions of the two major instincts and allowing generously for symbolic forms of satisfaction. On the other hand, they can employ the hypothesis of neutralization of instinctual-drive energies, which is designed to explain how energies become divested of their instinctual aims. I shall take up here the difficulties that result from broad definition; in the next section, the difficulties involved in the concept of neutralization.

It could be said by an advocate of Freud's instinct theory that in what I have thus far written I have disregarded the very broad meanings Freud gave to Eros and Thanatos. In speaking of anxiety, for instance, and of adaptive behavior I have not allowed that Freud meant to include all self-preservative strivings under the heading of Eros. I have treated libido in too narrow a context of sexuality, and aggression in too literal a sense of destruction. This champion of the instincts could remind me that the aim of Eros "is to establish ever greater unities and to preserve them thus—in short, to bind together"; whereas the destructive instinct aims "to undo connections" (Freud, 1940, p. 20). And I should have to admit that binding together and pulling apart cover just about everything, except perhaps leaving things as they are, which does not sound like an instinctual aim at all. But let us see what happens when we adopt the principle that all behavior is to be classed as either erotic or aggressive or both. I shall use by way of illustration the playful and exploratory behavior that is so basic to adaptation.

We can start with the idea advanced by Kardos and Peto (1956) that play is an expression of infantile sexuality. Their position is based on an earlier paper by M. Balint (1936) entitled "Eros and Aphrodite," in which Eros, a playful juvenile, is identified with forepleasure and Aphrodite, a mature woman, with end pleasure. Balint considers that forepleasure and end pleasure are fundamentally different, both as experiences and in their biological significance. Whereas end pleasure is serious and purposive and has a sharp pattern of rise and decline, forepleasure is playful and indefinite, ever present and arousable, capable of continuing more or less indefinitely, and, since it has no executive organs of its own, always attached to ego functions. Balint pictured forepleasure as a primal function of the body, inseparably connected with all somatic functions such as nutrition, sense perception, and muscular activity. This is the basis on which Kardos and Peto place their theory of play. "The characteristics of primitive play are identical with those of infantile sexuality. The ebb and flow of play is fully applicable to infantile sexuality with its easy change from narcissistic positions to object positions, from auto-erotic to object-erotic activities" (1956, p. 107).

A somewhat similar conception appears in a theoretical discussion of play by Alexander (1958). Play is an expression of surplus libidinal energy. It is to be distinguished from utilitarian forms of motivation by the fact that it is aimless and seems to be an end in itself. Alexander thus agrees with Kardos and Peto in finding the energy of play in pregenital libido, but he is aware that his formulation creates a curious clash with Freud's chief contribution to the theory of play, which emphasized the repetition compulsion and the mastery of painful situations by a shift from passivity to activity (Waelder, 1932). Alexander admits that playing can be problem solving in the interests of mastery and that this introduces a highly utilitarian function. But when this happens it is not true play, done for itself as when a colt romps about; the same activities have been captured for a serious purpose, as when the colt flees from danger. We have to conclude, I think, that for Alexander Freud's contribution to the meaning of play was not about play at all.

These views are alike in relating play to pregenital libidinal energy. Play which is not perceptibly erotic, such as manipulation of objects and locomotion, is thus ranged beside play which is clearly erotic, such as thumb sucking, stroking the body, and masturbating; the ultimate source of energy is held to be the same. The basis for identity is found in certain very general characteristics such as the pattern of arousal, the ebb and flow of activity, and the indefinite, aimless direction that can be described as doing something as an end in itself. Identity of instinctual aims, of course, cannot be demonstrated; nothing akin to the erogenous pleasure of sucking the thumb can be shown for activities such as playing with a rattle or building with blocks. The hypothesis here is intended to reach beyond what can be demonstrated.

Turning now to the destructive instincts, we find that Hartmann, Kris, and Loewenstein (1949) and Hoffer (1950) have selected motor activity as the chief early outward channel for aggressive energies. If these energies are conceived, following Freud, to be first directed inward, their externalization is vital for survival, and this service is performed by hitting, biting, scratching, and then the manipulative activities that flower so richly during the second half of the first year. Hartmann, Kris, and Loewenstein undertake to elucidate the adaptive and the organizing aspects of the aggressive drive, which lie in the circumstance that "Musculature and motility, apparatuses for the discharge of aggression, contribute decisively to the differentiation between self and environment and, through action, to the differentiation of the environment itself" (1949, p. 23). These authors use the concept of neutralization, but in Spitz's more detailed exposition (1953) it is made clear that at least the earlier manifestations must be understood as straightforward expressions of aggressive energy. Initially, then, the interpretation is entirely symmetrical with the one concerning erotic energies.

Spitz describes as follows the situation that develops in the course of the first year.

> Perception and thought initiate the discharge of the drive into aim-directed activity. Sensory organization, musculature and motility here function as apparatuses for the discharge of aggression. Aim-directed aggression is now placed in the service of acquiring mastery over objects of the environment as well as for the acquisition of skills, among which grasping is one of the first and locomotion the

second. The function of grasping in the discharge of aggression becomes clearly evident in the second half of the first year [1953, pp. 130-131].

It should be understood that we include in the manifestations of the aggressive drive also those activities which are not experienced as hostility, for instance grasping, etc. [p. 132].

The last sentence is disconcerting. What is to be the criterion for classifying behavior as aggressive if hostility is a matter of no consequence? In a later paper (1958) Spitz deals with this problem by invoking Freud's most general property of the destructive instincts, pulling things apart.

There cannot be any doubt that at the oral biting level, the aggressive drive will find its outlet in a number of destructive, hitting, tearing, and particularly biting and chewing activities. Experimental psychologists have remarked on the predominance of these activities in the second half of the first year, when the child seems bent on reducing everything he can reach into its smallest component parts. At the same time, however, the aggressive drive is placed into the service of sensory discrimination, and it may not be too fanciful to point out that here also, in the visual field, one percept is being dissociated and distinguished from the other [1958, p. 388].

It will be clear from this brief exposition, I believe, that a large number of activities have been counted as manifestations of both instincts. The playing child, expressing pregenital libido, is at the same time the grasping and manipulating child, expressing destructive energy; whole ranges of behavior have been taken as evidence for either Eros or Thanatos. It is not hard to make the discrimination if we choose placid thumb sucking, with its long-sustained stimulation of a sensitive zone, and angry screaming and thrashing, with their blindly violent muscular action and evidence of acute affect. But when we extend the range to activities that lack these clear characteristics, what is to be the criterion whereby one draws a line and decides, for instance, that a certain bit of behavior does not express erotic energy but does express aggression? Are we to hang onto the distinction between pleasurable stimulation of body surfaces and active motor patterns? If so, it must have been a mistake to include manipulation and locomotion under pregenital sexual activity. Are we to insist on cutaneous and other sensory inputs as contrasted with skeletal muscular output? If so, it must have been a mistake to call sensory organization and discrimination "apparatuses for the discharge of aggression." Are we to take Freud's final step and define the distinction in terms of what happens to entities, whether they are joined together or pulled apart? Then when we see an infant picking up a block, thus binding hand and block together, and putting it down again, thus separating them once more, we must suppose that the two forms of instinctual energy are flowing out in short alternate spurts.

The alternating-spurt hypothesis can of course be given a semblance of legitimacy by relating it to Freud's idea of instinctual fusion. Certainly no one can object on principle to the conception that the infant's playful and exploratory activities express more than one need, even in rapid succession. But it is hard to see how the instinctual aims of erotic joining and destructive separating could ever be truly fused, in the way that the products of the hot and cold water taps are fused to a tepid temperature in the washbowl. In effect, then, the determination to perceive playful behavior in terms of the outflow of erotic and aggressive energies means looking for characteristics that resemble those of indubitably erotic or aggressive acts, be they only such generalized ones as the ebb and flow of activity or the joining and separating of entities. It is important for theorists to realize how loosely these characteristics have been defined and how badly they serve to distinguish one instinctual drive from another. But the main point I want to make is this: *the search for these characteristics produces a failure to observe the behavior in its own right, directing attention away from its intrinsic meaning and adaptive significance.* This is another instance of a conceptualization doing positive harm. It was once a great illumination to be shown latent erotic and aggressive urges behind behavior where their presence had not been suspected. But if this analysis is generalized and assumed to apply everywhere, the observer is discouraged from looking at things in any other aspect. The search for latent meaning in playful and exploratory behavior has interfered with grasping its manifest meaning.

To Spitz's suggestion concerning "aggressive" separation of percepts in the visual field one must reply that this is indeed very much too fanciful: it leads to a false description of the perceptual process. The learning of visual forms, as Hebb (1949) has shown, is as much a matter of joining parts together as it is of separation. Circles and squares, for example, cannot be discriminated until there has been a long apprenticeship involving eye movements, successive fixations, recognition of angles, and the building up of a knowledge of forms. The growth of perception is a constant interplay between organization and discrimination. Manipulation, too, passes constantly between joining and separating: the description given in Chapter 3 of a child's play with a clothespin shows kaleidoscopic changes from mouthing to twisting to examining visually to passing between the hands to dropping to picking up to throwing away. These two examples could be multiplied endlessly, but they suffice to make the point. These activities are not illuminated by an analysis in terms of hypothetical discharges of erotic and destructive energies; they are simply misperceived. What is significant about them is sensorimotor, not sensory *vs.* motor; it is joining *and* separating, not joining *vs.* separating; it is, above all, discovering how to deal with things—finding out what kind of perceptual effects can be produced by what kind of exertions. When we see any example of playful or exploratory activity as a whole, rather than fragmented into two instinctual classes, it seems to me that the hypothesis of independent ego energies is vastly more suitable. This enables us to reserve the assumption of erotic or aggressive energies for those occasions, frequent enough, when the behavior exhibits unmistakable signs of a gratifying autoerotic or aggressive element, or when it is possible to infer a symbolic meaning, as in the child so astutely observed by Freud.

DIFFICULTIES OF NEUTRALIZATION

We take up finally the concept of neutralization of instinctual-drive energies. Independent ego energies are neutral in the sense intended here, so the issue can be stated quite simply: is it more valuable to assume that neutral energies are there from the start, as part of the natural endowment of the living being, or is it more valuable to assume that only the two classes of instinctual energy are there from the start, and that they can be transformed later into neutral energies? The divergence between positions here is not as great as it was in the last section. Those who use the idea of neutralization admit the shortcomings of a universal analysis in terms of erotic and aggressive urges. They allow that it is not appropriate to force behavior which has no discernible erotic or destructive aim into the two categories of instinctual energy. But they continue to postulate an inherent relation between these energies and neutral ones: the latter are transformed from the former, and in special circumstances they may even be transformed back again.

I shall try to show that the theory of neutralization leads to grave difficulties, but I approach this argument with a certain diffidence, in the spirit perhaps of a diplomat whose opponent has made a great concession, so that the situation seems to call for an answering generosity. An observer might ask if I am not disposed to compromise and allow effectance to be derived from instinctual drives, now that we are all agreed on the necessity for a neutral energy. And this observer would be encouraged when he found me praising the influence the concept of neutralization has had upon psychoanalytic ego psychology, especially in the hands of Hartmann and of Rapaport who have spoken so strongly in behalf of adaptive behavior and the growth of psychic structure. But the poor peacemaker is doomed to disappointment: he is going to find me stubborn about the origins of neutral energy. Perhaps he will persist in his attempt at arbitration by reminding me that both Hartmann (1955) and Kris (1955), in their contributions to a symposium on sublimation, seem prepared to attribute real importance to a primary ego energy that is not derived from the instincts. Hartmann discusses the possibility "that part of the mental energy—how much or how little we can hardly estimate—is not primarily drive energy but belongs from the very first to the ego, or to the inborn precursors of what will later be specific ego functions" (p. 25). Kris wrote: "When Freud hinted at the existence of such energy sources, it seemed difficult to find a place for them in psychoanalytic thinking. Now this assumption seems to have become eminently useful" (pp. 32-33). Now surely, with so much granted, I must be prepared to reach a settlement. It would be nothing short of cantankerous to deny merit to the hypothesis of neutralization.

If this is so, the reader will have to put up with my being cantankerous.

The theory of neutralization asserts that instinctual-drive energies, defined initially as having aims, can be deflected from these aims and so come to direct their force toward entirely different aims. Such a statement is full of implications about the nature of energy and the mechanism of transformation. I shall argue (1) that it won't work, and (2) that we don't have to try to make it work, because the hypothesis of independent ego energies makes the concept of neutralization superfluous.

The Meaning of Neutralization

The original idea comes, of course, from Freud, who introduced it in *The Ego and the Id* (1923) in explanation of certain rather special phenomena, and promoted it in *Inhibitions, Symptoms and Anxiety* (1926) to a general operating principle. We should probably be a little wary of these rapid generalizations; as we have seen, the same thing happened to identification, with rather disastrous results. Perhaps wariness is the more justified when we remember Freud's partiality to the libido theory: his fully developed idea was that the ego ran on desexualized libido, and he made no serious move in the direction later followed by Hartmann to apply neutralization symmetrically to the destructive instincts. But let us consider the idea more directly on its merits.

According to Hartmann, "We call neutralization the change of both libidinal and aggressive energy away from the instinctual and toward a noninstinctual mode" (1955, p. 18). There are many degrees of such change; it seems probable "that there exists a continuum of gradations of energy, from the fully instinctual to the fully neutralized mode" (p. 19). Full neutralization implies complete detachment from instinctual aims. "Once the ego has accumulated a reservoir of neutralized energy of its own, it will—in interaction with the outer and the inner world—develop aims and functions whose cathexis can be derived from this reservoir," which means that they do not always have to "depend on ad hoc neutralizations" (p. 20). What phenomena stand in need of this hypothesis?

> . . . it already clearly appears that neutralization . . . plays a decisive part in the mastery of reality. The formation of constant and independent objects, the institution of the reality principle, with all its aspects, thinking, action, intentionality all depend on neutralization. . . . if we accept Freud's statement that self-preservation, in man, is mostly taken care of by the ego, we come to understand neutralization also as a powerful help to this central biological aspect of man, not as its opponent as has occasionally been described. Besides reality testing and the mechanisms of adaptation, the integrating (or synthetic, or organizing) functions share in the maintenance of self-

preservation and they too are not purely instinctual in character but mostly belong to those that work with neutralized energy [pp. 24-25].

In an earlier paper Hartmann (1953) had applied the concept to schizophrenia, suggesting that a central part might be assigned to a failure of the capacity for neutralization, so that libidinal and aggressive urges appeared in behavior in unmodulated forms. When aggression was thus insufficiently neutralized it could be of no service in creating or maintaining a defensive system.

Hartmann makes it clear that neutralization does not mean the sexualization or "aggressivization" of ego functions. These two processes imply something quite different: the impairment of an already operating ego function because it acquires an additional sexual or aggressive meaning. Thus if at a certain age the function of speech comes to have highly aggressive significance, speech itself may pick up the inhibitions surrounding aggression and stuttering may ensue. This is quite a different matter from the use of energy neutralized from aggressive sources to supply power for the growth of speech. The process of neutralization not only changes the aim of this energy but also frees it from any prior inhibitory vicissitudes. Hartmann's concept of degrees of neutralization seems designed to allow that instinctual energies in their support of ego activities may retain some generalized portion of their aims, though surrendering the focal goals of erogenous stimulation or hostile destruction. Freud (1923) and Nunberg (1931) suggested that the synthetic functions of the ego exhibited one of the most general characteristics of Eros, that of binding and uniting separate entities into wholes, and Hartmann (1955) calls attention to an element of fight or hostility in defensive anticathexes, the energy for which may therefore be attributed to partially neutralized aggression. But it is equally clear that neutralization can go the whole way, so that both libido and aggression can drain into a reservoir that is freely at the disposal of ego aims. This last postulation frees us from the difficulty discussed in the previous section. It is not necessary to search all ego activities for latent erotic or destructive directedness; when neutralization is complete, only ego aims will be present.

To this extent the theory of neutralization is clear, for which we should be grateful to Hartmann. But I think it is fair to say that in this form it is still a pre-theory, a somewhat metaphorical statement of how we might possibly suppose things to happen in terms of energy. Neutralization refers to what is, when we stop to think of it, a pretty drastic change in energy. The concept can hardly advance from being a magic word unless the conditions and processes of this change can be specified. It is in the nature of instinctual drives, by definition, to press toward instinctual aims, and we recognize that they continue to do this throughout life. Under what conditions, then, can they be prevailed upon not merely to deflect themselves through roundabout channels, not merely to accept modified but still satisfying forms of their goals, but to release a part of their force from all connection with original aims and make it over without obligation to the ego?

Hypotheses About Energy Transformation

This is where trouble starts. Freud dealt with the problem only in the form of desexualization, and he related this to the replacing of a libidinal object choice by an identification, which implied "transformation of object-libido into narcissistic libido" with "abandonment of sexual aims" (1923, p. 30). Narcissistic libido was thus Freud's first version of neutral energy, and when a little later he produced his structural conception of the ego he tried to elevate the desexualization mechanism into a general principle of ego development, with the unhappy results I have already examined in my discussion of identification. It seems impossible to use the sequence of object loss and identification as a paradigm for the neutralization of instinctual-drive energies, especially if aggressive drives are to be included. The most that can be done with Freud's idea is to relate neutralization in some way to frustration of direct discharge.

Working along this general line, Rapaport (1951, 1960) evolved an idea of neutralization that started from drive frustration and anticathexis. With the establishment of defenses, instinctual drives become differentiated into

> ... a variety of derivative motivations. If we now consider that the same defense development will occur in relation to one or more of these derivative motivations, we are envisaging the process by which the whole hierarchy of derivative motivations originates.
> ... It is plausible that the originally peremptory discharge tendency of instinctual drive energy is increasingly hampered by the layers of structure superimposed on it. Thus, the higher in the hierarchy

of mental structure a derivative motivation appears, the more scaled
down its peremptoriness and appetitiveness: in other words, the more
neutralized it is [1960, pp. 212-213].

While this description provides for a scaling down of instinctual
urgency, it does not imply an end point at which aims are fully
abandoned and a pool of neutral energy created. It also leads, I
believe, to a serious chronological trap. It cannot dodge the shaft
directed at instinct psychology by Kardiner, Karush, and Ovesey
(1959), who point out the fallacy of giving instincts executive
functions as well as energic ones. Rapaport derived anticathexis
directly from instinctual dynamics, producing out of the opposition
of two energies the structures that would begin the process of neutralization. As we have seen, this is an unworkable scheme; defense
against instincts must be established through some responsiveness
to reality, some modicum of knowledge that expression is inappropriate or dangerous. This is fatal to the chronology of the scheme:
reality testing precedes the forming of those structures which ham-
per and neutralize instinctual energy, yet reality testing is also
alleged to be one of the things accomplished by neutral energies.
One cannot deny to Rapaport's idea a certain metaphorical effectiveness, suggesting as it does the cumulative nature of growth, but
it does not achieve what can be accepted as a fundamental elucida-
tion of the conditions and process of neutralization.

A tendency appearing in the recent literature makes it seem to
me less and less likely that any such fundamental statement will be
possible. Increasing reflection has shown that if neutralization is to
do the work set out for it, the process must start quite early in life.
When one thought in terms of relinquished object cathexes, identifications, and a fully formed knowledge of the constant and impersonal properties of the outside world, the image of an initial
predominance of instinctual drives giving way gradually to neutralization did not seem implausible. But with increasing attention
to early child development, with research being directed even at
the first days of life, we have all been reminded that the child
begins his exploration of the world very early, that sensory and
motor coordinations are in practice just about from the start, and
that action, reality testing, intentionality, and the mastery of objects
have clear beginnings in the first months of life. It has been necessary to push neutralization back earlier and earlier until we find

Lustman (1957), whose research is on newborn infants, arguing
that neutral energy must be present from the start. Lustman has
demonstrated that as early as the third day infants give differentiated
responses to auditory, tactile, and electrical stimulation. He takes
this perceptual repertory as evidence for a rudimentary ego, and
assigns it to the "conflict-free sphere," showing that it is altered and
even suppressed when nursing is going on or when pain is experienced. Lustman uses Hartmann's phrase, "primary ego energy,"
to account for his findings, and calls attention to Jacobson's argument (1954) with regard to an early undifferentiated phase of
energy.

It is clear, I think, that the further back in life we push neutral
energy the less reason we have for assuming that it is neutralized
out of something else. Jacobson's postulation that all energy is
neutral in the beginning, becoming differentiated later into libidinal
and aggressive drives—a postulation I have already criticized on
the ground that early oral eroticism seems so clearly libidinal—
leads to an extraordinary redundancy of explanations. It would be
necessary to explain first how this energy becomes deneutralized,
then how its two differentiated forms again become neutralized;
would it not be simpler to suppose that part of it stayed neutral all
along? It seems to me that the hypothesis of independent ego energy
gets us out of this whole set of conceptual difficulties about energy
transformation. Effectance (an urge toward sensory and motor
activity), eroticism (an urge toward pleasurable stimulation of
sensitive zones), and aggression (an urge toward forceful destruc-
tiveness)—not to mention the avoidance of pain and anxiety—
are all available pretty much from the start, and although we must
be shrewd in studying their interaction we need not ever perform
the feat of turning them into one another.

What is there in the roster of functions performed by neutralized
energies that cannot be performed equally well by independent ego
energies? We have only to tick off Hartmann's list—adaptation,
reality testing, mastery of reality, formation of constant and independent objects, defensive organization, thinking, action, intentionality, the synthetic function—to see that they are the very things
I have discussed in this essay. But let me undertake one more brief
confrontation of the two hypotheses, choosing Kris's account of
easel painting by nursery school children (1955). This will permit

us to see a little more concretely what is meant by neutralization, with the added advantage of bringing before us the concept of sublimation.

Easel painting is made available in all good nursery schools, according to Kris, because "The structure of the activity . . . supplies an incentive for increased neutralization" (p. 38). For the child of two to three standing at the easel,

> There are significant and typical moments: There is the first stroke and its result. The transposition of the kinesthetic experience of the arm movement with the big brush onto the trace on the sheet is to some two-and-a-halves a significant experience. It is not a totally new experience; the principle is familiar from the handling of pencil or crayon. But the broader scope of the movement, the larger and brighter result on the sheet is bound to attract interest. There something has been done; dare we say "created"?
>
> Some children are, as it were, soon captured by the expansiveness of the movement. . . .
>
> . . . I shall neglect many alluring sideroads and concentrate on the problem with which almost all those who stay with the easel for their nursery years meet at one point: the battle against the impulse to smear which the medium itself stimulates. . . .
>
> The battle against smearing starts not at once and its intensity is subject to great variations. . . . The smearing may start after ten or more minutes of work, and then an explosive process may take over, sometimes supplemented by excited stamping, clutching of the genitals and rhythmical rubbing of the brush against the sheet—briefly by a passionate outburst [1955, pp. 34-35].
>
> On later stages the fantasy content becomes elaborate, stories may be expanded, and some of those faithful to the easel achieve what seemed to attract them when the first stroke of the broad brush created that bright trace on paper: but now their product is "organized," they "make" a world of things. This progress requires renunciation of direct discharge. The neutralization of energy can, as it were, be watched [p. 37].

This is a beautiful account, but does the concept of neutralization have any essential function in it? The observations are clear as crystal. The child first discovers gratification in a surprising bit of efficacy, the possibility of using arm, hand, and brush to produce a bright stroke on the paper. This answers in every way to what I have said about effectance and the feeling of efficacy. But the medium stimulates urges that are not neutral: the libidinal and probably also aggressive urge to smear is aroused. Kris makes the interesting observation that this occurs regularly without any discernible relation to the stage or conflictedness of bowel training. If it is not correlated with these events, we might expect it to bear some relation to the degree of frustration experienced by the child in achieving coordinated, effective action with hand and brush. At all events, in many cases the satisfaction of producing coordinated forms, of picturing an organized world, triumphs over the pleasure of smearing; the original joy at creating the first line can be amplified endlessly as one's growing competence permits the portraying of more and more complicated scenes. What is the basis for assuming that this set of functions, which operated gratifyingly under its own steam before the urge to smear was aroused, thereafter requires the additional support of neutralized "smearing energies"?

This example illustrates with great clarity, it seems to me, the difficulty created for psychoanalytic theory by the lack of a sufficient concept of independent ego energies and of the kinds of satisfaction to which they lead. The theory of instincts sets up the supposition that all satisfying experience will represent libidinal or aggressive discharge, even if the channel be extremely roundabout and the form be altered out of all recognition (fully neutralized). A gifted and sensitive observer like Ernst Kris did not let this theoretical supposition obscure what he saw, so he faithfully described the child's initial and subsequent experiences of efficacy in easel painting. The energy implications pass unnoticed because they are so much a matter of common sense. Then something libidinal and aggressive comes on the scene, and *after that* a necessity is felt to relate all further gratification to instinctual energy. The result is two explanations where one would suffice. The successful easel painter is securing the satisfaction of (1) efficacy and an increasing sense of competence, and also of (2) neutralized instinctual energies, which, if fully neutralized, have lost their original aims in favor of ego aims—and how can these be defined in terms any different from efficacy and competence? Given an adequate idea of independent ego energies, the concept of neutralization is wholly redundant.

This is not for a moment to argue that instinctual energies simply drop out of easel painting after a brief disruptive appearance. They may continue to confer something of their own meaning upon it and may even secure a limited amount of discharge. But when we say this we are not claiming that they are neutralized. They may be carefully controlled and narrowly channeled, but their push is still toward some derivative form of smearing. The controlling influences come partly from social demands for certain kinds of performance, partly from the desire to master the medium and work with it efficaciously—the motive that Kris saw budding in the first brush stroke. These motives, and especially the learned structures to which they give rise, serve to limit severely the outlets for instinctual impulse and force it to be content with fantasied or symbolic satisfactions. Only if the ration is unbearably small will the impulse assume strength enough to disrupt adapted performance.

Easel painting can easily be taken as an example of sublimation. The dismal estate of this concept has been much discussed, particularly by Glover (1931) and Levey (1939), and I do not believe that Hartmann (1955) has restored it to conceptual clarity by relating it to neutralization. The sublimation of instinctual urges implies a successful channeling into lines of action that are socially desirable. By definition these are likely to be strongly oriented toward social actualities and to involve a good deal of practiced skill and experience. The common conceptualization in psychoanalytic theory tends to slip into the error already mentioned, that of giving instinctual drives executive functions and assuming that they conjure into existence the lines of interest and action that harmonize with physical, social, and moral actualities. When independent ego energies are taken seriously the problem appears in a different light. Sublimated activities do not have to be powered by the meagerly discharged energies of aim-inhibited instincts. Current satisfaction is provided not only by social rewards but also by interest in increasing one's sense of competence in the task itself. In other words, sublimation represents a special sort of cooperation between, on the one hand, interests with an enduring capacity to engage and satisfy effectance, and, on the other, instinctual impulses that can find in the same activities some measure of aim-inhibited gratification.

Inconsistencies in the Concept

To repeat: given an adequate conception of independent ego energies, the concept of neutralization is wholly redundant. And is it, in any event, a legitimate conceptualization, just in terms of internal consistency? Is it possible to imagine any kind of energies which first have aims, then lose these aims, then resume them again during periods of regression? The final difficulty of the concept of neutralization, it seems to me, is that it requires an idea of energy that leads to intrinsic absurdities and that cannot be squared with what is known about energies in the nervous system.

The absurdities arise largely from the use of an unfortunate metaphor, that of a flowing liquid. It was Freud who introduced the hydraulic analogy, and it continues in Rapaport's references to flowing streams and Hartmann's image of a reservoir. If we were dealing with one energy, one water that tends to flow downhill, the trouble would be less, but when we start with two streams representing different *kinds* of energy—a distinction "which presupposes physiological processes running in opposite directions" (Freud, 1923, p. 43)—when we let them flow together and become one kind in a reservoir of neutralized energy, and when we add the proviso that they can flow out again and resume their original characters, our imagery begins to dance like that of a delirium. Once the waters of the White Nile and the Blue Nile have joined in a common stream, is there any way to draw them out and conduct them back to their original beds, taking care that no blue is sent back to the white or white to the blue, which would imply that erotic and aggressive energies could be transformed into each other? But let us not fuss over the logic of a metaphor that was innocently intended to be helpful in picturing things. The real trouble is that psychoanalytic theory has been slow to transcend metaphor and cast its theory of energies more nearly in contemporary terms.

Energy is a very general concept referring to whatever accomplishes work or produces action. It manifests itself in the varied forms of heat, light, electricity, mechanical motion, and it is what lies behind the specific manifestations of directed forces such as those that run waterwheels, clocks, cars, or electrical machinery. When Freud perceived the extraordinary mobility of sexual urges, with their power to create fantasies, slips, symptoms, and sublimations as well as pressing for more direct discharge, he naturally created an energy concept (libido) that emphasized this capacity for fluid transformation. Yet, as we know, he also insisted that the energy was sexual in nature, that it had an intrinsic connection with pregenital and later with genital aims, and that it had somatic sources in erogenous zones. To this extent it did not signify all the energy within the person but was seen as a specific, differentiated force. Freud's entire treatment of libido throughout his life betrays, it seems to me, an abiding uncertainty as to just how much he wanted to mean by it. As a consequence he gave it, as occasion demanded, the attributes of a virtually free energy and those of a distinctively bound instinctual force. Jung was wrong when he tried to make it a general interest-energy; libido was sexual, and Freud meant sexual. But then there was the problem of "neutral" ego interests, for which libido had to be desexualized, and Freud meant desexualized.

The fatal inconsistency in the concept of neutralization springs, it seems to me, directly from this blurred spot in Freud's treatment of instinctual energies. It was perhaps a wise tactical move on his part to build a theory of psychic energies unhampered by the limited physiological knowledge of his time. But he certainly did not intend to argue for a permanent separation between the realms; he hoped that the somatic sources of instinct and the chemical nature of libido would presently become clear. Today we are no longer justified in maintaining a sharp separation between psychical and physiological concepts. Some progress, at least, has been made toward understanding the physiology of instinctual drives in animals and of the operation of the nervous system in man. Can the neutralization of drive energies find any plausible counterpart in neurological terms?

As it stands today, the doctrine of neutralization seems to perpetuate certain assumptions long discarded from neurology. It involves the assumption that a fairly sharp distinction can be made between energy and apparatus, the latter resting inert until infused with some quantity of the former. It also involves the assumption that energies operating in the apparatus can be of different kinds. Both of these assumptions enjoyed high favor during Freud's years in physiological research. The great Helmholtz had but lately proposed the analogy between the nervous system and a telegraph system and had developed considerably the idea of specific energies in nerves, a concept that seemed to be needed to explain the different qualities of sensation generated by different sensory systems (Boring, 1929, Ch. 5). Both ideas are today hardly more than historical curiosities.

In the first place, the Helmholtz analogy has yielded to the realization that the "apparatus" is alive, that it is composed of living cells rather than inert wires, and that these cells contain the energy that makes the system operate. A certain amount of energy is constantly being generated within the cells and is quietly undergoing discharge even during sleep. Energy enters the system from outside through internal and external sense organs, but the work of the sense organs consists not of transmitting force directly but of releasing the energy inherent in sensory nerves. Thus it is impossible to conceive of libido as being introduced like electricity to energize and operate a mechanical apparatus.

In the second place, research on the nature of the nervous impulse has gone wholly against the idea of specific kinds of energy. The process of transmission seems to be everywhere identical, consisting of a sequence of electrochemical events that have the same character in all nerve cells. Differences in the quality of experience and in the behavior that ensues cannot be laid to characteristics of the energy; they have to be sought in neural patterns and neural locations. The nervous system contains an enormous number of possible interconnections, but we have to remember that it also contains an enormous number of fixed spatial arrangements. This is obvious in such instances as sensory and motor nerve roots in the spinal cord or localized sensory and motor areas in the cerebral cortex. Recently it has become strikingly obvious in experimental work on the hypothalamus in animals, where destruction of a small area will knock out whole instinctual functions such as feeding or sexual behavior (Stellar, 1954). New importance clearly has to be attached to nervous centers in the brain stem in the arousal and control of instinctual drive. In connection with the sex drive in animals, hormone levels appear to be of considerable significance (Beach, 1951), but even here it is a question of releasing the intrinsic energies of a particular subsystem rather than an introduction of energy into the apparatus as a whole.

Seen in this light, an instinctual drive does not function with its own *kind* of energy, but with neural energies released in particular *places* (centers) and organized in particular *patterns*. Energy can be called sexual, for instance, only by virtue of the fact that certain somatic sources or hormonal conditions activate certain nerve centers which in their turn activate a characteristic pattern of excitations in skin, genitals, and elsewhere. As Lashley expressed it, motivation in general implies "a partial excitation of a very specific sensorimotor mechanism irradiating to affect other systems of reaction" (1938, p. 468). Aggressive energy is differentiated from sexual by the places and patterns that are central in the excitation. An ego interest, such as learning the skills necessary for an occupation, is neutral in the sense that its places and patterns are not those of either eroticism or aggression.

While this knowledge of specificity in the nervous system has been derived rather heavily from experiments with animals, we have no right to assume that human behavior is organized on completely different principles. It should be noticed that nothing in this account stands in the way of simultaneous and related activity in several different localities by several different patterns. Sexual and aggressive energies, active simultaneously, can be in conflict or can fuse with respect to certain objects. Either can irradiate its sequential excitations into an aroused ego interest, possibly disrupting it (sexualization, "aggressivization") or possibly strengthening it (overdetermination, sublimation). Irradiation covers the spread of sexual energy into the diversity of channels that led Freud to speak of mobility. I do not see that this picture of neural functioning need in the least weaken or obscure the great historic insights of psychoanalysis. But there is no place in it for the notion of neutralization of instinctual-drive energies. The neuron systems that form the sexual pattern cannot pluck out their intrinsic energy and deposit it in the neurons involved in a pattern of ego interest. No meaning whatsoever can be attached to the statement that the energy of an active ego interest was once sexual but is not sexual now, or that the energy of a given expression of aggression was for a while neutral but has now become aggressive again. Such transformations are simply not possible in the system as we have come to know it.

There is no doubt in my mind that the concept of neutralization of instinctual-drive energies will simply have to be abandoned. I can see no future for a concept of energy transformation for which no convincing mechanism has been proposed, which contains such serious metaphorical absurdities, which is so incompatible with current knowledge of brain function, and which is being betrayed by its best friends as they push it further and further back to the first weeks and days of life. But I cannot feel that anything is lost if we make full use of independent ego energies in some such way as I have tried to do in this essay. This concept can easily take over, with more convincing detail, everything that has been attributed to neutralization, and it can far outstrip that idea in its power to explain the facts of reality testing and ego development. Only one real concession is required by the change in conceptualization. We cannot continue to say that erotic and destructive urges comprise the entire push behind human behavior. It could be argued that Freud in effect expanded this list when he conferred vast power upon the avoidance of anxiety. At any rate, I hope that the arguments advanced here will make it appear that a persistent interest in efficacy lies as deeply embedded as anything in human nature.

Concluding Note: Effectance and Structure

A last word should be said about the status of effectance as an energy concept. In speaking of the concept in this way and in suggesting a name for independent ego energies I am aware of taking certain risks. It would be unfortunate, I can see, if using the word "effectance" should generate a vivid image of a flowing liquid, a Red Nile to put with the Blue and the White, and lead to sterile speculation about the doings of this energy when outward signs are lacking. It would also be unfortunate if it became a lazy man's short cut in clinical descriptions, as has happened to neutralization. Furthermore, concepts of general energy tend to be discarded in physiological research as knowledge of processes and structures becomes more precise, and psychoanalytic research, as Colby (1955) has shown, must advance in the same direction.

I have used an energy concept in this monograph because psychoanalytic theory is based on instinctual energies, and because independent ego energies already existed as a postulate, though a poorly developed one. But I should call attention to the fact that my thesis is inherently structural. The importance of effectance as energy does not lie in direct confrontations with instinctual energies, in battles of cathexis and anticathexis, or in conflicts between measurable charges of force. Its importance lies in its suggestion that apart from instincts the human organism is still a restless creature, constantly directing itself toward its surroundings and learning through experience the effects that can be produced upon the environment—the kind of relations that can be sustained with it. The energy leads to exploring and testing reality. It thus contributes to the forming of those dynamic structures which we describe variously as abilities, skills, patterns of coping and mastering, defensive organizations, and knowledge. It is these learned dynamic patterns that constitute the representation of reality within the mind and the main instrument of control over instinctual impulses. Our knowledge about the energy is derived entirely from playful and exploratory behavior and its structural products. It is on this account that I have alternatively called my thesis one of action and its consequences, and it would be no discomfort to me to see the word "effectance" quickly wither on the vine provided the image remained of that active, probing, learning, coping, adapting aspect of ourselves that seems a necessary complement to instinctual drives.

9

IN A NUTSHELL

To condense a long argument is to run the risk of sounding unduly arbitrary. Yet in a time when so much is being published there is an obligation to prospective readers to put down somewhere the gist of the thesis. A summary may also be regarded as a proper offering to those who have patiently made their way along the winding trail of the whole work.

1. *Statement of Purpose*

This essay can be described as an attempt to develop the psychoanalytic concept of independent ego energies in order to improve our understanding of the relation between ego and reality. It is based on the belief that recent research on animal behavior and child development provides the basis for a coherent conception of such energies and of the contribution they make to ego development. This conceptualization, which emphasizes learning through action and its consequences, is held to improve our comprehension of reality testing, early ego deviations, identification as a growth process, self-esteem, and ego strength. It is held to be helpful, moreover, in resolving a number of difficulties in the psychoanalytic theory of energies.

2. *The Content of Psychoanalytic Ego Psychology*

When Freud was hardly more than on the brink of those discoveries that were to change forever our ideas about human nature, he began to construct what we would call today a psychological theory of personality. As the discoveries progressed from one triumph to another, revealing whole ranges of disguised and unsuspected motivations, the most fitting concepts appeared to be those of instinctual drive and energy, and for a time this aspect of the

theory dominated all others. But soon the searching eye of psychoanalytic technique began to rest on the forces that control instinctual drives. The result was a fresh series of discoveries concerning defense mechanisms, and the beginnings of a theory of the
ego as a structural system. As matters were left by Freud, the erotic
and destructive instincts provided the power for all action, including
that of the ego apparatus.

Since Freud's death the psychology of the ego has been the most
active growing edge of psychoanalytic theory. Freud had assigned
to the ego as its decisive function the maintaining of relations with
reality. Hartmann presently pointed out that the performance of
such a function raised the whole problem of adaptation, and required concepts of structure and of learning that were not well
supplied by a theory centered upon instincts. An examination of the
chief proposals for developing psychoanalytic ego psychology reveals a surprising unanimity about the needed content. Everyone
is agreed that attention must be paid to the growth processes
whereby man's complex repertory of adaptive behavior comes to
be put together. This means that the facts of exploration, manipulation, locomotion, language, the practicing of motor skills, the
growth of cognition, the development of plans and intentional actions, and the emergence of higher thought processes all become
building stones for an adequate ego psychology. Such facts have
long been the domain of academic child psychology, and they are
by no means best observed in psychoanalytic therapy. Yet only by
their inclusion is it possible to reach Freud's goal of a complete
theory of personality.

Admitting this body of facts to psychoanalytic theory raises difficult theoretical problems. On the face of it, the adaptive processes
just listed do not press toward erotic or destructive instinctual aims.
Some theorists have thought that this discrepancy was only a matter of appearance. If one stretched the definitions of the two instincts sufficiently, and if one made generous allowance for unconscious and symbolic forms of gratification, perhaps all behavior
could be brought under the twin scepters of Eros and Thanatos.
Such a view was found wanting by Freud himself, who amended it
by postulating a process whereby libido could be desexualized and
thus made freely available for the neutral aims of the ego. This
hypothesis, expanded by Hartmann and his associates to include the

neutralization of both kinds of instinctual-drive energy, provides the ego with its own allowance, so to speak, but reminds us that this came from the pockets of the parent instincts. Other workers, finding the transformation of energy implausible, have preferred to postulate an independent source, a case in point being Hendrick, who proposed an instinct to master.

The position taken in this essay is located somewhere between Hartmann's and Hendrick's. It agrees with both that the energies behind adaptive activity must be neutral with respect to instinctual aims. It does not, however, require a transformation of energies originally instinctual, nor does it assume a new instinct in any ordinary sense of the word. The theory advanced here, curiously enough, fits a niche already provided in the edifice of psychoanalytic theory, but one in which no statue has ever been placed. It corresponds roughly to the idea mentioned by Freud, but never more than casually, that the ego apparatus might have intrinsic energies of its own and that there might be a natural satisfaction in the exercise of ego functions. In this essay the idea of independent ego energies is taken seriously and pursued through several of its chief developmental implications.

3.   A Way of Conceiving of Independent Ego Energies: Efficacy and Competence

Recent trends in animal and child psychology are decidedly helpful in forming an idea of independent ego energies. Among experimenters with animals there has been a sharp revival of interest in manipulative behavior, curiosity, and exploratory play. When all known drives are at rest, rats will examine new objects and explore new territory, kittens will find their way to toys, monkeys will manipulate whatever is at hand, and chimpanzees will subject novel objects to searching scrutiny and testing. In the absence of such opportunities animals will seek them, and they can learn maze pathways and other habits to serve them in reaching such rewards. It seems impossible to connect all of this behavior with aims of food, sex, or avoidance of pain, and some workers have postulated additional drives to account for it.

These observations can be matched and made in much greater detail on children. Before the end of the first year the child typically spends long hours in the manipulative exploration of objects, and in the course of time there will be intensive testing of locomotion, experimenting with sounds and verbal forms, and involvement in the whole expanding realm of interests that we refer to as the child's play. Observations by Piaget show that during the second year some of this play takes on a character that deserves to be called scientific investigation: objects are explored systematically with the child's whole repertory of actions, and their potentialities are tested by putting them in different positions. Such activities are pursued with concentrated attention, with persistence, often with chuckles and other signs of satisfaction, and sometimes, when the object proves refractory, with unmistakable evidences of frustration. It is impossible not to characterize this kind of behavior as motivated, but most of it has no plausible relation to the aims of instinctual drives.

The playful exploratory and manipulative activities of children provide the basis for a theory of independent ego energies. Examining them closely, we can see that more is involved than a random overflow of activity. It is noticeable in young children—indeed even in young animals—that attention is given longest to objects upon which it is possible to have large effects. Studies of preferences show that the most interesting objects are the ones with which the most can be done. Even when an external stimulus obviously starts the transaction, the response tends to have the character of a series of varied actions producing whatever effects are possible. Noticing this interest in effects, Groos in his study of play attributed to the child a "joy in being a cause." Recent workers have begun to see the significance of these facts for learning to deal effectively with one's surroundings. It is proposed here to refer to the energy behind such behavior as *effectance,* and to the affect that attends it as *feeling of efficacy*. Effectance thus refers to the active tendency to put forth effort to influence the environment, while feeling of efficacy refers to the satisfaction that comes with producing effects.

Independent ego energies and their satisfactions are conceived to be just as basic as the instincts. They are not, however, related to particular somatic sources or to consummatory patterns of discharge. Conceivably they can be equated with the inherent energy of the nervous system. But their significance for development lies in their direct relation to the formation of psychic structure. Effectance is a prompting to explore the properties of the environment; it leads to an accumulating knowledge of what can and cannot be done with the environment; its biological significance lies in this very property of developing *competence*. Instinctual energies, of course, likewise produce action, effects, and knowledge of the environment, thus making a contribution to competence. But their contribution is necessarily narrower than that of neutral energies which stand ever ready to promote exploration for its own sake. It will be noticed that this conception of independent ego energies tends to reduce the sharp metaphorical distinction between energy and structure. If we conceive of structure as competence, we are giving it the dynamic character of patterns of readiness for future action.

Competence is the cumulative result of the history of interactions with the environment. *Sense of competence* is suggested as a suitable term for the subjective side of this, signifying one's consciously or unconsciously felt competence—one's confidence—in dealing with the various aspects of the environment. It is easier to describe these concepts in transactions with inanimate objects, but they apply equally well, and more importantly, to interactions with other human beings. Human objects present the same problem of finding out what can and cannot be done with them, a problem that is not fully covered by instinctual aims, and we can assume that great importance will always be attached to one's *sense of interpersonal competence*.

4. *Reality and Its Testing*

In psychoanalytic theory the ego is given the function of representing reality and of assuring that behavior is governed by realistic considerations. According to the thesis of this essay, reality testing —finding out about reality and being guided by it—comes about through attempted actions and their consequences. Reality is not passively received; it does not imprint itself on the mind. It is slowly constructed through active, varied, and persistent exploration, and what is learned about it is how to deal with it: what actions produce what effects on what objects.

This conception has by no means been overlooked in psychoanalytic theory. Freud used it explicitly to explain how one learns to distinguish between inner and outer stimuli. But the systematic application of an action theory to reality testing has been greatly impeded by attempts to work wholly with instinctual energies and to derive the entire course of events from hypothetical first situations. This tendency is shown in Freud's account of the transition from the pleasure principle to the reality principle, a change which he described entirely in terms of instinctual frustration and an unwilling reckoning with reality as the frustrator. It is shown in the idea that defense originates from a splitting of instinctual energy into cathectic and anticathectic components, with structure arising in layers from their repeated collision. These are unsuitable concepts for understanding the relation between ego and reality. They can be dressed up to plausibility only by the belated smuggling in of those ideas about action and structure which a theory of independent ego energies seeks to make explicit from the start.

According to an action theory, reality testing is not undertaken solely because of instinctual frustration. Exploration occurs in its own right, and reality can be interesting and satisfying as well as frustrating. Even in Freud's model situation it seems clear that frustration leads to action and that the pleasure principle is transcended through the discovery of some action, like crying, which influences the environment and can be used to influence it again. Tolerance of delay depends on a confidence, born of experience, that something efficacious can be done if need waxes painful.

The reality principle is thus learned by slow degrees. This applies equally to the distinction between self and not-self: it is a cumulative growth depending upon extended exploration of one's own body and its sensations as well as of sensations proceeding from external objects. This unavoidable conclusion plays havoc with much that has been written about early introjection, projection, and the externalization of libidinal and aggressive energies. Most of this speculation presupposes that self and not-self have been discriminated once and for all almost from the beginning. But many of these hypothetical events stand to gain from reconsideration.

An action theory is most particularly needed to account for the construction of a world of permanent objects having independent causal relations. If we knew the world wholly through instinctual cathexes, we would forever see objects in relation to our needs, not in impersonal relations to each other. On this point Piaget's detailed developmental studies are highly illuminating. His observations fill in the successive steps of what would otherwise be a hypothetical course of development. Growth of the concept of permanent objects is traced by means of experiments in which objects are covered and put out of sight. Before eight months, out of sight is out of mind, even if the object has been concealed only by placing a handkerchief over it. The child first looks for the hidden object when he has already begun the action of reaching for it at the moment when the cover is put down. Having learned in this way that it can be found, he can then slowly learn to transfer his action when the object is hidden under a different cover, and by the middle of the second year he can take fairly elaborate account of its successive movements. What is going on in this sequence is the disconnecting of the object from any one action and location, thus gradually constructing the idea of its independent existence. Piaget describes in like sequential fashion the growth of the concept of causality apart from one's own effort. In such fashion the child works and plays his way toward knowledge of an enduring world with impersonal causal relations.

Additional evidence for this way of thinking is provided by studies of older children's perceptions and memories of places they have visited. Werner, pointing out that the child's world long remains a world of action, reports experiments in which children of different ages brought back from places such as a canal dock or a department store entirely different descriptions depending upon what they had found to do in these locations.

The objective stable world is thus best conceived of as a construction based upon action. Knowledge about the environment is knowledge of the probable consequences of action. It is a system of readinesses for action which can properly be conceived of as patterns of facilitation and inhibition in the nervous system. This is the form in which reality leaves its record, and instinctual drives are governed by it—become bound by it—because they have to use the nervous system as their means of expression, complete with its acquired facilitations and inhibitions. There is no need to assume that cathexis plays any necessary part at all in knowledge of reality.

5. *Early Deviations in Ego Development*

Following a suggestion of Freud's that the psychoses would shed helpful light on the ego, psychoanalytic workers in recent years have given much attention to disorders in early childhood and have conceptualized them as failures in ego development. This means in particular a deficiency in social responsiveness and object relations, a failure to achieve stable defenses, and an inadequate growth of reality testing and active mastery. The causes of these disorders were first thought to lie in the mother, who was thus assigned a position of virtual omnipotence in her child's adaptive growth. This one-sided picture was later made more interactive by allowing for constitutional deficiencies in the child and response to them by the mother.

Introduction of the concept of independent ego energies permits a closer analysis of what goes wrong in these interactions. It allows us to tighten with appropriate developmental detail the loose connections between weak ego growth and maternal coldness or deprivation. Our question comes to be phrased as follows: what happens to obstruct the infant's tendency to explore and interact with his environment, blocking the usual pathway to reality testing and structuration? In other words, what goes wrong with the expression of effectance, feelings of efficacy, and the growth of a sense of competence?

These concepts allow us, in the first place, to recast the picture of what normally goes on between mother and infant. On the mother's side, we can see that the sense of maternal competence— the ability to perform the socially vital task of bringing up children —is agreeably enhanced when the child develops well, but gravely challenged when his behavior is deviant. Children who are unusually passive, venturing little, and children who are overactive, achieving no stability, each in their own way seriously frustrate maternal competence and thus evoke some of the excessive compensations that have been described in "schizophrenogenic" mothers. On the child's side, we can see that in ordinary circumstances effectance prompts manipulative and exploratory action which is rewarded by feelings of efficacy. Such action is inherently independent, hence sometimes at odds with the mother's wishes and convenience; it does not draw its original power from maternal encouragement and reward. In normal growth the mother thus does not stand as the central motive force in ego development, though she may help or hinder it in important ways. In abnormal cases it must be shown how this development comes to be seriously obstructed.

Concepts of efficacy and competence thus allow us, in the second place, to schematize the causes of the inhibition of effectance. (1) When deprivation and anxiety are very severe, so that the infant when awake is constantly yearning for instinctual gratification and security, exploratory play, the spare-time activity between periods of crisis, may simply be swamped and crowded out. (2) There may be a specific obstruction of socially directed effectance. This is probably the situation in the autistic child whose mother, described as cold and mechanical in her ministrations, never responds to his initiative and thus permits no feelings of efficacy. (3) There may also be a specific obstruction of exploratory play with inanimate objects, though this will not usually occur alone. Such a result could be produced by circumstances that connected play with isolation, fear, or pain.

6. *Identification as a Process of Development*

Of late years the concept of identification has run riot through the clinical literature. The metaphor of undisciplined riot is not out of place: identification has been used in several quite different senses, applied to quite dissimilar phenomena, and never clarified with respect to implicit underlying processes.

We are obliged to lay this confusion at Freud's door. In different writings he used identification (1) as a mechanism in melancholia, where it occurred as a regression from lost object cathexes; (2) for the little boy's admiring imitation of his father, where it was conceived of as a primitive type of object relation; (3) for the internalizing of parental values during resolution of the oedipus complex; (4) for relations among siblings, where it developed as a reaction formation against rivalry; and (5) for the aim-inhibited tender tie among the members of an adult group. The most serious inconsistency in these usages is between identification as the copying of a model, based on wanting to be like the model, and identification as an emotional tie, based on loving and wanting to be close to the model. Freud clearly stated that identification meant only the first, but he frequently used it in the second sense as well.

The difficulty here is that if copying a model is taken as the central idea, then the emotional tie must be a variable, hence inessential, feature. This became clear in Anna Freud's concept of identification with an aggressor, where the imitation was of someone feared and hated. While the literature since Freud's death shows a tendency toward blurred and reckless extension of the concept, there have been attempts to restrict identification to a single clear meaning. This has been done most successfully when a firm distinction is drawn between identification and introjection. The latter then moves back chronologically to the oral stage, carrying with it the connotation of an emotional tie in some such form as a wish for union and merging with the mother. This leaves identification as an imitative process which comes to its first peak during the phallic stage and continues to influence development in the manner described by Erikson.

Thus restricted, identification signifies copying a model whose competence is admired. It is done for the sake of creating that competence in oneself. Like simpler forms of imitation, it implies that the child already has in his repertory the acts he now wants to increase and integrate. The great flowering of make-believe and dramatic play occurs only when the child is mature enough to copy fairly elaborate adult patterns. Identification must be conceived of in terms of attempted action, though this does not exclude dreaming about actions beyond the range of present possibility. Through action and its consequences the child finds out which identifications will work and which ones are doomed to fail.

It will be clear that this formulation does not require any genetic connection between introjection and identification. The two things are psychologically very different. Introjection, if it is not literally modeled on oral incorporation, at least must signify an attempted restoration of the total nursing situation with its feeling of closeness, a relatively passive state not characterized by feelings of efficacy. Identification happens actively in the interests of competence, its chief reward being an increased sense of competence. To call it a partial incorporation is to confuse two things that have no psychological resemblance.

Superego formation and the resolution of the oedipus complex, furthermore, cannot be conceived of simply in terms of identification. Several adaptive processes are at work simultaneously in a complex situation. In so far as the boy accepts prohibitions against a sexual interest in his mother he is actually abandoning part of the identification with his father and learning to act unlike him. Identification applies well to those parts of the process in which parental behavior is copied. It does not apply to the internalizing of prohibitions against behavior still allowed to the parents. But there is certainly no need to capture superego formation in a single formula.

7. *Self-Esteem, Sense of Competence, and Ego Strength*

Psychoanalytic theories of self-esteem are generally cast in terms of instinctual energies and infantile fantasies. When Freud discovered narcissism he made self-regard a function of narcissistic libido, which obscured the possibility that it might have to be differentiated from self-love. In Ferenczi and Fenichel one finds the idea that self-regard is related to fantasies and feelings of omnipotence, which have their origin in the immediate gratification of all needs in the womb. From this comes the conclusion that the level of self-esteem is regulated by the inflow first of oral supplies, later of narcissistic supplies. The theme is continued in the theory that the ego ideal becomes the repository of narcissistic omnipotence. Level of self-esteem can then be conceived of as a reflection of the difference between the ideal and the actual.

Other psychoanalytic theorists, notably Silverberg, have related self-esteem to the success of one's activities directed toward the environment. In the terms used in this essay, self-esteem is correlated with sense of competence, hence ultimately with experiences of efficacy. This view of the matter rescues self-esteem from confusion with self-love by relating it primarily to independent ego energies rather than to narcissistic libido. It also suggests that Ferenczi set up the wrong image for the starting point of omnipotence when he chose a situation of instant passive gratification without a hint of efficacy. Self-esteem has its deepest root in the experience of efficacy. It is not constructed out of what others do or what the environment gratuitously provides. It springs rather from what one can make the environment do by crying, by signaling, or by coordinated acts of competence. Fantasies of omnipotence can be based upon the infant's experience of commanding the environment to serve him (the master who rings for the servants) or upon his experience of mastering it by his own efforts (Robinson Crusoe, Superman).

This account of self-esteem, which locates its inner source in efficacy and the sense of competence, is not intended to crowd out the esteem income that may or may not be provided by others. This is a very real factor, but we must remember that supplies of esteem are not bestowed whimsically; they have some relation to what the person has done. Esteem is constantly involved in a transactional process in which effort expended and encouragement received work in a complementary fashion. It is valuable to distinguish between esteem supplies (respect) and narcissistic supplies (love).

Ego strength must also be seen as clearly related to acquired competence and sense of competence. This concept, useful in clinical practice, has generally been defined negatively as the absence of crippling anxiety or of anticathectic defense processes. Such a view neglects the positive contributions of effectance, which is at work building up adaptive capacities that help in coping with dangers, and a sense of competence that opposes the development of anxiety. This work is constantly going on between times of crisis —in conflict-free situations—and its results may be highly significant when the next crisis occurs. This view of ego strength as an active, cumulative achievement is valuable in understanding the stages of development, in forming a genetic theory of psychopathology, and in explaining those not infrequent cases in which good adjustment seems to have sprung miraculously from a childhood loaded with pathological influences. A psychoanalytic case of the latter kind, presented by its author as an example of healthy growth, reveals the need to supplement psychoanalytic theory with concepts of action and efficacy. The early circumstances, impulses, fantasies, and defense mechanisms disclosed by the analysis offer no basis for predicting the relatively successful adjustment found in middle life. But the riddle can be solved if one pays careful attention to the way in which defenses adopted in crises led to actions of an efficacious sort which worked well upon the particular environment and thus became the basis for a continuing growth of competence and confidence.

8. *Further Considerations of Energy: Anxiety, Cathexis, Neutralization*

Freud came to regard the instincts as the very foundation of psychoanalytic theory. He was highly partial to explanations in terms of instinctual energy, and as between the two basic instincts he was further partial to the libido, a concept to which he remained loyal throughout his life. His preferences are shown by several facts: that he never really worked out the implications of the death instinct, that he continued to use cathexis as if only libido were involved, that he gave anxiety increasing importance without letting it be an energic rival of the instincts, and that he nipped independent ego energies in the bud by producing the hypothesis of desexualized libido. His decisions with respect to energies were not the only possible ones, and they have led to serious difficulties.

When he revised his theory of anxiety in 1926, Freud created a greater revolution than he knew. Anxiety was detached from its previous status of converted libido and assigned great power over the outflow of instinctual-drive energies. Freud did not, however, represent this power as an instinct or drive, as academic psychologists have generally done. In his conception anxiety was merely an affect giving a signal of danger, and the real power in the production of defenses lay with the pleasure-pain mechanism, to which the instincts themselves were subject. There is no way to read this account without concluding that in fact he had invoked a very strong driving force, the avoidance of anxiety, and had brought it into direct conflict with instinctual drives over the use of the pleasure-pain mechanism. One can only note with regret how much better the problems of anticathexis and defensive structure could have been solved if Freud had realized the full implications of what he had done.

Cathexis, an apt concept for describing a loving interest in objects, has come to be used in psychoanalytic theory to signify any kind of positive attitude. It is thus customary to refer to the cathexis of external objects, of the self, and even of ego functions, always with the implication that these things can be of no interest unless they are cathected. Two difficulties result. One is the question of cathexis by aggressive instinctual energy. This is surely a legitimate concept in a dual instinct theory, but it implies that cathexis can be destructive, and the word is practically never used in this sense. The other is that objects must have a permanent cathexis if they are to be conceived of as having a permanent existence. This creates difficulty for the idea that instincts have a periodic character. These difficulties can be resolved by returning cathexis to its original meaning of an investment of libidinal energy, and by introducing independent ego energies to account for a "neutral" or nonlibidinal interest in objects. Such interest is related to feelings of efficacy, and the permanence of objects is assured by the permanence of the acquired patterns for influencing them. The concept of the libidinal cathexis of ego functions is perhaps not an impossible one, but libido is not required to make the ego run.

Difficulties have resulted from the attempt to interpret all play and exploratory behavior as a manifestation of erotic or aggressive instinctual energies. Since erotic and aggressive aims are by no means regularly apparent, it becomes necessary to stretch the meaning of the two energies to such generalities as binding things together or pulling things apart. This analysis is fatal to an understanding of the meaning of exploratory acts. Joining and separating occur in lightning alternation in manipulative behavior, for example, but pointing out this superficial fact obscures the real meaning of the behavior, which is to find out what can be done with objects. On this point effectance and efficacy yield a more penetrating analysis than instinctual drives.

It was in part to deal with difficulties of this kind that Freud introduced the idea of desexualized libido and Hartmann expanded it to include a parallel process of neutralization of aggressive energies. The concept of neutralization contains the implicit recognition that the adaptive activities of the ego cannot be forced into the categories of instinctual aim. The assumption is made that energies originally distinguished by their aims can divest themselves of these aims and become part of a neutral reservoir available to the ego for its own purposes. There is the further proviso that during regression the energy may be reconverted to its original aims. If this idea is considered in neurological terms, it will not work. If it is accepted as a vague hydraulic analogy, it still will not work. Telling very much against it is the fact that no real progress has been made in detailing the conditions under which the remarkable transformations take place. Even more serious for such a theory is the growing evidence that neutral energy is manifested early in life, even during the first days and weeks. If energy that is neutral in the psychoanalytic sense is conceived to be active so early, the hypothesis that it is transformed from the instincts is superfluous and the case for independent ego energies becomes virtually self-evident. But nothing

is lost, because independent ego energies, adequately conceptualized, can do everything that neutralized energies could do, except
to deneutralize themselves.

Freud's fundamental concepts were formed under the influence of
the tremendous discoveries he made by means of the psychoanalytic
method. They have the character of magnificent metaphors designed
to capture these discoveries. But he also hoped to formulate a complete theory of personality, and for this it is necessary to include
wide ranges of facts not readily observed by the psychoanalytic
technique. His goal remains worthy, and the present essay is designed
to be a step in its direction.

BIBLIOGRAPHY

Alexander, F. (1958), A Contribution to the Theory of Play. *Psychoanal. Quart.,* 27:175-193.

Allport, F. H. (1924), *Social Psychology.* Boston: Houghton Mifflin.

Allport, G. W. (1943), The Ego in Contemporary Psychology. *Psychol. Rev.,* 50:451-478.

Alpert, A., Neubauer, P. B., & Weil, A. P. (1956), Unusual Variations in Drive Endowment. *The Psychoanalytic Study of the Child,* 11:125-163. New York: International Universities Press.

Baldwin, J. M. (1895), *Mental Development in the Child and the Race.* New York: Macmillan.

Balint, M. (1936), Eros and Aphrodite. *Primary Love and Psycho-Analytic Technique.* London: Hogarth Press, 1952, pp. 73-89.

———— (1937), Early Developmental States of the Ego. Primary Object-Love. *Primary Love and Psycho-Analytic Technique.* London: Hogarth Press, 1952, pp. 90-108.

Beach, F. A. (1951), Instinctive Behavior: Reproductive Activities. In *Handbook of Experimental Psychology,* ed. S. S. Stevens. New York: Wiley, pp. 387-434.

Bender, L. (1953), Childhood Schizophrenia. *Psychiat. Quart.,* 27:663-681.

Benedek, T. (1938), Adaptation to Reality in Early Infancy. *Psychoanal. Quart.,* 7:200-215.

Berlyne, D. E. (1950), Novelty and Curiosity as Determinants of Exploratory Behaviour. *Brit. J. Psychol.,* 41:68-80.

———— (1960), *Conflict, Arousal, and Curiosity.* New York: McGraw-Hill.

Bettelheim, B. (1943), Individual and Mass Behavior in Extreme Situations. *J. Abn. Soc. Psychol.,* 38:417-452.

Bibring, E. (1936), The Development and Problems of the Theory of the Instincts. *Int. J. Psycho-Anal.,* 22:102-131, 1941.

Bing, J. F., McLaughlin, F., & Marburg, R. (1959), The Metapsychology of Narcissism. *The Psychoanalytic Study of the Child,* 14:9-28. New York: International Universities Press.

Boring, E. G. (1929), *A History of Experimental Psychology.* New York: Appleton-Century-Crofts, 2nd ed., 1950.

Bornstein, B. (1951), On Latency. *The Psychoanalytic Study of the Child,* 6:279-285. New York: International Universities Press.

Bühler, C. (1954), The Reality Principle. *Amer. J. Psychother.,* 8:626-647.

Bühler, K. (1918), *Die geistige Entwicklung des Kindes.* Jena: Fischer, 4th ed., 1924.

Butler, R. A. (1958), Exploratory and Related Behavior: A New Trend in Animal Research. *J. Indiv. Psychol.,* 14:111-120.

———— & Harlow, H. F. (1957), Discrimination Learning and Learning Sets to Visual Exploration Incentives. *J. Gen. Psychol.,* 57:257-264.

Carr, R. M., & Brown, W. L. (1959), The Effect of Sustained Novelty upon Manipulation in Rhesus Monkeys. *J. Gen. Psychol.,* 61:121-125.

197

Cho, J. B., & Davis, R. T. (1957), Preferences of Monkeys for Objects Other than Food. *Amer. J. Psychol.*, 70:87-91.

Colby, K. M. (1955), *Energy and Structure in Psychoanalysis*. New York: Ronald Press.

Cooley, C. H. (1902), *Human Nature and the Social Order*. New York: Scribner's.

Eisenberg, L. (1957), The Fathers of Autistic Children. *Amer. J. Orthopsychiat.*, 27:715-724.

Erikson, E. H. (1950), *Childhood and Society*. New York: Norton.

——— (1946-1956), Identity and the Life Cycle. *Psychological Issues*, 1(1). New York: International Universities Press, 1959.

——— (1962), Reality and Actuality. *J. Amer. Psychoanal. Assn.*, 10:451-473.

Eysenck, H. J. (1953), *The Structure of Human Personality*. London: Methuen.

Fenichel, O. (1937), Early Stages of Ego Development. *Collected Papers*, 2:25-48. New York: Norton, 1954.

——— (1938), Ego Strength and Ego Weakness. *Collected Papers*, 2:70-80. New York: Norton, 1954.

——— (1945), *The Psychoanalytic Theory of Neurosis*. New York: Norton.

Ferenczi, S. (1913), Stages in the Development of the Sense of Reality. *Sex in Psychoanalysis*. New York: Brunner, 1950, pp. 213-239.

French, T. M. (1952), *The Integration of Behavior*, Vol. 1. *Basic Postulates*. Chicago: University of Chicago Press.

Freud, A. (1926), *The Psycho-Analytical Treatment of Children*. New York: International Universities Press, 1959.

——— (1936), *The Ego and the Mechanisms of Defence*. New York: International Universities Press, 1946.

——— (1952), The Mutual Influences in the Development of Ego and Id: Introduction to the Discussion. *The Psychoanalytic Study of the Child*, 7:42-50. New York: International Universities Press.

Freud, S. (1895), Project for a Scientific Psychology. *The Origins of Psycho-Analysis: Letters to Wilhelm Fliess, Drafts and Notes: 1887-1902*. New York: Basic Books, 1954, pp. 355-445.

——— (1905), Jokes and Their Relation to the Unconscious. *Standard Edition*, 8. London: Hogarth Press, 1960.

——— (1911), Formulations on the Two Principles of Mental Functioning. *Standard Edition*, 12:218-226. London: Hogarth Press, 1958.

——— (1915a), Instincts and Their Vicissitudes. *Standard Edition*, 14:117-140. London: Hogarth Press, 1957.

——— (1915b), Repression. *Standard Edition*, 14:146-158. London: Hogarth Press, 1957.

——— (1915c), The Unconscious. *Standard Edition*, 14:166-204. London: Hogarth Press, 1957.

——— (1917, [1915]), Mourning and Melancholia. *Standard Edition*, 14:243-258. London: Hogarth Press, 1957.

——— (1920), Beyond the Pleasure Principle. *Standard Edition*, 18:7-64. London: Hogarth Press, 1955.

——— (1921), Group Psychology and the Analysis of the Ego. *Standard Edition*, 18:69-143. London: Hogarth Press, 1955.

——— (1922), Two Encyclopaedia Articles. *Standard Edition*, 18:235-259. London: Hogarth Press, 1955.

——— (1923), The Ego and the Id. *Standard Edition*, 19:12-66. London: Hogarth Press, 1961.

——— (1925a [1924]), A Note upon the 'Mystic Writing-Pad.' *Standard Edition*, 19:227-232. London: Hogarth Press, 1961.

——— (1925b), Negation. *Standard Edition*, 19:235-239. London: Hogarth Press, 1961.

———— (1926), Inhibitions, Symptoms and Anxiety. *Standard Edition,* 20:87-172. London: Hogarth Press, 1959.

———— (1932), *New Introductory Lectures on Psychoanalysis.* New York: Norton, 1933.

———— (1940 [1938]), *An Outline of Psychoanalysis.* New York: Norton, 1949.

Fromm, E. (1947), *Man for Himself.* New York: Rinehart.

Gesell, A., & Ilg, F. L. (1943), *Infant and Child in the Culture of Today.* New York: Harper.

———— ———— (1946), *The Child from Five to Ten.* New York: Harper.

Glover, E. (1931), Sublimation, Substitution and Social Anxiety. *Int. J. Psycho-Anal.,* 12:263-297.

Goldstein, K. (1940), *Human Nature in the Light of Psychopathology.* Cambridge: Harvard University Press.

Groos, K. (1901), *The Play of Man.* New York: Appleton.

Harlow, H. F. (1953), Mice, Monkeys, Men, and Motives. *Psychol. Rev.,* 60:23-32.

Hartmann, H. (1939), *Ego Psychology and the Problem of Adaptation.* New York: International Universities Press, 1958.

———— (1953), Contribution to the Metapsychology of Schizophrenia. *The Psychoanalytic Study of the Child,* 8:177-198. New York: International Universities Press.

———— (1955), Notes on the Theory of Sublimation. *The Psychoanalytic Study of the Child,* 10:9-29. New York: International Universities Press.

———— (1956a), The Development of the Ego Concept in Freud's Work. *Int. J. Psycho-Anal.,* 37:425-438.

———— (1956b), Notes on the Reality Principle. *The Psychoanalytic Study of the Child,* 11:31-53. New York: International Universities Press.

———— Kris, E., & Loewenstein, R. M. (1946), Comments on the Formation of Psychic Structure. *The Psychoanalytic Study of the Child,* 2:11-38. New York: International Universities Press.

———— ———— ———— (1949), Notes on the Theory of Aggression. *The Psychoanalytic Study of the Child,* 3/4:9-36. New York: International Universities Press.

Hebb, D. O. (1949), *The Organization of Behavior.* New York: Wiley.

Hendrick, I. (1934), *Facts and Theories of Psychoanalysis.* New York: Knopf, 2nd ed., 1939.

———— (1942), Instinct and the Ego During Infancy. *Psychoanal. Quart.,* 11:33-58.

———— (1943a), Work and the Pleasure Principle. *Psychoanal. Quart.,* 12:311-329.

———— (1943b), The Discussion of the 'Instinct to Master.' *Psychoanal. Quart.,* 12:561-565.

Hill, L. B. (1955), *Psychotherapeutic Intervention in Schizophrenia.* Chicago: University of Chicago Press.

Hoffer, W. (1950), Development of the Body Ego. *The Psychoanalytic Study of the Child,* 5:18-23. New York: International Universities Press.

Holt, R. R. (1963), Two Influences upon Freud's Scientific Thought: A Fragment of Intellectual Biography. In press.

Jacobson, E. (1954), The Self and the Object World. *The Psychoanalytic Study of the Child,* 9:75-127. New York: International Universities Press.

Jones, E. (1955), *The Life and Work of Sigmund Freud,* Vol. 2. New York: Basic Books.

Kagan, J. (1958), The Concept of Identification. *Psychol. Rev.,* 65:296-305.

Kanner, L. (1943), Autistic Disturbances of Affective Contact. *Nerv. Child,* 2:217-250.

Kardiner, A., Karush, A., & Ovesey, L. (1959), A Methodological Study of Freudian Theory. *J. Nerv. Ment. Dis.*, 129:11-19, 133-143, 207-221, 341-356.

────── & Spiegel, H. (1947), *War Stress and Neurotic Illness*. New York: Hoeber.

Kardos, E., & Peto, A. (1956), Contributions to the Theory of Play. *Brit. J. Med. Psychol.*, 29:100-112.

Kassebaum, G. G., Couch, A. S., & Slater, P. E. (1959), The Factorial Dimensions of the MMPI. *J. Consult. Psychol.*, 23:226-236.

Katz, D., & Katz, R. (1928), *Gespräche mit Kindern*. Berlin: Springer.

Klebanoff, L. B. (1959), Parental Attitudes of Mothers of Schizophrenic, Brain-Injured and Retarded, and Normal Children. *Amer. J. Orthopsychiat.*, 29:445-454.

Klein, M. (1955), On Identification. In *New Directions in Psychoanalysis*, ed. M. Klein, P. Heimann, & R. E. Money-Kyrle. New York: Basic Books, pp. 309-345.

Knight, R. P. (1940), Introjection, Projection and Identification. *Psychoanal. Quart.*, 9:334-341.

Kris, E. (1955), Neutralization and Sublimation: Observations on Young Children. *The Psychoanalytic Study of the Child*, 10:30-46. New York: International Universities Press.

Lashley, K. S. (1938), Experimental Analysis of Instinctive Behavior. *Psychol. Rev.*, 45:445-471.

Levey, H. B. (1939), A Critique of the Theory of Sublimation. *Psychiatry*, 2:239-270.

Levy, D. M. (1955), Oppositional Syndromes and Oppositional Behavior. In *Psychopathology of Childhood*, ed. P. H. Hoch & J. Zubin. New York: Grune & Stratton, pp. 204-226.

Loewald, H. (1951), Ego and Reality. *Int. J. Psycho-Anal.*, 32:10-18.

Lorenz, K. Z. (1952), *King Solomon's Ring*. New York: Crowell.

Lustman, S. L. (1957), Psychic Energy and Mechanisms of Defense. *The Psychoanalytic Study of the Child*, 12:151-165. New York: International Universities Press.

Macfarlane, J. W., Allen, L., & Honzik, M. P. (1954), *A Developmental Study of the Behavior Problems of Normal Children Between Twenty-one Months and Fourteen Years*. Berkeley: University of California Press.

Maenchen, A. (1953), Notes on Early Ego Disturbances. *The Psychoanalytic Study of the Child*, 8:262-270. New York: International Universities Press.

Mahler, M. S. (1952), On Child Psychosis and Schizophrenia. *The Psychoanalytic Study of the Child*, 7:286-305. New York: International Universities Press.

────── & Elkisch, P. (1953), Some Observations on Disturbances of the Ego in a Case of Infantile Psychosis. *The Psychoanalytic Study of the Child*, 8:252-261. New York: International Universities Press.

────── & Gosliner, B. J. (1955), On Symbiotic Child Psychosis: Genetic, Dynamic and Restitutive Aspects. *The Psychoanalytic Study of the Child*, 10:195-212. New York: International Universities Press.

Mark, J. C. (1953), The Attitudes of the Mothers of Male Schizophrenics Toward Child Behavior. *J. Abn. Soc. Psychol.*, 48:185-189.

Maxwell, G. (1960), *Ring of Bright Water*. New York: Dutton.

McDougall, W. (1908), *An Introduction to Social Psychology*. Boston: Luce, rev. ed., 1923.

Miles, R. C. (1958), Learning in Kittens with Manipulatory, Exploratory, and Food Incentives. *J. Comp. Physiol. Psychol.*, 51:39-42.

Mittelmann, B. (1954), Motility in Infants, Children, and Adults. *The Psychoanalytic Study of the Child*, 9:142-177. New York: International Universities Press.

Montgomery, K. C. (1954), The Role of the Exploratory Drive in Learning. *J. Comp. Physiol. Psychol.,* 47:60-64.

Mowrer, O. H. (1950), *Learning Theory and Personality Dynamics: Selected Papers.* New York: Ronald Press.

Muchow, M., & Muchow, H. (1935), *Der Lebensraum des Grossstadtkindes.* Hamburg: Riegel.

Munroe, R. (1955), *Schools of Psychoanalytic Thought.* New York: Dryden Press.

Murphy, G. (1947), *Personality: A Biosocial Approach to Origins and Structure.* New York: Harper.

Murray, H. A., & Kluckhohn, C. (1953), Outline of a Conception of Personality. In *Personality in Nature, Society, and Culture,* ed. C. Kluckhohn, H. A. Murray, & D. M. Schneider. New York: Knopf, 2nd ed., pp. 3-49.

———— & Morgan, C. D. (1945), A Clinical Study of Sentiments. *Genet. Psychol. Monogr.,* 32:3-149, 153-311.

Nunberg, H. (1931), The Synthetic Function of the Ego. *Int. J. Psycho-Anal.,* 12:123-140.

Piaget, J. (1927), *The Child's Conception of the World.* New York: Harcourt, Brace, 1929.

———— (1936), *The Origins of Intelligence in Children.* New York: International Universities Press, 1952.

———— (1937), *The Construction of Reality in the Child.* New York: Basic Books, 1954.

———— (1945), *Play, Dreams and Imitation in Childhood.* New York: Norton, 1951.

Piers, G., & Singer, M. B. (1953), *Shame and Guilt: A Psychoanalytic and a Cultural Study.* Springfield, Ill.: Thomas.

Preyer, W. (1888), *The Mind of the Child.* New York: Appleton.

Rank, B. (1949), Adaptation of the Psychoanalytic Technique for the Treatment of Young Children with Atypical Development. *Amer. J. Orthopsychiat.,* 19:130-139.

———— & MacNaughton, D. (1950), A Clinical Contribution to Early Ego Development. *The Psychoanalytic Study of the Child,* 5:53-65. New York: International Universities Press.

Rapaport, D., ed. (1951), *Organization and Pathology of Thought.* New York: Columbia University Press.

———— (1960), On the Psychoanalytic Theory of Motivation. In *Nebraska Symposium on Motivation,* ed. M. Jones. Lincoln: University of Nebraska Press, pp. 173-247.

Reich, A. (1958), A Character Formation Representing the Integration of Unusual Conflict Solutions into the Ego Structure. *The Psychoanalytic Study of the Child,* 13:309-323. New York: International Universities Press.

Riesman, D. (1950), *The Lonely Crowd: A Study of the Changing American Character.* New Haven: Yale University Press.

Ritvo, S., & Provence, S. (1953), Form Perception and Imitation in Some Autistic Children: Diagnostic Findings and Their Contextual Interpretation. *The Psychoanalytic Study of the Child,* 8:155-161. New York: International Universities Press.

Rochlin, G. (1953), Loss and Restitution. *The Psychoanalytic Study of the Child,* 8:288-309. New York: International Universities Press.

Ross, A. B. (1955), A Schizophrenic Child and His Mother. *J. Abn. Soc. Psychol.,* 51:133-139.

Sandler, J. (1960), On the Concept of Superego. *The Psychoanalytic Study of the Child,* 15:128-162. New York: International Universities Press.

Sanford, N. (1955), The Dynamics of Identification. *Psychol. Rev.,* 62:106-118.

Schachtel, E. G. (1959), *Metamorphosis.* New York: Basic Books.

Schilder, P. (1935), *The Image and Appearance of the Human Body*. New York: International Universities Press, 1950.

Sheffield, F. D., & Roby, T. B. (1950), Reward Value of a Non-nutritive Sweet Taste. *J. Comp. Physiol. Psychol.*, 43:471-481.

Shinn, M. W. (1898, 1907), *Notes on the Development of a Child*. Berkeley: University Press, University of California Publications in Education, 1 & 2.

Silverberg, W. V. (1952), *Childhood Experience and Personal Destiny*. New York: Springer.

Solomon, R. L., & Wynne, L. C. (1954), Traumatic Avoidance Learning: The Principles of Anxiety Conservation and Partial Irreversibility. *Psychol. Rev.*, 61:353-385.

Spitz, R. A. (1945), Hospitalism: An Inquiry into the Genesis of Psychiatric Conditions in Early Childhood. *The Psychoanalytic Study of the Child*, 1:53-74. New York: International Universities Press.

—— (1946), Anaclitic Depression: An Inquiry into the Genesis of Psychiatric Conditions in Early Childhood, II. *The Psychoanalytic Study of the Child*, 2:313-342. New York: International Universities Press.

—— (1953), Aggression: Its Role in the Establishment of Object Relations. In *Drives, Affects, Behavior*, ed. R. M. Loewenstein. New York: International Universities Press, pp. 126-138.

—— (1958), On the Genesis of Superego Components. *The Psychoanalytic Study of the Child*, 13:375-404. New York: International Universities Press.

Stellar, E. (1954), The Physiology of Motivation. *Psychol. Rev.*, 61:5-22.

Stern, W. (1914), *Psychology of Early Childhood*. New York: Holt, 2nd ed., 1930.

Stott, D. H. (1961), An Empirical Approach to Motivation Based on the Behaviour of a Young Child. *J. Child Psychol. Psychiat.*, 2:97-117.

Sully, J. (1896), *Studies of Childhood*. London & New York: Appleton.

Thistlethwaite, D. (1951), A Critical Review of Latent Learning and Related Experiments. *Psychol. Bull.*, 48:97-129.

Tolman, E. C. (1943), Identification and the Post-War World. *J. Abn. Soc. Psychol.*, 38:141-148.

Waelder, R. (1932), The Psychoanalytic Theory of Play. *Psychoanal. Quart.*, 2:208-224, 1933.

Watson, R. I. (1959), *Psychology of the Child*. New York: Wiley.

Weil, A. P. (1956), Some Evidences of Deviational Development in Infancy and Early Childhood. *The Psychoanalytic Study of the Child*, 11:292-299. New York: International Universities Press.

Welker, W. I. (1956), Some Determinants of Play and Exploration in Chimpanzees. *J. Comp. Physiol. Psychol.*, 49:84-89.

—— (1961), An Analysis of Exploratory and Play Behavior in Animals. In *Functions of Varied Experience*, ed. D. W. Fiske & S. R. Maddi. Homewood, Ill.: Dorsey Press, pp. 175-226.

Werner, H. (1926), *Comparative Psychology of Mental Development*. New York: International Universities Press, 3rd ed., 1957.

White, R. W. (1952), *Lives in Progress*. New York: Dryden Press.

—— (1959), Motivation Reconsidered: The Concept of Competence. *Psychol. Rev.*, 66:297-333.

—— (1960), Competence and the Psychosexual Stages of Development. In *Nebraska Symposium on Motivation*, ed. M. Jones. Lincoln: University of Nebraska Press, pp. 97-141.

Wolff, P. W. (1959), Observations on Newborn Infants. *Psychosom. Med.*, 21:110-118.

Woodworth, R. S. (1958), *Dynamics of Behavior*. New York: Holt.

INDEX

Abraham, K., 71, 106
Action, 2, 35, 50, 53, 66, 67, 69, 70,
  97, 109, 118, 119, 126, 133,
  136, 140, 150, 153, 168, 171,
  172, 183, 186-188, 193
  and child's conception of causality,
  35, 36, 51, 64
  and its consequences, 34, 38, 46-
  51, 53, 69, 134, 181, 182, 186,
  189, 191; and reality testing, 59-
  68
  and knowledge, 46-47, 59, 65, 68
  and objects, 50, 60-65
Activity, 3, 105, 128, 132, 146, 147,
  149, 162
  pleasure in, 37, 38, 42, 48
Actuality, 67-68
Adaptation, 13-16, 18, 21, 22, 24,
  36, 38, 41, 42, 44, 45, 67, 68,
  78, 92, 141, 142, 161, 162, 165,
  167, 168, 172, 183, 184, 189
Adler, A., 14, 151
Aggression, 42, 92, 93, 103, 129,
  149-153, 156-158, 161, 162,
  164, 165; *see also* Drive, aggressive; Energy, aggressive
Aims, 20-22, 29, 32, 36, 42, 55, 153,
  158, 161, 163, 165, 167-171,
  174, 176, 183-186, 195
Alexander, F., 162
Allport, F. H., 109
Allport, G. W., 81
Alpert, A., 84
Anger, 158
Animal behavior, 25-29, 33-35, 182,
  184
Anticathexis, 3, 56, 57, 169, 171,
  180, 187, 193, 194; *see also*
  Countercathexis
Anticipation, 17, 45, 46
Anxiety, 7, 8, 15, 17, 26, 40, 57, 70,

90, 102, 103, 113, 123, 138,
  140, 146, 148, 152-156, 159,
  161, 180, 190, 193-194
Aphrodite, 162
Assimilation, 116
Attention, 6, 7, 32, 58, 61
Autism, early infantile, 72-74, 82,
  85, 87, 140, 190
Autonomy, 113

Baldwin, J. M., 95
Balint, M., 160, 162
Beach, F. A., 178
Bender, L., 75
Benedek, T., 46, 105
Berlyne, D. E., 26
Bettelheim, B., 99
Bibring, E., 7
Binding, 7, 55, 57, 58
Bing, J. F., 126
Boring, E. G., 177
Bornstein, B., 123
Brown, W. L., 28
Bühler, C., 47, 51, 160
Bühler, K., 37
Butler, R. A., 26-27

Carr, R. M., 28
Cathexis, 7, 56, 57, 153, 157-161,
  180, 187, 188, 193-195
  aggressive, 157, 158,
  attention, 58, 61
  bound, 55-56, 58, 70
  externalization of, 53, 54
  libidinal, 127, 158, 159
  narcissistic, 49, 130
  object, 49, 54-55, 60, 70, 97, 194;
  abandoned, 100-101, 104; regression from, 102
Causality, 35, 36, 51, 53, 61, 64, 188
Child psychology, 21, 183, 184

203

ABOUT THE AUTHOR

ROBERT W. WHITE received the Ph.D. in psychology at Harvard University in 1937. Previously he had taught at the University of Maine and at Rutgers University. Since 1937 he has taught at Harvard, serving at different times as Director of the Psychological Clinic (1946-50) and Chairman of the Department of Social Relations (1957-62). He is the author of *The Abnormal Personality* (1948, 1956, 1964), *Lives in Progress: A Study of the Natural Growth of Personality* (1952), and, with M. Brewster Smith and Jerome S. Bruner, *Opinions and Personality* (1956).

ABOUT THE AUTHOR